HERE
AND
GONE

Coming of Age As My Father Comes Undone

ERIKA VARGAS

Note to the Reader:
This memoir includes detailed descriptions of mental
and physical health issues. Please read with care.

This is a work of creative nonfiction. The events are portrayed
to the best of my memory. While all the stories in this book
are true, some names and identifying details have been
changed to protect the privacy of the people involved.

To Mom,
for everything

Prologue

The anticipation is intolerable. I creep around the side of his building, my heart thumping in my chest. *Please no one see me. Please no one see me.* The last thing I need is the cops called: *Hi, yes, there's a young woman suspiciously peeping through an elderly man's blinds.* I don't know what I'm about to see. My father—injured, helpless? His dead body, lifeless on the floor?

It's clearly been a while since the windows have been cleaned; pollen clouds my view. I frantically clear a small circle with my fingertips until, within seconds, I see what I need to see.

He's there on his bed—fully intact, alive, thank God. He's sitting up—white ribbed tank top hanging off his skeleton; khaki pants on, but loose; his belt at the foot of the bed. I wonder how long he's been there. Was he trying to get up to buzz me in after I feverishly rang unit number 16 four times over a ten-minute span? Or was he just . . . sitting? He turns his head and sees me—his previously blank, empty eyes instantly spewing anger, disappointment, disgust. *Why?*

Fight or flight. I run back around to the entrance of the building, up the concrete front steps, press 16 again, wait, allowing ample time for him to make it to his buzzer. Three minutes pass. I buzz again and wait until finally I am granted access. After hours of ignoring my calls and buzzes, he's conceded, and now I can get some answers. I hear him unlock the kitchen door, but it remains closed, daring me to let myself in. He's standing by the dining room table when I enter, and I'm surprised he made it there so quickly; that ten-foot journey usually takes a full minute, not mere seconds. He's pushing himself today.

I offer him a quickly rejected hug as I blurt out, "Are you okay? My god, I've been so worried. You knew I was coming. Why didn't you answer my calls?"

He steadies himself and turns away from me. His hand grabs his belt loop, securing his pants.

"I didn't want to talk to you," he says. Then for minutes, familiar attacks shoot at me like bullets: *You're a liar. I am ashamed. You have no respect for your father. You don't care. You're selfish.*

The juxtaposition of how worried I've been and his accusation of me caring so little overwhelms me; my brain overheats, exploding at the contradiction. I'm used to this, but today, I snap. The adrenaline that has been building in my body since five unanswered calls ago becomes too much; it bubbles up, begging for release. Heat rises to the surface of my skin, my fists clench, my brows press together. The thought that has been nagging me for months escapes my throat before I even realize what I'm saying: "You make me want to die! You make me want to kill myself!"

A pause. A tendon in his shoulder twitches.

"Then we'll bury you," he says.

BEFORE

1.

"Up?"

I'm staring high into the sky—actually only a few feet, but to my toddler self, my dad seems as tall as the highest tree. He smiles back at me and scoops me up with his strong arms, throwing me above his head and catching me as we erupt into belly laughs.

. . .

Toys are everywhere. The tree lights sparkle next to us, and we're so used to the smell of pine that we barely notice it. Christmas Day is so special—while everyone else is at church or tolerating family or throwing together an elaborate home-cooked five-course dinner, I am with my two favorite people on earth. It doesn't matter that they've been divorced for almost three years; they get along just fine, and I love holidays when we all spend time together. I'm four and a half years old (well, four and three-quarters, *thank you very much*), and I'm happy as a clam sitting in my living room amid wrapping paper and bows, playing with my mom and dad.

"Erika Vargas, star of the circus!" my dad announces, cupping his hands around his mouth as I twirl a Hula-Hoop on my arm and talk into my fabulous new toy microphone using my other hand. My mom is recording all of it on a camcorder. This will become a cherished memory. My father's energy is contagious. Even when the moment has passed, I can feel it.

· · ·

It's thirty minutes to midnight. My eyelids struggle to stay open even though a rerun of my favorite *Rugrats* episode is on. My dad sits next to me, a smile permanently on his gentle tan face. He is reading the newspaper, and we just finished sharing a giant bowl of vanilla ice cream covered with excessive chocolate sprinkles. Curled up beside him, I'm wearing his Exxon shirt, "José" embroidered on the patch. I wore it to school today after all. It was Hero Day, and my classmates and I dressed as someone who means a lot to each of us. I dressed up as my daddy, my face marked up with paint to mimic his five-o'clock shadow. People say I'm the spitting image of him—petite stature, large brown eyes, a round face, thick dark eyebrows that form a crease when we are thinking really hard. He is strong, he is hardworking, and he is my hero. I gave a speech about why he inspires me, how he drives big trucks and climbs up a ladder to the tippy top of the oil towers at work. How *brave* my daddy is, my daddy who takes me to Canobie Lake Park every summer for his company picnic and watches, beaming, from the ground while my friend and I ride the roller coasters, loop-de-looping and stomachs turning. He never joins us, of course, because he is afraid of heights—something his coworkers would never know.

I'll be asleep within minutes, and he will carry my little eight-year-old body upstairs to my very own room in his beautiful town house just one town over from where my mom and I live. Even though tomorrow is Saturday, I'm likely to wake between six and seven o'clock naturally—a horrible night's sleep for a child my age. But it's our thing—I stay up late, and I eat all the foods my mom won't allow me to have for fear they will rot my teeth.

Fridays are my glory days because I get to spend them with him—the routine we've kept since my parents divorced when I was just under two years old. When the bell rings at the end of the school day, I burst through those front doors and run out to find his bright red car parked among those of the other parents. I always spot him leaning against the back door, clad in his perfectly-ironed polo shirt and khaki pants, arms crossed, patiently waiting to greet me. When we lock eyes, our faces both brighten.

We often start our afternoon at the playground. Full of pride, he watches as I learn the monkey bars. He teaches me to ride a bike and puts a bandage on my first scraped knee from trying without training wheels.

Sometimes we walk around the mall. We develop Beanie Baby Fridays, where a new stuffed toy joins my collection each week. It's no secret he spoils me. After all, I'm his little girl—his only daughter, the only child he raised. I cuddle my new toy while he tries on a pair of steel-toed boots he needs for work. Once in a while, he lets me invite a friend to join us and treats us to Auntie Anne's giant soft cinnamon sugar pretzels.

We always end the afternoon at the grocery store and toss boxes of sugary cereal, orange sherbet, and Jell-O into the cart. Before bed, we boil water and mix it with red gelatin crystals, stirring and stirring until it magically turns into a delicious strawberry mold by morning.

One weekend, we decide to enter a local craft store's Dress-a-Tomato contest. During our weekly grocery store trip, we meticulously select vegetables to make a Mr. Potato Head version of a tomato: baby corn for the arms, peas for the eyes, a tiny carrot shred for the smile. We create a toothpick and veggie masterpiece and are sure we will win the contest . . . until my dad drops the plate, ceramic shattering and tomato splattering across his pristine white kitchen floor. We just stare at each other for a moment—mouths open, eyes wide—until we keel over with laughter. Instead of bringing a crushed tomato person to the contest, we play Nintendo for hours, attempting to get Mario or Luigi to rescue the princess, to no avail.

On Friday evenings, he cooks me one of the three meals he can prepare: spaghetti, ravioli (do these count as different meals?), or steak. I hate the steak and one day announce that I have become a vegetarian, much to his dismay. As a born and raised Peruvian carnivore, he genuinely cannot understand why someone would willingly avoid meat, something so central to his culture. He is always grabbing my skinny, little arm, saying, "We need to put some meat on these bones!"

As an eight-year-old girl, I am served the same amount of pasta as him—a fifty-one-year-old man. Saturday morning breakfast consists of a banana, a bagel with cream cheese, the Jell-O we prepared the night before, a bowl of cereal with whole milk, and a large glass of orange juice. I am full, but not *too* full. I know he wants to fuel me up so I am strong for soccer—a sport I am truly terrible at. I live in fear of the ball. One time, I score for the wrong team by accident, but it's okay—he cheers for me anyway. I know it thrills him to watch me play, so I stick with it for a while.

Sometimes he reads me to sleep, his thick Peruvian accent making the story more interesting when he puts the wrong emPHAsis on the wrong syllABle. Our favorite bedtime story is "The Grasshopper and the Ants." I love the singsong way my dad tells the story of the hardworking ants who prepare all summer by finding and hiding food for the cold winter months so they can relax and enjoy the fruits of their labor. I always laugh at the grasshopper, who just sings and plays, the ants reminding him to *never put off for tomorrow what you can do today!* My dad is like the ants—a self-made, well-prepared man who works hard all week so he can relax on the weekend. He is never unprepared like that silly grasshopper. There isn't anything he can't handle.

. . .

On a rainy Saturday morning, my father decides it's time to teach me how to stand up to bullies now that I'm in third grade. He stands behind me, as if we're in a line, and pokes my back with his finger.

"Hey!" he yells. I turn around, giggling. He doesn't break character. "Give me your lunch money!"

We repeat this over and over until I loudly and firmly say "No!" without missing a beat. Finally, he lets himself smile with me, confident I can protect myself at school and keep myself safe against those stereotypical lunch-money-stealing bullies.

With him, I feel safe. With him, I'm prepared for anything.

. . .

When my mom and I go to Upstate New York on three-day weekends to visit family friends, my dad and I miss our special day. He primarily works the overnight shift, so we can't just swap for another night of the week.

On one of those long weekends when I'm in fourth grade, I miss him unbearably. His car hasn't been working, and I imagine him housebound, channel surfing all alone in his living room while eating a pizza from Domino's and missing me too. I love the trips to New York. My mom and I sing along to Disney and Beatles CDs and play the Alphabet Game (she's good, but I always win). But when the song "Maybe" from the musical *Annie* blares through the car's speakers, I find myself blinking back tears, staring out the window so as not to hurt my mom's feelings. I picture my dad, shoveling a path alongside the highway through thigh-high mounds of snow, yelling, "Erika, I'm coming for you!"

. . .

My mom and I walk in the door to our two-bedroom apartment, buzzing about my upcoming play. She'd signed me up for the town drama program in fourth grade and encouraged me to stick with it when I wanted to quit because the slow song in *Bye Bye Birdie* made me cry. After that, I fell in love and signed up again every season.

I'm *so* excited because I have my first speaking role. I'm eleven. I've been acting for two years now, and I finally get to be heard onstage!

My mom will be there opening night. My dad will be there too, sitting next to my mom, as close to the front row as they can get.

We are getting ready to cuddle up in her bed to watch *Friends*, and Mom checks the answering machine. One message. I hear my dad's voice.

"Hello, my love. This is Daddy . . . ," he starts out, as per usual.

But this time, it's different. He pauses. His voice begins to crack.

"I'm sorry," he wails, and I know he is unnecessarily apologizing for sounding anything less than strong. "My mother has died. I have to go to Peru. I'm so sorry, Erika, but I will miss your play. Te quiero mucho."

My heart stops.

ERIKA VARGAS

I've never heard my father cry. In fact, I wasn't sure he was capable of crying. What do I do? How do I take care of someone who has always taken care of me? Whenever I fall and scrape my knee, he helps me up, kisses me on the head, and holds me until the pain stops and everything is okay again. How do I return the favor?

2.

One day, when I'm in eighth grade, my father announces that he is going to buy my mom and me a house. He's been saying he's wanted to for years; but somehow, in this moment, I know he is serious.

As I've grown older, I've started to observe that none of my friends' families live in apartments, only houses—many of them gigantic. So having a house of my very own sounds better than living at Disney World. My mom and I went to a showing of a tiny two-bedroom ranch last year, and I saw tears in her eyes as she told me on the drive home it wasn't going to work out. I've heard her exasperated sighs while balancing her checkbook and paying the monthly rent. Most of my friends have two parents who work, so I know saving money must be hard for my mom. But ever since I heard that my boyfriend, Parker, allegedly referred to the two-bedroom apartment I share with my mom as a "shit shack" behind my back in the lunchroom, I've grown self-conscious about where I live and wish for a house even half as nice as my friends' homes.

I excitedly tell my mom about my dad's plan, and her eyes shift to the floor as she says, "Okay." I wrinkle my nose, irritated that she doesn't mirror my excitement.

"Just don't get your hopes up, sweetie," she says. "Buying a house is a big deal." It's clear she doesn't believe it will happen.

I believe it, though. Every Saturday morning, my dad and I eat our big breakfast, red pens in hand, as we scan the real estate

9

section of the newspaper, looking at ads for available properties in Natick, the town where my mom and I live. We drive around town, sometimes just ogling the outsides of on-the-market houses, sometimes stopping in for an open house. My eyes are drawn like magnets to For Sale signs on front lawns. It becomes a routine for us, another fun way of spending time together.

We see house after house after house, and after many months, I feel exhausted by the ongoing disappointment of not moving forward with any offers. I'm starting to understand why my mom didn't believe my father's plan would come to fruition. We see one house in West Natick with a finished basement (a house with a place I can hang out with my friends is high up on my wish list), hardwood floors (though I don't understand what all the fuss is about), and a decent-sized yard. I'm in love.

"Thanks, I don't think this is the house for us, though." My dad shakes the Realtor's hand on our way out.

Angry tears rush down my face the second I'm out of the Realtor's line of vision. What's wrong with the house? It's perfect! It's small, so it can't be too expensive, right?

As I whip open the car door, I tell my dad that I'm losing hope, that I wish he never promised us this stupid house because I feel like that dream is being crushed, that it will never happen, that I was totally content in the apartment with my mom until he swooped in and tried to save us from a life that didn't need saving.

Even midmeltdown, I know I sound ridiculous. I'm crying like a little brat to a father about to spend hundreds of thousands of dollars on his daughter and ex-wife, and the only benefit he will reap is seeing me slightly happier than I already am.

He waits until he knows I've gotten it all out, then calmly speaks. "Erika, the Realtor told me there's an issue with the water pipes," he says, handing me his blue plaid handkerchief to wipe my nose. "It would be too much extra work to repair."

After a few minutes of pouting, I apologize.

About a year later, we find The House. It is perfect. It's a raised ranch on a cul-de-sac. It has a pink front door and a pink mailbox, and I hate pink, but I don't even care because this house is everything. There are three bedrooms, and the tiniest room has a full-sized wall print of a waterfall; that will be the computer room. The downstairs is finished and perfect for having lots of friends over, something I don't do often; ever since the "shit shack" comment, I've been hiding my home from everyone other than my best friend, Angela. The downstairs bathroom features an accent painting of green ivy against the stark white walls. There's a huge porch, and a quarter-acre yard lined with lush pine trees.

And—best of all—we can get a dog! Our apartment complex is not pet-friendly, so it's always been out of the question. But now it's only a matter of months until a tiny, little puppy can be ours.

Now I understand patience. This is why he said no to so many other houses. Unlike me, he didn't see something shiny and say "Mine mine mine!" Rather, he took a breath, said "No, thank you," and walked away with the grace and patience of a man who trusts his spot-on judgment.

He meets with his mortgage people and closes on the house while I am at school. I run to the bathroom halfway through my history class to call him and ask how it went, muffling my excited scream with my palms.

My mom hasn't even seen it yet! She trusts us to choose a home that we can all love, even though my dad, of course, won't be living there with us. Thank goodness I don't have any homework because I spend all night on the computer designing a replica of the house for her in *The Sims* computer game so I can show her all of the details. This feeling is euphoric. I have never ever been so grateful.

On a beautiful spring Saturday, my mom and I move in. Natural light flows through the windows, illuminating the living room like it's a palace—*our* palace. My house becomes the place my friends hang out on weekends. I proudly show it off to my new boyfriend, and we spend summer nights watching movies on the downstairs couch. I learn what it is like to love a dog, an Australian shepherd mix we name Freckles. I (begrudgingly) learn how to mow the lawn. Angela sleeps over almost every other weekend, and we don't worry whether our giggles will wake up my mom because we are all the way downstairs and she is all the way upstairs. Angela and I tan our skin on my back deck, run through the sprinkler in the yard, and wash my mom's minivan in the driveway on hot summer days. We trim each other's bangs in the tiny half bathroom off my bedroom. I watch midnight lightning storms through the bay window overlooking the front yard. My mom, dad, and I spend Christmas morning in the bright, cozy living room.

The house makes my high school years *that much more* incredible. And I have my father to thank for it. He's shown me that hard work pays off. He left his five siblings and his mother behind in Peru to come to Boston at age twenty-one, hoping to achieve the American dream. I want to be like my dad. I want to save money, invest it, be patient when I am making big purchases, provide for my family, and be independent and fancy, but frugal. This home represents so much to me, and I won't ever let it go.

3.

Since middle school, I've received a weekly allowance of $20 from my dad, much to my mom's discontent. She's more of a "you should work for your money" type of gal, and my dad is more of a "show your love with Benjamins" (more like Jacksons, technically) type of guy. Having worked as hard as he has to earn his wealth, he wants to share it with those he loves, regularly sending money to his siblings in Peru as well. My mom knows it will cause a fight if she tells him to stop giving me money; plus my dad is stubborn, so he would probably just keep doing it anyway. And being a sixteen-year-old with a group of adventurous friends, I'm certainly not going to advocate for a lower allowance.

As I've grown older, my time with my father has looked different—instead of watching Saturday morning cartoons, he teaches me how to drive a stick shift in a vacant school parking lot, remaining patient when the day comes for me to take the car on the main roads and I stall at intersections, panicking about how to get back in gear. When we've both reached our limit for the day, we move on to job hunting. He grew up working from a young age, often with little to no pay, and wants to instill a strong work ethic in me. Driving around looking for Now Hiring signs in storefront windows is our new favorite hobby, reminiscent of the days we used to scan the roadside for For Sale signs in the front yards of houses. These little road trips also help drive our conversation, which seems more limited as I've gotten older. I'm certainly not gabbing to him about my boyfriend (although he finds out about him when he sees me kiss him on the lips after school, much to my embarrassment, and demands that I let him take us to lunch the next day, which fortunately is only mildly awkward) or how I'm starting to be curious about drinking.

After a few unsuccessful "Are you hiring?" drop-ins to stores around neighboring towns, I find an adorable little bakery in Wellesley and give it one last-ditch effort. They're hiring; in fact, they pretty much hire me on the spot.

I run back to the car where my dad is waiting and open the door, shrieking, "I got the job! Well, kind of . . . I have to fill out this paperwork and bring it back, but they basically said I have it and can start as soon as possible! They want me Saturday and Sunday mornings, and the pay is amazing, and I get my license soon, so you or Mom won't have to drive me!" I give him a massive hug; he smiles and tells me he is *so* proud of me and he knew it would work out. He's a great actor, though. The sorrow behind his smile is palpable once my excitement dies down, and he's quieter than usual on our drive home.

Within weeks, I stop sleeping over his house. My Fridays become about going to the movie theater with friends or getting a good night's sleep before an early Saturday morning at the bakery. My father and I still have the occasional Friday afternoon mall trip and get lunch some Saturdays after my shift, but otherwise, our time together becomes limited—our grocery trips, drives around town, and giant Saturday morning breakfasts become a thing of the past.

After a few weeks of work, I tell my father I don't want an allowance anymore and thank him for the years he's provided me with one. My pay rate at the bakery is great; plus I get excellent tips from the wealthy croissant-eating, latte-consuming patrons of Wellesley Hills. I can no longer, in good conscience, accept the weekly money from my father. I feel proud, mature, and happy with my decision. The corners of his mouth turn upward as he says, "Okay." But the moment his smile fades, I feel his energy shift the same as it did the day I got the job—there's a sadness in his eyes, like he's lost something.

4.

I wake up with a low-grade fever but have to head to my high school to take the SAT IIs. I've been studying my butt off for the chemistry subject test, and I feel confident.

On the way to the test, my mom's phone rings. I can tell by her voice that something is wrong, and I implore her to tell me what the call was about.

"We'll talk about it after your exam, honey. Go ace it!"

It was a nice try, but I push and push. I am crawling out of my skin with curiosity and worry.

She concedes, gently places her hand on mine, and explains to me that my dad is in the intensive care unit at the hospital. He was rushed to the ER last night, underwent emergency gallbladder surgery, and experienced some complications. I burst into tears. I don't really understand what the surgery entailed; all I know is my father is sick in a hospital bed while I have a stupid exam.

I rush through the multiple-choice questions and go straight to the hospital. Upon entering the building, I am overwhelmed by the intense smell of hand sanitizer and sickness. Everything is blurry, and I can't tell if it's because of my fear or my fever. A nurse in blue scrubs assesses my symptoms and leads me to my father's room. "Wear this," she says, handing me a surgical mask. "You're sick. You'll infect him."

Tears rush down my face as soon as I see him. Because of my fever, I'm not allowed to even squeeze his hand. I'm afraid to even speak. I don't trust this flimsy mask. My once-strong daddy is helpless. He's barely conscious, almost motionless, attached to tubes and machines. The man who climbs towers despite his fear of heights cannot even lift himself up.

DURING: PART I

5.

Within a few months of my new job starting, our Friday glory days gradually ending, and his gallbladder surgery, my father's close friend John MacIsaac passes away. My dad is sixty, and his friend was in his eighties. My father, in addition to driving for Exxon, has a number of odd jobs near the properties he owns in West Roxbury, where John MacIsaac lived. He spends many a weekday morning landscaping, which is how he met his buddy John MacIsaac. John MacIsaac has one of those names that you can't say just part of—it's a package deal. Just "John" would sound too weird, too disrespectful. He was always Mr. MacIsaac or John MacIsaac. He was a war veteran who gave me his hat from the army and who always invited us in for tea, handing me a wrapped strawberry candy from the antique bowl forever on his entryway table. His apartment had the stale smell of an old man's living quarters—a musty combination of dust, licorice, and Irish Spring soap. We both loved him dearly, and his death leads to an endless mourning period in my father's life.

More things begin to change. My father retires from his job. Even without having all the details, I know that age sixty is earlier than most people retire, particularly someone like my father, who loves his job and is the hardest-working person I know. Now he spends all day at home; when I call, I can always hear the murmur of his television in the background, the sports announcer's excitable tone in stark contrast to my father's, which

21

has become increasingly more monotonous. One day, he calls me, asking if my boyfriend and I can go grocery shopping for him. My father has never asked me—or anyone else probably—for a favor his entire life. He is too proud. I start helping him with grown-up errands that I don't even do for myself yet: depositing checks, paying bills, picking up stamps from the post office. On our car rides, the radio does much of the talking; my father sits in the passenger seat beside me, staring out the window, only speaking to instruct me where to turn.

For most of my junior year of high school, I know something is wrong and begin to recognize that he seems depressed. I hope and assume it will pass, that he will get help, that his depression will lift and he will emerge as himself again—like the spring sun through the clouds after a dark, dreary winter.

But the depression doesn't lift. A year later, he sells his town house to move into a tiny lifeless condo in Natick, just a little over a mile from my house. The smaller sadder apartment matches my smaller sadder father. He's grown so thin over the past year that I can't imagine him packing and lifting and sorting all on his own. I rally help from my best guy friend, Brendan. Moving day arrives, and we're there with bells on, laughing as we carry box after box until I notice my father's hands are shaking. I furrow my brow and quickly try to think of other things, like how to arrange his furniture and what we might order for lunch. Brendan turns to me, his hand on my shoulder as he calmly, supportively whispers, "I think I know why he's shaking . . . early signs of Parkinson's."

I don't give it another thought—he's arrogant, he's only eighteen, he knows nothing. Just because his grandfather had the disease doesn't mean he can go around diagnosing people. His grandfather was well into his eighties while my father is only sixty. Impossible. *Since when is he an expert?* I think to myself, helping my father lift a box labeled "Fragile."

6.

Sweet, meaningful moments with my father grow fewer and farther between. Some days, he invites me to get lunch with him; and we laugh about old memories, like summers at Canobie Lake Park or the nights we fell asleep playing Nintendo. But most days, he sits in silence and blankly stares at the television while I try to make conversation. As his depression worsens, my mood begins to parallel his. I feel hopeless, worried, and scared about what is happening and what could happen; and I wonder if things will ever be the same.

Following a gut-wrenching breakup last year, I'd dabbled in some disordered eating behaviors: trying to make myself throw up after small binges on food I had deemed "unhealthy," restricting myself of calories so I could watch the number on the scale—and myself—grow smaller and smaller. It started as a little weight-loss experiment with a friend that we intended to be temporary. Julia and I would stand guard for each other as we took turns kneeling in the high school bathroom stalls, shoving our fingers down our throats to no avail. We attempted diets that we found in pro-anorexia forums online, encouraging a specific alternating calorie intake each day to "trick" our metabolisms. We wrote each other whimsical notes, joking about the times we chewed and savored our favorite candy, only to spit it out into a napkin before swallowing in an attempt to avoid the calories turning to fat on our teenage bodies. Within weeks, Julia developed full-blown anorexia and successfully began purging whatever she ate. This scared the shit out of me, so I stopped everything; her spiral served as my wake-up call. I swallowed fear and guilt and scribbled notes begging her to stop, slipping them into her hand as we passed each other in the hallway between classes.

Even after I break free, the restrictive eating and attempted purge behaviors often resurface when I'm upset, which, come senior year, is much of the time. Between the change in my dad's mood, the increased stress of keeping up with working a few weekday afternoons and weekend mornings at the bakery, taking three Advanced Placement classes, attending meetings for National Honor Society and Peer Leaders, running lights for the school play, and applying to colleges, I feel overwhelmed and deeply sad most days.

Generally, my mom is one of my main supports. We call ourselves the Vargas Girls; as an only child and a single mom, our bond is unshakeable. In so many ways, we're different—she prefers the "natural, no makeup, quick comb through her hair, casual T-shirt, jeans, and sneakers" look, whereas I cover my acne-prone skin with COVERGIRL foundation, wear black dress pants and frilly shirts, and wake up early to run a straightener though my hair each day. She's a die-hard Patriots football fan, whereas I'm not 100 percent sure what a "down" is. But she often says, "Erika got José's looks and my personality!"—and this is spot-on. Both of us can talk to anyone who will listen, constantly eager to move the thoughts out of our brains and through our lips as quickly as possible, and we're fluent in sarcasm. She is unapologetically herself, and this gives me permission to be the same. She is always showing up for the people she loves, especially me. In elementary school, she volunteered at the last minute to be my Girl Scout troop leader after the original mom backed out. She sits in the front row for all of my school plays (even when I'm just in the chorus) and leaves work early to attend my tennis matches (even though I'm sidelined for most of them, only playing when the varsity girls finish). She let me cry in her arms when our first bunny, Lopsy, died in his sleep; and I'd collapsed into her soft, warm body after my first big breakup.

During times of high stress, though, we both struggle to stay calm and levelheaded. It is clear I'm my mother's daughter—short-fused, easily overwhelmed. Her emotions are quickly triggered when I'm upset, and this often comes out as frustration and invalidation versus compassion. It's like she just wants to *fix* how I'm feeling by telling me I *shouldn't* feel that way.

"Erika, you're always so stressed. You need to learn to let it roll and to not let things get to you so much," she'll say.

"Oh, okay, yes, because that's *so easy* to do," I'll retort.

My mom will huff as she says, "You know, Erika, I guess I never say anything right! I'm on *your* side here, but you *never* want to talk about anything!"

My teenage attitude then rears its ugly head through eye rolls and more snide remarks, and my mom loses her temper, which only further fuels the beast within me. What could be easily brushed off instead turns into battles—doors slamming and wails emerging from our respective bedrooms. We are also both incredibly sensitive, so after our arguments, we always end up apologizing, our cheeks stained with teardrops. But until the inevitable instances of "I love you, I'm so sorry" come, I use my terrible moods as a weapon against her, a way to punish her by depriving myself, even if she never knows about it. I journal about our arguments, angrily typing, "Anyway, at least I don't have an appetite now!" and "Hey, thanks for making me not want ice cream anymore!"—as if I am ever the optimist, able to find the silver lining in each crushing episode.

When my emotions peak to a point that feels beyond my control and I feel like I can't breathe or function or calm myself down, I sometimes take tweezers to my wrist, scratching the skin to a raw shade of pink. I'm too scared to use anything sharper. I've always been squeamish, and I am afraid to bleed too much for fear I will pass out. I am diligent in hiding this from my mom, suspecting she would be angry with me if she discovered I am intentionally harming myself. Self-harm is my own little secret, my own provocative "Fuck you" to everyone and everything when I am in a negative headspace.

The only person with whom I discuss my own spiraling mood is Brendan. Despite initially feeling annoyed that he tried to diagnose my father, the fact that he saw my dad in his new weakened state makes him closer to the situation than anyone else in my life besides my mom. We've known each other since we were twelve, and he has some strong bullshit radar—the kind of annoyingly helpful person who calls you out when you're trying to feign happiness. In the fall of senior year, we spend a lot of time driving around town, procrastinating on our AP Physics homework; and I don't know how, but he sees right through me when I'm trying to pretend I'm fine.

Talking about it with only one person is great. The less I talk about it, the less I'll think about it . . . right? Plus I don't want to burden people. Julia is a grade below me and not part of my main friend group, and typically, I feel safest with her when it comes to personal stuff. I trust her with anything; she listens without breaking eye contact, empathizes, and keeps secrets—the kind of friend who'd bury a body with you, no questions asked besides "Are you okay?" But she is deep in her eating disorder; she has enough to worry about without holding my shit too.

When my dad and I pick up Angela for one of our occasional lunch outings, I watch her eyes widen as she opens the car door and sees a much smaller, much paler version of the man she has known since we were kids. My father treats us to a meal at TGI Fridays like he used to when we were young; he picks at his chicken wings while Angela and I share nachos and speak in mostly inside jokes.

When he drops us off at her house after lunch, she plops down next to me on the couch in her den and places her hand on my forearm.

"Girl," she says gently, "is everything okay with your dad?"

Though I appreciate her concern, I'm caught off guard; she isn't usually this direct. She and I have been inseparable since middle school, and she's become something of a second daughter to him. I feel obligated to protect his image as a strong, confident, cheerful man; but evidence to the contrary is right in front of us. I casually mention that he's been having a tough time and seems depressed. She hugs me, and it is understood that I can bring it up again if needed.

I am lucky to have a hilarious and fun group of friends—Angela, Cassie, Alex, Laura, Tessa, Seth, Mason, Colin, and Kyle—with a deep mutual love for one another. We spend weekends piled on the futon in Kyle's basement to watch Will Ferrell movies or squish together on the old, but comfortable couches in the downstairs of my house to play board games. Though we usually hang as a group, one of my favorite activities is going for long one-on-one drives; the end goal is a burrito from Anna's Taqueria in Brookline, and the forty-minute commute allows for great conversations. During some of these drives, I share with a select few that my dad has gone through some mood changes but leave it at that. I love my friends, but my god, can we be judgmental of one another. I've witnessed—and participated in—the vent sessions about "how *sensitive* she was!" or "what a *weird* thing he said!" I'm afraid if I share too much about what's happening with my dad (and, subsequently, with me), they'll think I'm being too dramatic. I don't want to be a downer.

I go through the motions of preparing my college essay and working my ass off to get the straight A's I know will make my dad (and me) happy. But at the end of the day, as I try to slip off into sleep, my mind can't help but try and process what is happening to my father. I toss and turn, imagining what I could say, what I *should* say, questioning what my role is as his daughter. I turn my wandering mind into a nightly prayer ritual. I'm not particularly religious, but something about this feels grounding, a way to reflect on the day and my life from a zoomed-out lens. Every night, I pray my dad will get better. I pray his pain will end and he will regain the happiness and sense of humor he has lost. I pray things will go back to how they were before depression crept into his brain. I thank God for happy moments with my dad and his intermittent smiles, for keeping my family safe, for my mom and my friends and my dog; and I say "Amen."

I press repeat on "Wonderful" by Everclear over and over because the lyrics about missing your old life send me into a flood of cathartic tears, making me feel the tiniest bit more at peace—at least for the night. I write and I write and I write; my emotions spill out into words, and this is the outlet that keeps me afloat on the hardest days.

7.

My parents never worked out a solid system for exchanging money. As a child, my mom often asked me to get the child support check from my dad during our time together; and when I did, my dad would sneer, shaking his head as he scribbled the numbers dictated by their divorce agreement. I never understood why this caused tension or why I was involved at all. I hated being their liaison. Their divorce never bothered me since I had no memory of them as a couple, and they were all smiles when we'd get together for holidays. But I learned at a young age that money brings out a different side of people.

This only intensified once we moved into the house as not only did my dad already owe my mom child support, but my mom also began to then owe him monthly rent. There is also a family cell phone plan bill somewhere in the mix. The ideal exchange would involve one check in which the child support due to Mom is subtracted from the rent and phone bill check written to Dad, but for some reason, this doesn't happen even when it is suggested by one to the other over and over. I remain in the middle, communicating to each parent what is due and when, and I never stop hating this role.

One month, my father turns to threats; after my mom deducts the child support he has failed to pay from her monthly rent payment to him, he leaves her a voicemail, grumbling, "Thanks for not paying the full rent . . . really appreciate that . . . You'll be sorry." As if in disbelief, we play the message again; the check exchange has always been tense, but not like this. After dinner, I flip through my vocab flashcards in a futile attempt to study for tomorrow's English quiz, my mind replaying the voicemail, wondering what he meant.

My father's mood continues its downward spiral; and his body grows thinner, weaker, sicker. The handwriting on his checks becomes smaller and more wobbly. He eventually asks me to write the checks for him, but even his signature becomes illegible. I notice him wince in defeat with each attempted signing of his name, and I am quick to act as if I didn't see it. I don't want to elicit more shame than what I can see he already feels. Acknowledgment, especially from his own daughter, would feel so shameful to him. My head spins with questions about what is happening: How much—or how little—is he eating? Is his blood sugar low? Is that why he's shaking? But how do you ask someone why they're seemingly degenerating? My psychology class certainly has not prepared me for this.

I call him after school one day to ask if he wants to get lunch tomorrow. I have a half day, and it's been a while since we've spent time together.

"I have a doctor's appointment tomorrow," he says. "How about Wednesday instead?"

Relief washes over me. This is the first I've heard that he is seeing a professional. The doctor has to address the weight loss, the shaking, the obvious desolation . . . right?

"Erika?"

His voice snaps me back to the present moment.

"Sorry, I got distracted . . . I have a huge calc test Thursday, so I should study Wednesday. Another time soon, though, okay?"

Later in the week, my father calls the landline after I miss his call to my cell. By the time I pick up the downstairs phone, my mom has already answered upstairs. So unbeknownst to them, I hear the first part of their conversation.

"How was the doctor, Tuco?" She's always called him by his nickname. "Erika mentioned you had an appointment scheduled the other day, right?"

"Nancy, I . . . I don't know what's going on." His voice breaks. "I'm depressed, my best friend has died, I'm losing Erika, I'm losing my mind . . ."

"I know things have been hard, Tuco," my mom empathizes. "Did the doctor say what he thinks it is?"

He continues, "I don't know. I just feel so . . . depressed. I feel nervous to drive. I have headaches, and the doctor doesn't know what's causing them. I'm just . . . I'm going to sell everything and give it to you two." He begins to cry. This is the first time I've heard him cry since his mother died six years ago. His candor and gentleness toward my mom catches me off guard; he'd seemed so angry in that recent voicemail.

"Do you think you should see another doctor? Maybe it'd help to get some more answers, you know?" My mom is so gentle. He continues to weep. "Tuco, I don't think Erika should talk to you when you're like this," she says calmly.

My mom has always tried to protect me; she cares for him, but I know she fears that hearing my father in this fragile state will scare and upset me. She's right, but I don't think she realizes this has become somewhat of a new normal; he is always sad, weak, vulnerable around me now—not the dad I once knew. Their conversation is too much for me to bear, so I gently, quietly hang up the phone. I wait for my mom to call down for me to pick up the phone, but she doesn't. Instead, within a few minutes, she explains that she just spoke with him, that he isn't feeling well, and that she offered to bring him something to eat. So we do.

A few weeks pass without much change; my dad and I talk about every other day, and I bring him to Roche Bros. to pick up groceries every so often. I return home from school one day, toss my backpack on the floor of the computer room, and begin my afternoon ritual of signing on to Instant Messenger and logging in to my email. My inbox alerts me that I have a new message from my father that was sent yesterday—he hasn't emailed me in years.

Erika, I'm afraid I might croak.

Do not worry about me, my love, I will be okay.

I don't want to leave you.

The juxtaposition of these seemingly contradictory statements is very confusing. I don't know how to make sense of the situation. Before I know it, my fingers are click-clacking on the keyboard, typing "I hope you are okay, Daddy"—the name reminiscent of our glory days that I can't bring myself to stop calling him, no matter how old I am. "I don't want you to leave me either, I love you." Then as if to escape the messenger, I immediately log out of my email and lie on the floor of my bedroom with my physics textbook, hoping the complexity of the lab report I have to write will distract me from thinking of the words "I don't want to leave you."

Around 5:45 p.m., I hear the garage door open. Then a knock on my bedroom door.

"Hi, honey. How's your homework?"

"Not too bad, just some calc left. How was your day?"

"Interesting," my mom says as she sits on my bed and pats the spot next to her. I sit by her side. "Daddy actually called me a bunch at work, and I want to tell you what's going on so you aren't caught off guard if you hear from him." My abdomen tenses.

"He's in the hospital, and he's okay now. They found six bleeding ulcers in his stomach, which were actually pretty easy to treat."

I gulp, my eyes stinging as I ask, "So he's definitely okay?"

"Yes," my mom answers. "Ulcers are a horrible thing to go through, but he'll recover. He also had an MRI and an EKG to check some other things, and he said they came back normal. We'll visit him tomorrow, okay?"

I tell her about the emails, and her soft green eyes widen in response.

"Oh, honey, I wish he hadn't said those things. It's all going to be fine, okay?"

I nod my head yes, but I don't believe her—how could I?

Every time I check my email, I find myself short of breath, fearing that more daunting messages might appear in my inbox.

After he's discharged from the hospital, my dad doesn't call me for a few days, and it quickly becomes clear that it is now my responsibility to initiate contact. Our calls become shorter, his answers to my questions clipped. I try to make small talk, but it's becoming harder. On an evening call, when I ask what he did today, his tone instantly changes from sadness and apathy to a biting anger.

"I couldn't do *anything*, Erika. I had no one. You're never around to help me."

The only time I've heard him speak this way was in the message he left my mother: "You'll be sorry . . ."

Surprised by his tone, I stumble over my words, finally spitting out, "Daddy . . . I had school today and then work. I got home at, like, seven and had to do homework, which is what I'm doing now. But I took a break to call y—"

He cuts me off with a "pfft," pauses, and says, "Sometimes I'd rather be dead."

Hearing those words knocks the wind out of me. How can I be so terrible that I make my father want to *die*? What happened to the sentiment from last week's emails—fear of leaving me, fear of death . . . but now finding some type of comfort in it?

My mom hears me crying, so I tell her what he said. She immediately calls him and firmly tells him he cannot speak to me and guilt me that way—he's always encouraged me to work hard at school and my job, which is what I'm doing. She reminds him that she has offered to help him when he needs it, but he doesn't reach out.

She shakes her head as he replies. With a calm firmness in her voice, I hear her say, "Okay, Tuco, I'm ending this conversation." Then she places the phone on the receiver with an exasperated sigh.

"What happened? What did he say?" I ask, sniffling.

"Well . . ." My mom closes her eyes for a few seconds, seemingly deciding whether to share. "He said I'm cold-blooded and have no compassion. He thinks I'm making you work so much . . . I don't know where he gets this or what's going on with him. Last time we talked, things felt civil . . ." Tears fill her eyes, and we sit on her bed, speechless.

His moods change rapidly. The next day, he sends me an apologetic email. Whether this acknowledgment is genuine or in response to the call from my mom, it doesn't matter—it feels good to not be crying. Maybe now things will be okay.

And for a time, they are okay. But whenever it's check time, the tension returns. On the first of the following month, since I'm going to visit him anyway, my mom asks me to bring him his mail, which occasionally comes to us since the house is in his name. She asks me to please get the child support from him while I'm at it.

Our visit starts out nicely; we sip Dunkin' Donuts coffees and share a glazed donut while watching *Seinfeld* reruns. But as soon as I ask him for the check, his eyebrows fold together; and he angrily accuses me of only coming by to get the money, telling me that's all I ever do. He is relentless as he calls me *"Spoiled!"* *"Selfish!"* *"Unappreciative!"* *"Just like your mother!"* I leave in tears and immediately call my mom, screaming, "I will *never* be in the middle of this again! *Never!*" Ever since he told me I'm never around to help him, getting him to see that I love him and care for him is hard enough; there is no room for error. Even through the phone, I can feel my mother's face fall. She apologizes and never puts me in that position again.

8.

As a hardworking student, I've always been anxious about school, but now my anxiety is rapidly developing into a monster that makes me fear all interactions with my dad. I call every two or three days; but each time, he barks at me, saying that I "never" call. When I visit, he says I "don't care enough" to see him, that I "don't like" him. If I so much as hint at my mother's existence, he tells me "she can go to hell."

Sometimes I cry into my mom's arms on the couch, trying to fight the impending visit, telling her I know I'm just walking into the lion's den.

In an effort to give me perspective, my mom asks me to consider how I would feel if *something happened* and I hadn't called or seen him or if we ended our last conversation on bad terms. It's a nice attempt, but the sentiment really messes with my head. I become afraid of ending things with anyone on anything less than positive terms. My guilt grows and grows as I live in constant fear that if I express my feelings, if I tell someone I am hurt, if I am fighting with someone and it is left unresolved, they will die; and it will be on my conscience that during our last conversation, there was conflict. It's a principle that can be helpful. I truly do see the merit—*live each day like it's your last! Don't sweat the small stuff!* But what happens when that gets in the way of living genuinely? What happens when the person is hurting you, crushing your spirit? Do you just smile and act like everything is fine? What do you do with the burgeoning resentment resulting from all that suppression?

I try this approach, but sometimes it's impossible; my adolescent brain vibrates with pain in response to his accusations, and I hang up the phone or walk out of his apartment after forcing an angry, ungenuine "I have to go now, I love you" out of my mouth. I question how depression can alter his sense of reality so deeply. Does he really think I don't call? Can depression make someone so hostile, so cruel?

No matter how warranted or how long I wait, apologies from my dad never come. Even as a child, when we fought, we rarely discussed it after and instead just resumed normalcy until it felt genuine. Now a few hours after blowout conversations during which I cry so hard I can barely see, he will call and ask if I want to get coffee, and we will. Then everything will pass and be fine—until the next time. Sometimes we fight, and the next day, I get a call: "I left something outside for you," and I come home to find a carton of fresh strawberries or a pack of yogurt or an iced coffee on my front steps. There is no note with an apology, but I come to understand that these small gifts are his way of making amends. It is his way of saying "I love you. I'm sorry. I still want a relationship, and I don't understand what is happening" when he cannot find the proper words.

9.

As a truck driver, my dad always had to have a special license since he operated gigantic eighteen-wheelers full of gasoline. He is aware and patient and remains calm while driving. I've always felt safe with him.

As his body and mind change, so does his driving. He asks me to drive when we go on errands because he feels a bit shaky behind the wheel. Now the man who always seemed to possess a natural compass gets lost and needs directions often.

I'm driving home from school on a chilly November afternoon, and I pull onto my street. A car veers onto my side of the road, and I honk and quickly swerve, my seat belt catching me as I catch my breath. I look up and see my father in the driver's seat. He drives away.

As soon as I step into my house, I call him, concerned. "Was that you?"

"Oh, Erika . . . Did I just almost hit you? Was that *you?*" He pauses, not needing an answer; he already knows it was me. "I don't know how this has happened to me, Erika," he cries helplessly.

I don't know exactly *what* has happened, and it seems he doesn't either.

"I'm so sorry," he continues. "I'm seeing the doctor again soon."

"It's okay, Daddy. I'm worried about you," I offer, hoping this gentle acknowledgment of my concern doesn't feel too shaming. "Why were you on my street anyway? You know I'm just getting out of school."

"I was just hoping for a glimpse of you."

These words echo in my mind.

As my father faces more driving difficulties, I am driving more than ever, using it as a coping skill whenever I need to clear my head, which is often. I spend nights driving around town, blaring music, sobbing ugly tears as I wonder how my father, my mood, my life—everything—changed so goddamn quickly.

10.

The pit of guilt in my stomach following our most recent interaction is impossible to shake. It's clear that he misses me, so I make a commitment to myself to spend more time with him, even as his mood and treatment of me continue to be erratic. I pick him up for a breakfast date one morning during one of my free periods from school; we nibble our omelets without much conversation.

"Have you trimmed the bushes next to the driveway?" he grumbles, wiping a flake of egg from his lip.

"No," I confess. "I've had a lot going on."

"Well, then I guess I'll have to hire a landscaper. More money out of my pocket!" He stabs his fork into a home fry.

"Daddy . . . I'm only seventeen. I have school and work and play rehearsal and—"

"Erika, I had an infection and could have died a few weeks ago, and you can't even keep up with the house! Maybe I should sell it . . ."

I know this is an empty threat; he's just angry. Before I can craft a response, a busser asks if we're done with our meals. I nod as my dad requests the check, and we exit silently, my father leaving a $20 bill on the table.

After dropping him at his apartment, I call my mom at work.

"Expense Payables, this is Nancy." The familiarity of her voice is so comforting and activates the tears I've been holding back.

"Hi, Mom." My voice quivers. "He's just . . . He's just *so sick* looking, so old and shaky. And he's just *angry*, like I'm doing something wrong just by sitting there, just by existing. Today was hard, like . . . I want to spend time with him because he looks like he could die any second, and I know he's sad, but . . ." I take a breath, realizing I haven't for a minute. "I don't get it. I just don't like being around him, and now I somehow have to get through school . . ."

My mom sighs and lowers her voice. "I wish we knew more about what's going on with his health, honey. I'll talk to him and try to get more information."

I tell her "okay," but I don't feel confident she will get very far. Ever since she set a limit with him about how he was speaking to me a few weeks ago, his anger toward her has cemented.

That evening, me by her side, listening, she calls him to check in; he answers the phone. "What do you want?"

"I'm just calling because we haven't spoken in a while, and I wanted to see how you've been feeling . . ."

"Yep," he barks. The tension is palpable.

After a few seconds, he breaks the silence. "I'm sick, Nancy, and all you care about is my money . . . Even when you visited me in the hospital, you wished me dead! You're disgusting, and you don't want Erika to see me, her sick father!"

My mom waves me away, not wanting me to hear anything else he says. In my room, I stare at the ceiling above my bed, trying to make sense of what he just said. My mother has never wished him dead. When we visited him in the hospital, he was kind to her, thanking her for coming.

I know it must be hard for my mom—they're divorced; she doesn't have to help, and she's not obligated to check in on him. In a way, though, there is an odd sense of comfort in hearing him speak to her this way; it makes me realize I'm not the only one bearing the brunt of it.

Just weeks ago, he was reaching out to her to share medical updates. If he stops communicating with her, I fear I'll never get an understanding about what's going on. He complains of headaches from time to time and is obviously depressed, but otherwise, he just keeps referring to himself as "sick."

After they hang up, my mother opens my door and sits beside me, hugging me tightly. "I just can't forgive him for the way he's treated you, honey. I know he talks to you just as badly, if not worse. He's crushing your spirit. I can see it. I know I've been pushing you to keep a relationship, but part of me wonders if it'd be easier for both of us to take some space . . . I know he's sick in some way, but he doesn't have to be so *nasty*. I've seen him act like this before . . . This is how he was during our divorce, and it was awful."

She doesn't see it, but I roll my eyes at her referencing her past marriage to him; it's not the same. It's normal for parents to fight, but he's my sweet, silly father who has always spoiled me with love. I don't have it in me to say anything, though. I can't handle conflict with both of my parents at once. The more my mom has witnessed the shift in my father's personality and treatment of me, the more she's been the one keeping me grounded, which has meant fewer door slams and tearful arguments between us.

We sit and cry and hug and think. As it turns out, the ever-sensitive Vargas Girls are not ready to write him out of our lives. It would have to take something really, really big for it to come to that. Instead, it's death by a thousand cuts—not one major incident, but still enough shallow pain to constantly bleed.

11.

At school, college applications are all anyone talks about: Where are you applying? What was your SAT score? Have you visited the school? What's your safety? What's your reach? When do you think you'll hear back? I've applied to four schools: Brandeis, Fairfield, Sacred Heart, and, of course, Boston College. When I was twelve years old, for a short time, my father lived in West Roxbury, a Boston neighborhood just a few miles from Chestnut Hill, Massachusetts, where the beautiful BC campus sits. We would drive past it often, and it was love at first sight—for both of us. I don't know much about the school. I just know it's gorgeous; has a proper campus; is close to home, but not in my backyard; and is hard to get into. That's all I need.

Over the summer, I'd briefly dated a Harvard boy whose dad asked me my SAT score and scoffed when I shared it. "For BC? That's a reach." For a public high school, Natick is very competitive; and I want to prove to myself, to my dad (and a little bit to that kid's dad) that I can do this, that I'm good enough for Boston College. Every decision I've made in high school, every extracurricular, every AP class, every late-night project or study session has led up to this point. I apply early action, seal the envelope, and nervously place it in the mail just a few days before the November 1 deadline.

Even with all the strain on our relationship, I see my father's subtle smile, the tiny twinkle in his eye whenever I mention BC.

He's been saving for my college education ever since I was born, and just knowing I've applied to a prestigious school means he can brag about me, which I know is important to him. He didn't go to college, which is why it's so essential to him that I take advantage of the amazing education opportunities the United States, particularly the Northeast, boasts. When he left Peru and hopped on that plane to Boston as a young adult, he never looked back. Once here, he struggled to learn the language, which is hard for me to imagine because his English was fantastic by the time I was old enough to talk. One time, he asked if I'd ever played "shoe horse", and we laughed and laughed, realizing he sometimes translates directly, placing the adjective second. After learning enough English to get by, he decided not to pursue an education and instead began to find success doing odd jobs. Like many immigrants who come from developing countries, he measures his success financially, and he worked long and hard hours to be as successful as possible. He made his money mowing lawns, repairing toilets, and shoveling snow. One day, he lied and told a woman for whom he worked, "Yes, I can paint a shower," with the ulterior motive of meeting my mom, who was the woman's tenant.

My father's first steady American job was driving trucks for Arco, which later became Exxon. One night, when I was ten, he took me for a ride in his Exxon truck, honking the horn while I giggled in the passenger seat.

By the time I started middle school, my father had realized his American dream. He'd learned English, become a US citizen, started a loving—albeit unconventional—family, and achieved financial success. He was a respected employee at Exxon and moved from driving trucks to working in the plant. And he'd invested his money wisely. He owned three condominiums in West Roxbury, a town house in Ashland, and, of course, the house where my mom and I live. It wasn't easy for him, though, and he wants it to be easy for me.

For as long as I can remember, he'd preached about why I should attend business school! Law school! Become a banker! An accountant! An attorney! He is disappointed when I show no interest in business or law school, though he can get behind me wanting to go into advertising; there's good money there. He seems as excited and nervous about college applications as I am.

One night, in mid-December as I'm walking out of my house to go babysit, my mom stops me. She just checked the mail, and there is a big envelope from Boston College with my name on it. Hands shaking, I tear it open (it's a miracle the letter stays intact); and sure enough, I've been offered early admission. We jump up and down, Freckles nervously running laps around our raucous cheers. As we start crying, I realize I am going to be late to babysit; so I hop in the car, still in shock. I had convinced myself I didn't have the qualifications to get in early, so my admission is an instant confidence boost. As I pull out of the driveway, the first thing I do is call my dad.

"Hi, Daddy. I only have a minute because I have to go babysit—"

"Erika, slow down, slow down! Are you okay? I can't understand you."

"Yes, yes, I'm fine! Sorry . . . I'm just calling to tell you I got into BC! I only have a minute to talk, but I had to tell you first!"

"Oh, Erika . . ." He pauses, and I can tell there is a lump in his throat. "You have made me so proud today!"

I will remember this moment forever: Driving up the Mill Street hill as he answers the phone. Blinking back tears as I approach the intersection with Route 135. The butterflies in my stomach as he tells me how proud he is—something I haven't heard from him in so long. I called with the hopes of bringing a ray of light to his day, and it is clear that I have. A year ago, he looked at my straight-A report card; and his only response, with a furrowed brow, was "What happened here?" pointing to the

A– I got in AP English. I know he will spend the night beaming, imagining himself watching me walk across the stage and accept a Boston College diploma in four years. I feel like we did it together; he encouraged the work ethic that helped me gain acceptance to my dream school, and I helped him reach his eighteen-year-long goal of making sure I received the education opportunity he was never afforded. For a moment, me in my little car and him in his little condo, I like to think we both find peace.

12.

During the first two years of high school, Valentine's Day was about boys. I had a boyfriend each of those years and loved dressing in red or pink, expecting a student council–sponsored rose delivered to my desk in homeroom and the overall feeling of love in the air.

Junior year, I was still on the mend from my first big heartbreak, but I was madly in love with my friends. I hosted a singles party in my basement, which had very fitting pink-striped walls. We drank too much soda because most of us weren't into booze yet, played a very platonic game of spin the bottle, and slept alone in our separate houses, our bodies crashing into sugar comas from chocolate chip cookies and candy hearts.

Senior year is a little different.

It's Valentine's Eve, a lazy Sunday featuring an early-morning bakery shift and nothing else. After work, my friend Alex and I decide to run some errands together; and after a quick outfit change and a few spritzes of body spray to mask the sour aroma of stale coffee that follows me after my shifts, I hop in her car. We're trying on clothes in the Target fitting room, chatting like we always do, when she gets a text message inviting her to our friend Kyle's house for a last-minute Valentine's party later that evening. I check my phone, expecting the same invite to appear on my cell phone screen, but it never arrives.

Alex is the perfect person to be with during this type of situation—she has a soothing, sweet, compassionate tone and puts others' feelings before her own, often to a fault. We slowly realize that my lack of invite is no error; and she comforts me, lets me air my confusion, and swears she won't go. I know I've spent less time with my friends lately—my mood's been awful, so I've isolated a bit. And I work the 5:30 a.m. Sunday shift at the bakery, so I'm in bed by 9:00 p.m. on Saturday nights. But I hadn't realized it had gotten to this point. Like a masochist, I ask if we can drive past Kyle's house on the way back home, where we see six of our closest friends' cars paralleled next to his snow-covered front lawn. I keep my feelings together, but the betrayal stings. I encourage her to go, to not worry about me; and she drops me at home, hugging me hard before driving away to join the party.

I walk in my front door, and the tears finally come. My mom greets me with a smile, but her expression quickly changes in response to mine. I pop into my room to connect my phone to the charger, then meet my mom back in the living room to fill her in. We are both confused. I've always prided myself on how great of a relationship I have with my friends, and since I hosted such a fun party last year, it hurts even more that they deliberately excluded me from this day. I fully embrace letting it out, and suddenly, I am overcome with emotion about all the changes this year has brought—my dad's unexplained illness, me overworking myself between the bakery and my new second after-school job at a day care, leaving for college in the fall—when, suddenly, we hear a sound like the rustling of papers coming from my bedroom.

When we enter my room, Freckles stares back at us, stunned. Her eyes widen, and she freezes in her tracks. We've caught her in the act. This morning, I used my employee discount to buy a dozen Valentine's-themed sugar cookies I planned to hand-deliver to each of my friends tomorrow at school. Apparently, I'd left them in a dog-accessible location in my room, and Freckles decided she too wanted some Valentine's Day love. Crumbs decorate her whiskers and lips; she ate every last one. We erupt into laughter. I reassure my mom that chocolate was not an ingredient in the cookies, and we let Freckles run around outside in the snow for an hour until she crashes into the same type of sugar coma I experienced with my friends just one year prior.

I chip away at some homework for a few hours and then sign on to Instant Messenger for a break. High off the comedic relief Freckles offered, I'd underestimated how hurt I still feel; and when I see my friend Colin's screen name on my Buddy List, I feel a pit form in my stomach. I want to leave it, but I just can't. I have been a central part of this group of friends; we never intentionally leave anyone out, and I want to understand.

Me: *Hey*
Colin: *hey*
Me: *how are you*
Colin: *Im ok you?*
Me: *im good*
I cut right to the chase.
Me: *how was kyles?*
Colin: *it was fun.*
Me: *im a little confused about why i wasnt invited?*
Colin: *it was a singles party. like last year. ur not single.*
Me: *what?*
Colin: *arent you getting valentines dinner with richard?*
Me: *yeah but I'm not dating him, we just hang out sometimes.*
Colin: *okay well this was for people who arent with anyone at all*
Now I can tell something is up. It feels very possible that they created a way to specifically exclude only me, given that two of our friends are hooking up with each other and they were both present. I have never not been invited; this feels fishy.

Me: *i just feel like this is a made up reason . . . like, tessa and mason were both there right?*

Colin: *Ok*

Me: *ok? come on colin. this really hurts, i dont get it. just please tell me the truth. why didnt you guys want me there?*

A long pause, then:

Colin: *youve just been kind of annoying some of us*

A short pause, then:

Colin: *youre melodramatic.*

Colin: *you never ask about anyone else*

Colin: *youre boy obsessed, u cant be single*

Colin: *youre annoyingly stressed all the time.*

Colin: *youre so self-centered.*

I can't keep up. I can't process this; the words are coming too fast, rapid-fire. I expected a reason, not a laundry list of my flaws. He continues, now giving specific examples:

Colin: *one time our friend told u she was fighting with her mom and u told her about how your dog bit u.*

I'm obnoxious, always interrupting, changing the subject to be about me, never showing enough compassion for my friends.

He ignores my pleas for him to stop, to converse instead of attack. But my flaws continue to appear next to his screen name, so I sign offline. It is too much to take. Learning the ugly truth about how the people you care about the most really view you feels unbearable. Sure, I have a mysteriously ill father who has become increasingly more verbally aggressive and accusatory, but at least I have my friends—except now I don't. I feel more alone than ever, and I start to wonder why I am even here. It's not just what he said—it's how quickly the words came out. How easily accessible everything was in his mind. I imagine our friends sitting around in Kyle's basement, one-upping one another with stories about what *shitty* and *annoying* thing Erika's done this week. It's no wonder I haven't opened up about what is going on with my dad, with me. This is the exact judgment I'd feared facing.

I need my mom. Even if I didn't want her help, there is absolutely no way I can hide my pain from her; my gasps for air between tears are audible from her bedroom. For the second time today, she holds me and tells me it will all be okay, though I don't believe her.

The next day, I shuffle through the halls at school in a daze. I didn't sleep well, and my eyes are still puffy; no makeup could help with that. My friends are nice to me, which I have a hard time accepting, given that I just found out all the shit they think about me. My guard is up, my skin thick. Julia knows what happened. I'd emailed her the night before once I'd calmed down a bit to vent to someone who I knew would understand. She meets me outside my first-period physics class with a handmade Valentine, temporarily brightening my mood. I am dreading fourth-period psychology as Colin is in the class, and it's going to be awkward as hell when we see each other. For survival, I'll probably just pretend everything is fine. *You're melodramatic.*

First period, second period, third period ends. I walk into psych, and the tension is palpable. We have assigned seats, and Colin and I are seated nowhere near each other, which helps ease the discomfort. When class is almost over, I become one of those rude students who starts packing up a minute before the bell rings, much to the teacher's discontent. I want to beeline it out of here.

Unfortunately, Colin is tall, fast, and closer to the door. He waits for me in the hallway.

"Erika?"

I stop and look at him, awkwardly smile, and take a deep breath, unsure of what to expect.

"Erika . . . ," he says again. "I'm so, so sorry. I don't know what came over me." Tears fill his eyes. It's clear he is being genuine, and it moves me. I hug him. We both try not to cry, and he walks me to my next class.

My friends end up telling me that right after our online chat, Colin emailed everyone except me, with the subject line: "tomorrow is valentine's day." He told them what he had said to me, sending them snippets of the conversation, owning that he was kind of a dick and asking them to be extra nice to me.

I forgive him, but the knowledge that this is how my friends view me isn't something that goes away. I remain guarded, my previously bubbly spirit infected by the labels hurled at me through the internet.

13.

Acceptance letters have arrived from Brandeis, Fairfield, and Sacred Heart. These letters end up in a pile of miscellaneous paperwork in the computer room, unlike the Boston College acceptance letter that hangs in a frame on my bedroom wall. The high of the acceptance, however, is soon blunted by the stress of financial aid applications.

I don't understand what the FAFSA actually is or what the forms are asking for. Fortunately, my mom does her research and fills out the forms immediately, well before the deadline, and submits them to the necessary places. Most schools, including BC, require the noncustodial parent to complete a financial aid supplement. I call my dad, and we make a plan to get cracking at the forms tomorrow morning.

We sit at his dining room table with Dunkin' Donuts coffees, staring at the paperwork. He adjusts his glasses, takes a large swig of French vanilla roast, and rubs his temple.

"This is asking for a lot, Erika. I'm going to need to look into it," he says, shaking his head.

"Okay," I acknowledge. "It's due in, like, two months, so we just need to make sure it's done by then."

"I *said* I would look into it, Erika!" His eyebrows press together.

The pattern of attempts to complete the forms only to be met with frustration and procrastination continues for three weeks, four weeks, and I continue to remind him that the deadline is approaching. He continues to tell me to calm down, with short-tempered anger in his voice. "It's fine! I'll get to them, Erika!"

The tension around seeing him increases as I constantly need to bring up the forms, and it always, *always* ends in an argument—a flashback to the child support struggle. Fairfield is the one school I've been accepted to that doesn't require the noncustodial parent to complete a form, and they have offered me a hefty merit-based scholarship and aid package. I start to reconsider my dedication to BC and wonder if choosing a school where I don't have to depend on my father is the wiser route. When I explain to him that I can go to Fairfield for $4,000 a year, he doesn't flinch, responding, "You're going to BC." Not a terrible predicament to be in—my father is in agreement with me attending my dream school. In fact, he won't have it any other way. For eighteen years, he's made it clear that he plans to pay, and he's well aware of BC's pretty price tag. But he doesn't realize that my faith in his mental state is dwindling, and I fear the worst-case scenario. Monstrous anxiety taunts me: *What if whatever is going on with him causes him to change his mind? His mood and behavior change so frequently—perhaps his promises will too! Maybe he'll just wake up one day and decide he really does hate you and doesn't want to pay anymore!*

That's okay, I reassure myself. *I can take out loans. It's what most people have to do anyway.*

The monster fights back almost immediately: *But if he never completes the forms, you won't even have a financial aid or loan package to fall back on!*

I try to silence the monster, but it is relentless: *You'll have to drop out and transfer, and you'll be behind socially and won't make any friends! And your friends from home already think you're annoying and dramatic and self-centered, so you won't have anyone who cares about you except your mom—and you'll probably annoy her too!*

My mom calls the Boston College Office of Student Services to ask if we can have the noncustodial parent supplement waived given my father's condition. We've started to accept that perhaps his brain is truly unable to make sense of what the forms are asking. The financial aid representative tells her we can get a letter from a third party explaining the situation, and Student Services will review the case individually. But there is no third party. There is me, there is her, and there is him. Despite my mother's attempts to offer help, to gain understanding, he won't allow his doctors to share any information with her. We can't just expect exceptions because my dad has seemed *really confused and depressed and angry and has lost a lot of weight*; we'd need a diagnosis, an explanation.

Ultimately, we do not apply for financial aid because the forms are never completed by him and instead collect dust on his kitchen table. He doesn't seem to mind.

14.

"Why did you ignore my call last night?"

Well, hello to you too, Daddy.

I'm in his living room, and before I can even take off my jacket, I'm defending myself. "I worked the late shift at the bakery, so I didn't have my phone on me. I called you back, though! Maybe you were asleep? You probably have a missed c—"

"I needed to go to the grocery store."

This will be a gamble. "Remember, Daddy, you can always call Mom. I know you seem to hate her lately, but she—"

He cuts me off again, saying, "Your mother doesn't care about me either! She doesn't want you to spend time with me because I'm sick! But she is making my condition *worse*!"

This is hardly an appropriate moment to ask for more information, but it feels important. I take a breath, straighten my back, and keep a calm voice. "What . . . *is* the condition, Daddy?"

He shakes his head. "You know I'm sick, Erika. You know I have a neurological condition, but you don't seem to care. You just let your father sit here, depressed. You're just like your mother—neither of you has any respect for me! None!"

Neurological condition? What does this mean? Is depression considered a neurological problem? Is he referring to the headaches he'd had on and off earlier this year? He must have gotten this term from a doctor. This doesn't seem like something he would just say.

Avoiding eye contact, he continues, "Erika, I don't want to see you anymore . . . unless you need something since that's all you come around for anyway!"

My stomach sinks. I blow through my lips in frustration. "If you hate me so much, why do you even ask me to come by? And why would you want to pay for college?" I ask him, slinging my purse over my shoulder, ready to bolt.

"Because I said I would!" he barks back.

I'm not sure how to interpret this—reassuring that he will pay, especially now that we have thrown in the towel regarding any type of aid, but there is no denial of hating his only daughter.

I walk out, rush home, and, with unsteady hands, take tweezers to my wrist to let them work their magic until I feel emotionally numb. I hear the roar of the garage door opening and tug at my sleeve to cover the fresh marks.

When I greet my mom, the blood vessels in my eyes reveal that I have just been crying. "He doesn't want to see me anymore," I announce. We revisit the idea of taking a break from him, but in my heart, I know I can't just cut him off. As painful as this is, he is my father, and no amount of avoidance will change that. I still love him, and my heart breaks for whatever is happening to his brain. *Neurological condition.* I tell my mom, and she seems as confused by the vagueness as I am. I tell her I don't want to talk about it anymore and push it out of my mind. I'm terrified to search the abyss of the internet. Deep down, it feels safer to hold on to the possibility this will pass, like the flu or a bad case of the common cold.

I know he didn't mean what he said, so I keep calling him every day to check in, and he keeps answering. We do the dance of acting like nothing happened, like everything is fine. Though it's never to ask for help, he still calls and leaves the occasional message for my mom on the landline, usually something about the house. My mom begins recording all messages from him "just in case." I don't know when she would need them, but I don't blame her. She also starts documenting every tear-filled interaction he has with me and every accusation he's made about her. It feels like we are preparing for a war we have yet to fully understand.

15.

Green Day's "Time of Your Life" is blaring constantly; graduation season has arrived. My uncle and aunt have flown in from out of state to watch me from the bleachers of my high school football field, and we have a party planned for later in the day. It is unthinkably hot for early June, and the three-hundred-plus students of the Natick High School class of 2005 sweat through our royal-blue gowns, faces flushed from the beating sun. After we parade onto the field and find our assigned seats, I tune out the graduation speakers as I scan the crowd for my dad.

I think back to how different things were just four years ago. I was ending eighth grade, which, at that point, had been the most amazing year of my life. I loved being the oldest in the school. I had a solid group of girlfriends . . . and I was absolutely terrified of high school. A friend's older brother had given us the sage advice to avoid eye contact with upperclassmen when you walk through the double doors your freshman year, and this kept me up at night. Like many parents, mine beamed with pride while simultaneously swallowing back tears that their baby girl was about to start high school. Despite their excitement, I begged and begged them to promise me they'd allow me to transfer to a different school if I hated it, needing the reassurance of a backup plan (ah, the early signs of a blossoming anxiety disorder). Fear consumed me. However, once I entered Natick High, I had the most amazing few years, and I never looked back.

When I reflect on that summer before high school, I remember how helpful my dad had been, how excited he had been, how he drove me to the high school for a tour for incoming freshmen the month before it began, how he took me to Staples, where I inhaled the comforting smell of new school supplies after my first day. It's weird to think back and remember such a different version of a person who is still in your life, someone who you don't expect to change. Of course, I look different—as a senior, I no longer have straight-across bangs and short hair that flips up at the ends where it hits my shoulders. I have grown into myself, my body; my mind has grown with new knowledge and new experiences. I've read my first epic novel, experienced my first deep love and subsequent heartbreak, and tasted my first sip of alcohol. We expect people to grow, to change, but we expect our parents to stay the same.

After a minute or so of scanning the bleachers, I locate my father in the audience next to Angela's family. When it is my turn to march across the stage to receive my diploma, he cheers and cheers. It is only after his enthusiastic response to my name echoing through the speakers that Angela's mom realizes she is right next to my father. I see her smile at him and say hello. They've interacted numerous times over the past six years—playdate pickups that later turned into sleepover pickups. But in this moment, he looks like a shell of himself. Not recognizing him is a mistake anyone could have made. His body has morphed into a physical representation of his spirit—dampened, frail, reminiscent of death.

After the ceremony has ended, my mom, aunt, uncle, and I make our way home to air-conditioned relief. Once we've finally cooled down a bit, we place plastic tablecloths and "Congrats, Grad!" banners on folding tables in the backyard. My friends, their parents, and a few of my favorite teachers begin to filter in, chatting over iced tea, Swedish meatballs, and thick slices of vanilla cake. I wonder if my father will come; he'd slipped out of the ceremony before I could say hello and remind him when to come by for the festivities.

Toward the end of the party, I see him slowly round the corner of the backyard; right next to him is his friend Ynes. I am struck with mixed feelings; it means so much to me that he came, but I know how uneasy he must be—I imagine he brought a friend for moral support as he knew he might otherwise feel (even more) uncomfortable and out of place. He stays within ten feet of the deck and away from the party masses the way kids stay close to the safety base during a game of tag. If you wander too far, you might get caught. If you stay close, immunity is certain. He avoids my mom, and she keeps her distance as well. She flashes me a smile from across the yard; she too is happy he came. He tells me he can only stay for a few minutes but wanted to congratulate me on my accomplishment. He kisses me on the cheek, gives me a gentle hug and a card, and then heads out.

The last time the three of us were at my house together, I was sixteen years old, and we were opening presents together on Christmas morning. My mom was offering my dad more eggnog while he tugged a rope with Freckles and sang along to José Feliciano's "Feliz Navidad." We were all smiles, healthy and happy in our own nontraditional divorced family dynamic and certain we'd be spending Christmas mornings together for years to come.

16.

Late spring melts into early summer; and I start the season with a brand-new boyfriend, Jim, who will also be going to BC in the fall.

The minute the graduating class of 2005 received our college email addresses, we signed up for Facebook and started friending everyone from our high school as well as random people we didn't know who were part of our soon-to-be college networks. I friended Jim, and we spent hours on Instant Messenger talking about our excitement for BC. We decided to meet in person, unsure whether or not it was a date. But sparks flew, and we ended the night making out in his car.

Jim is tall, incredibly smart, and has the most adorable subtle Southern drawl because his family spends a lot of time in Kentucky. He makes me weekly Counting Crows and Everclear mix CDs and passionately explains why he chose to include each song. He lives a few towns over from me, and we spend several days a week together, falling fast for each other and dropping the L-word earlier than my friends feel is appropriate. I feel safe with him, and he dries my tears as I tell him all about my father's depression, anger, and mysterious *neurological condition*. He meets my mom. I meet his parents. He brings me to his best friend Maya's birthday dinner at the Fairmont Copley in Boston. We drive to BC and run around the sprinklers that water the green space, lying in the grass, fantasizing about what our relationship will be like when we

live so close to each other. We are ecstatic when we learn that we
will be living in the same dorm; a short walk to each other surely
beats the thirty-minute drive we make to see each other now. Our
love feels pure, deep, unshakeable.

Midway through the summer, I pull some soul-crushing news
out of him: he recently made out with Maya, the same girl whose
birthday party I'd just attended. This happened a few weeks
after the party, when she found out she didn't get off the waiting
list at any of the colleges she'd applied to. He was at her house
comforting her, watching a movie (*Garden State*, my favorite) to
distract her from the sadness and shame she felt—and whoops!
They ended up rolling around on top of each other, making out
on the floor of her basement.

He defends it, saying, "You and I had *just* started dating! I
wasn't even fully ready for a relationship!"

"Then why did you ask me to be exclusive with you?"

"I didn't . . . I mean . . . I think you misinterpreted the
conversation!"

"Oh really? Then why did we change our Facebook statuses?"

The regular fighting starts immediately after I learn about his
indiscretion. We fight over money. I pay for most things; he says
that makes sense because I have a job and he doesn't.

We fight over alcohol. Alcoholism runs in his family, and
when I tell him that I took too many shots and puked in the yard
all night at Angela's eighteenth birthday party, he worries he can't
trust me around booze.

"Well, I can't trust you sober," I say, again throwing the
unfaithful makeout in his face.

Brendan and I take a long drive to the BC Bookstore one
Friday morning to treat ourselves to some new Eagles sweatshirts;
he's one of nine other Natick kids who will be attending alongside
me in the fall. About halfway through the drive, I tell him about
Jim's cheating.

"Are you fucking kidding? What a shithead. I knew I didn't like him," he offers. I'd brought Jim to a friend's graduation party earlier in the summer, and Brendan had gotten a vibe that hadn't sat well. "So you're gonna break up with him, right?"

I sink into the passenger seat and mutter, "No . . . I think it'll be okay. It really wasn't that big of a deal." *Liar.*

Silence, then a sigh. "Look," Brendan starts, "I trust you. But if he hurts you again, he'll need to answer to me. I care about you too much, and you're gonna meet so many better guys at school anyway."

I've always appreciated Brendan looking out for me like a sister. I know in my gut I should break up with Jim, but I don't. We have been together for only about two months—hardly enough time to build trust before it has been broken. But I really do love him; he has become *my person.* Plus it'd be awkward to live so close to each other and be broken up. And it was just a makeout—it's not like they had sex or anything! I tell no one else, afraid they will say the same thing as Brendan, so Jim and I keep riding the roller coaster through the sweet summertime.

17.

I fall even more in love with BC midsummer at freshman orientation. I spend two nights staying in a gorgeous dorm on Lower Campus, rooming with a girl named Vanessa, who I met in line during check-in. We become fast friends, stay up late chatting, and eventually decide to be roommates come fall. During the day, I mingle with other incoming freshmen, bonding during the icebreaker activities and promising to friend each other on Facebook as soon as we arrive home. I choose my classes and am thrilled to not have any before 9:00 a.m.! I feel a sense of relief when I think of the independence and sense of belonging college will bring—a feeling that is quickly compromised by the nagging fear that I might have to withdraw at any moment if my dad refuses to pay. But he promised me this wouldn't happen, and he is a man of his word.

Then, weeks before my freshman year is scheduled to begin, my dad and I have one of the worst fights of our relationship. It starts with the same old complaints: I don't call enough, I don't care about him. He asks about the financial aid deadline. I remind him that this has long passed and that payment for the first semester is due. "Well, I have a decision to make!" he barks. I furrow my brow in confusion, and he averts his eyes as he says, "Whether I am going to pay for college. I've already given you so much."

Panic ensues.

I should have chosen Fairfield—I should have *fucking* chosen Fairfield. My father has been incredibly dependable my entire life. He showed up for every soccer game and was early for every after-school pickup. He is right—he *has* given me so much. But now in the moment when it counts, when it feels too late to switch my intended school and I need *him* in order to apply for aid, he is backtracking. Why couldn't he have said this before? As crushing as it would have been a few months prior, I would have accepted it, submitted my intention to attend a different more-affordable school, and moved on.

I toss and turn at night, eventually sneaking into the computer room to search "schools still accepting applications for fall 2005," "last-minute scholarships," and "can I undecline admission?" I bite my fingernails raw from the moment I open my eyes to the second I fall asleep.

Another day of racing thoughts is followed by another night of little sleep. Given that my father's threat was based on me *not doing enough* for him, I know I have to call to check in. When I do—my face hot with anger and my teeth clenched with fear, a forced, fake, sickly, sweet "Hi, Daddy" escaping through my lips—my jaw drops when he suggests we drive to BC tomorrow.

"Sure . . . how come?" I ask, both hopeful for and terrified of his response, in desperate need of confirmation, reassurance—anything.

"To pay the bill," he says matter-of-factly as if my question was strange. "I'd prefer to do it in person."

Does he even remember what he'd said just a few days ago? I exhale, though not completely; a torturous anxiety reminds me that anything can change in twenty-four hours.

I pick him up early the next morning, a large Dunkin' Donuts coffee with his usual cream and two sugars waiting for him in the cupholder. My hands tremble as I start to drive, anticipating another change of heart. But we continue our drive to the school, where he proudly hands a check for the first semester's tuition and room and board over to a Student Services assistant. I breathe a sigh of relief and try to put my anxiety about payment on the back burner—at least until spring tuition is due.

Afterward, I take him to dinner and am pleasantly surprised when he makes it through the meal without insulting me; instead, we butter bread rolls, slurp spaghetti, and discuss how beautiful the BC campus is with its Gothic architecture and ample wide-open green space. The ride home is quiet. I drop him at his apartment, offering a hug and another *thank-you*, to which he responds with a humble smile before leaving the car.

As the days living under my mother's roof become numbered, she and I spend hot Saturday afternoons shopping the sales at Bed Bath & Beyond and Kohl's so I will be more than ready when that fateful move-in day arrives. I print over two hundred photographs to cover the cement block walls of my dorm room. At night, I curl into my bed and sort through the thick envelope of pictures, laughing while reflecting on the silly memories with friends and smiling at the moments I captured with my sweet Jim. My eyes well with tears as I hold the photos of my mom and me close to my heart, knowing the impending farewell is going to be hard on us both. It is only in this moment that I notice I didn't print any photos of my dad . . . and I'm okay with that.

But still, with only a few days to go, I plan a dinner with my father. Saying goodbye to him is complicated. I need distance from his anger, his mood swings, his threats. I need predictability, consistency. But my big heart worries about who will be there when he needs help. I know he *can* do many of his errands on his own . . . But should he? My mom reassures me she will continue to offer help, though we both know he will never accept it.

My father and I enjoy a meal at Ruby Tuesday, where we love the unlimited salad bar and eat so much produce that our bellies bloat.

"I'll see you soon, my love," he says sweetly; and to my surprise, he initiates a kiss on my cheek as he gets out of the car. Those last two words melt away the pain I've been feeling since our most recent fight. *My love.* My heart breaks knowing that—despite the issues we've had—he is going to miss me very much, and this makes me want to stay to protect him from his sadness, to keep being his little girl.

"Come visit. We'll get dinner, okay?" I say, and I mean it.

18.

It isn't until the night before move-in that it finally hits me that I'm leaving home and starting a new life. Even though I'll only be thirteen miles from home, I know it won't feel the same. I can't sleep, and I crawl into my mom's bed around 1:00 a.m., crying with her about how weird it will be to leave her. We've had our conflicts, but as my dad's condition has worsened, her support of me has been a consistent lifeline. Thinking about her at home all by herself breaks my heart. She never got back into dating, which I, as a child, was selfishly grateful for—I don't know how some kids of divorced families deal with their parents' new significant others. But now it just makes me sad to think of my mom all alone.

I finally get to sleep and wake up a few hours later—exhausted, but cleansed. The sob fest was cathartic, and I'm ready . . . at least for now. We pack her Ford Windstar to the brim and are on our way.

My nerves quell, and the first weekend is *awesome*. I meet a few girls on my floor but spend the first night with Jim at the freshman-class ice cream social and then trek back to his dorm room to watch *Fight Club* with his roommate. I sleep in my new extra-long twin bed in my new room with my new roommate, and the smells of cheap alcohol and floral shampoo linger in the halls of my new home. The next night, Jim and I head off campus for a Green Day concert we'd bought tickets for earlier in the summer.

After an incredible set, red and white confetti rains on us as we exit Gillette Stadium, and I've never felt more free.

As the weeks go on, though, that initial honeymoon phase of college fades; and I feel the dark loneliness of depression creeping back in. The opposite of what I expected to happen happens: The more time Jim and I spend together, the more his cheating starts to eat away at me. Like driving past a car crash and fighting the knowledge that you shouldn't look, I ask him for specific details about the makeout, using the logic that the more I know and the more I can picture it, the less my imagination will run wild and the less I will obsess.

"Did you really *only* make out? Is that really all it was? Or was there, like, touching?"

"No, I *swear* we just made out for a little!"

I huff; "for a little" cuts at my heart, reminding me this wasn't simply a quick mistake. I imagine them scooped up in each other's arms, eyes closed, breathing heavily, not being able to resist the temptation of the other's lips or tongue.

"Did you guys talk during it? Or after? Like . . . did you, like, tell her you *loved her* or anything?" I ask, seeking reassurance for the thousandth time that they're *just friends.*

Jim inhales and hangs his head, looking down at his squirming feet.

"Actually . . . yeah . . ."

"Yeah? What do you mean?" I ask. There must be some miscommunication—there's no way he means he said "I love you" to this girl.

"I told her I loved her . . . It was just an in-the-moment type thing . . ."

Well, shit.

I rush out of his room, seeking the comfort of my own. I scream into my pillow and take some time to process this information. Hours pass, my tweezers soothing me; and ultimately, I tell myself,

At least he was honest, willing my heart to believe that it's still *not that bad.*

Maya posts on his Facebook page from time to time, and I turn purple with anger, wanting her to just *GO AWAY.* It certainly doesn't help that she lives a town over, like a looming threat to our relationship. Even though we fight, I continue to spend most of my time with Jim, partly because he feels like my home base and partly to keep tabs on him. Sometimes things are okay. Sometimes I can forget about his summer slipup and instead get wrapped up in his silliness and his intelligence and our chemistry, so I stay.

Despite spending the majority of his time with me, Jim has managed to secure a bunch of friends from his floor. He's often out with the guys, grabbing pizza in Cleveland Circle while watching a football game, or stays in playing video games with his roommate. On these nights, I'm not sure what to do with myself. My roommate is awesome but has her own group of friends she met from moving in early for a leadership program. Other than her, I haven't quite connected with anyone since I spend most of my days and nights with Jim. Although I know I've put myself in this position, I'm not sure what to do about it. I watch girls dressed in cute heels and trendy outfits trip over one another as they drunkenly walk to Lower Campus for parties, and I feel like an outsider. Why would they ever want to be my friend? Most of the time, I'm in my own head about the cheating and my dad fading away. Why would anyone want to spend time with me anyway?

One night, when I am especially sad, I call my mom and confess to her that I've been unhappy most of the time. The *COLLEGE* life I'd imagined is not what it's cracked up to be. I ask my mom to come get me, and I'm grateful when she makes the drive so I can spend the weekend at home. I talk, I cry, we hug a lot. But when she drops me back on Sunday, I feel as flat as I did when I left.

I make an appointment at the campus counseling center, knowing that I need someone to talk to, to trust. The therapist assigned to me is warm, and I instantly feel comfortable.

"So tell me why you're here, Erika," she says, meeting my eyes.

This feels like a big question, so I say the first thing that pops into my head. "Oh, um, I have a boyfriend here, and we've been fighting . . . There's some trust stuff . . ." I pause, take a breath, and tell her the story.

I focus most of our sessions on my trust issues with Jim. I mention my dad here and there, but being away from home means the issues we've had are less in my face, whereas living a floor away from a boy I love but feel hurt by affects me every day. My therapist encourages me to think about what interested me in BC in the first place and challenges me to spend time with people other than just Jim.

Following this advice, I befriend the girls next door, Melissa and Katherine; and on a crisp October day, we take the 86 bus to Harvard Square, where we order giant Felipe's burritos with a side of chips and guac. The conversation starts out light. I share stories about my summer with Jim (but not *the* story), and they ooh and ahh over *how cute* our "how we met" story is. They talk about their own dating histories, and we all joke about how *heartbroken* we were when our first middle school boyfriends dumped us. After a few hours, once we've felt one another out, Melissa shares that she's struggled with her own shit; she used to cut and experiences on-and-off depression for which she's sought counseling.

Later in the week, Jim and I are walking back from dinner at the dining hall, and my phone rings. I don't recognize the number.

"Erika? Hi, it's Shauna. I got your number from Vanessa . . . I know we only met briefly, but I live down the hall from you . . ."

"Oh, hey! What's going on?"

"Okay, so I don't wanna freak you out, but something's up with Melissa. I don't know what happened, but she's kind of a mess right now and won't talk to anyone about what's going on . . . She doesn't look good, and she says she'll only talk to you . . ."

I've never been in a situation like this; but I somehow remain calm, hastening my step, hurrying Jim along. "I'll be right there. I'm just heading back from Mac. Gimme, like, five minutes."

I rush up the two flights of stairs to Melissa's room; her door is propped open, half a dozen of our floor mates gathered outside, mumbling with questions and concerns. When I walk in, Melissa is sitting on her bed, ghost white, wearing an oversized shirt and no pants.

"Hey." I sit on her bed and grab her hand. "What's going on? Are you okay? I came as quickly as I could."

"Thanks," she slurs. "I took something . . ." She motions to an empty prescription pill container. "I don't want to get in trouble," she pleads.

My eyes widen, and my fight-or-flight response kicks in, my fingers quickly dialing the number for Health Services. I help her put on pajama pants I find strewn in the corner of the room, and within minutes, a van arrives outside our building to transport us to the infirmary. I hold a paper bag as she vomits into it.

At the infirmary, the staff separate us, interrogating both her and me separately. She asks me if I've ever heard Melissa express thoughts of suicide.

"No . . . I know she's mentioned having depression . . . We're kind of new friends, so I don't know a ton . . . Is she okay?"

"She's going to be fine. The amount of benzodiazepines she took wasn't enough to threaten her life, thankfully. You did the right thing bringing her here. You can go in to see her in a moment."

Once I'm allowed in, Melissa hugs me, her shirt smelling faintly of vomit. "Thank you so much. I don't really know what happened. Today was just a weird day . . . and I just . . . I wanted to escape. I didn't really want to, like, die . . . just . . . escape . . . get some relief from the pain."

A thought in the back of my brain—*Maybe I could escape my pain too*—echoes so quietly that I barely hear it.

Once Melissa speaks with the psychiatrist on call and the infirmary staff are confident she's safe, the van transports us back to our building, where Melissa showers and goes to sleep. I offer to stay with her, but she assures me she'll be fine and will come get me if she needs me. I lie awake in my bed, thankful she's okay, grateful I could help, and shaken by how real shit just felt.

I plan regular lunch dates with Melissa and Katherine, and sometimes we venture across the river to MIT, where one of Melissa's friends from high school is a freshman. I go to my first frat party, playing flip cup and beer pong until the early hours of the morning.

Journalism had been among my favorite classes in high school, so I join the freshman mentoring program for the university's independent student newspaper, *The Heights*. At the first meeting, as we wait for the leaders to get started, the ten of us sit in silence. A boy with "Pete" written in bold black ink on his nametag glances at me and smiles. I am instantly struck by his large kind eyes and quiet confidence. An hour later, we walk out of the meeting together, talking about our hometowns and high schools, then sprint back to our respective dorms in an attempt to be the first to friend the other on Facebook. (I win.) Between my new club and some new friends, I finally feel as though I made the right choice in coming to BC over any other school. I feel my mood brighten the more I open my eyes to things on campus other than my relationship with Jim.

19.

My mom calls me on an early November morning, saying she misses me and asking if I want to come home for a bit tomorrow. The next day, as I'm finishing lunch at Hillside Cafe with Melissa and Katherine, I spot my mom's minivan pull up to the curb; and I run outside, beaming as I open the car door. It's only the second time we've seen each other since I've been away at school, and our eyes well with tears as we embrace. She's eager to hear about everything I've been doing, how my classes are, what *The Heights* program entails. Like Rory and Lorelai Gilmore, our mouths move a mile a minute the entire way home. We comment on the foliage and laugh about Freckles' latest antics and chat about how many trick-or-treaters came by the house this year compared to years past. We'll save the important stuff for when we are settled into the comfort of our living room.

My mom sits on the couch beneath the bay window, and I plop myself into the chair across from her. What a view, what a day—the gorgeous autumn leaves, my mom who I've missed so much, Freckles sitting next to me and panting with excitement that I'm home. It's perfect. I start rambling on about how much happier I've been at school, how I'm homesick sometimes, but mostly that I am in love with my boyfriend, my classes, my new friends, just *being* in college, it's amazing, I've found my niche on the newspaper, I'm thrilled I made the choice to go to BC . . . And then my mother starts to cry.

She had been smiling through my story, attempting to mirror my enthusiasm, but something about it didn't seem entirely genuine. My mom usually eats, sleeps, and breathes empathy for me . . . It's weird that she's not thrilled and even weirder that she's crying. It's not an "I'm so happy for you!" cry; it's a sad cry, a foreboding cry. I stop and ask her what's wrong, why I've upset her. I mentally review everything I've said and wonder if I somehow said the wrong thing.

"Honey, I'm so sorry, I have to tell you something . . ." She pauses and takes a deep breath. "Your father is selling the house." More tears erupt. "That's why I needed you to come home. I couldn't bear the thought of telling you any other way. I didn't want to tell you, God . . . You're so happy. Seeing you this way just kills me when I have such terrible news. Honey, I'm so sorry . . ."

Her voice fades into the background like I'm not even there anymore, like I'm in a separate world now. My chest tightens. No matter how deeply I inhale, I can't get enough air.

Why? Why would he do this? My body carries me to the couch next to my mom; we're hugging and sobbing. It's like I'm watching the scene as an outsider. Freckles tries to comfort us, placing her head on my knee.

My mom reviews the timeline. She received a certified letter in the mail. We have to be out by the end of the year, which is about two months from now. With every word, panic rises. I can't handle this. I'm a first-semester freshman in college. I'm still in transition. How can my brain hold this too? We are screwed. My mom can't afford another house. Where will Freckles go? Our old apartment didn't allow dogs. We'll be forced to get rid of her . . .

We sit together in silence, save for our cries. Minutes pass, and finally, I steady my breath and call Jim. I need to speak the words to believe them.

"I'm sorry, baby, that sucks so much," he says, his empathic "ughs" repeating through the phone as I share with him what my mother has shared with me. In this moment, it feels good to express my pain, to have someone hold it with me; but when we hang up, I don't feel better. Jim has lived in his house his entire life, and his family has never known financial stress. He does not, cannot get it. I call Angela; she has spent weeks at a time at my house over the past four years. She listens and tells me she loves me. My heart remains broken.

My mom drives me back to school, still in silence—what's left to say? I worry about her; she worries about me.

I have a stupid newspaper meeting that starts within an hour of my arrival back on campus. I can't miss it because I'm still new. I can't already be seen as a slacker. I try to put on a happy face but don't succeed. I enter the basement office, overwhelmed by the smell of printer ink and musty air. My new friend, Pete, asks me if I am okay; and of course, that question makes it impossible for me to keep it together. I respond with a "yeah" but blink back tears. My eyes meet those of Laura, the meeting leader, and I ask if we can talk in the hallway. I don't want to make a scene. I don't want to be *that girl*.

"Laura, I'm so sorry, I have some family stuff going on. I just found out that my dad is selling my house . . ." I'm not sure what to say, how to say it, and the words blurt out of me as the tears begin to flow more freely. She hugs me, says she completely understands, and assures me it is okay to leave.

The news from my mother consumes my every waking moment. The flame of anger that's been burning in my body for months transforms into a roaring fire.

20.

I wait a few days before calling my father even though I know this may only add fuel to the fire. I don't really care. I'm struggling to digest the news, to accept it, and my head is continually spinning. In a way, the anxiety about the logistics of finding a new home and moving is a nice distraction from the fact that, deep down, the whole thing feels like a giant "fuck you" from my dad.

I know how much money he has. Although he is a man of humility, I saw some of his tax forms and bank statements when we attempted financial aid, so I know more than the average daughter about her father's finances. I know he has a wealth of stocks, owns his condo outright, owns our house and two properties on the outskirts of the city, and has a very healthy bank account. I can't imagine how selling the house is justified from a financial standpoint. It dawns on me that spring semester tuition is due in less than a month, and I'm going to need to remind him about this too.

I finally pick up the phone to call him.

"Hello, Erika!" he greets me, unusually upbeat. *Why now?* Why does he always answer with a grunt, but today of all days, he's in a good mood upon hearing from me? Clearly, he doesn't know I know.

"Daddy, I need to talk to you . . . Earlier this week, Mom told me about the house . . . Please, please don't do this. Please. I don't know what we're going to do . . ."

His initial warmth turns to ice. "Erika, the house is expensive—"

I'm prepared. "I'll transfer schools so you can save money! I can go to UMass instead. In-state tuition is way cheaper!" My heart skips a beat at the thought of leaving BC, but I only started loving it a few weeks ago. I can totally readjust elsewhere. The house has priority.

He doesn't waver. I beg. His anger rises. I beg more.

Finally, he says firmly, "Erika, my decision is *final*."

Through shaky breath, I try one last-ditch effort and ask him if we can get dinner tomorrow to talk about it more. To my surprise, he agrees, so I don't feel like it's a lost cause quite yet.

The next day comes, and he is an hour late. He gets lost. He calls me, confused, struggling with the directions I provide. This same thing happened once in September, when he came to pick me up for a meal. This normally breaks my heart; it forces me (and, I imagine, him) to face the reality of how much of himself he's lost. But tonight, I'm just pissed; and the tardiness delays my studying, which further stresses me out. He finally arrives, and we drive in silence to Uno's. I'm not hungry.

A doe-eyed hostess greets us and seats us, and we peruse our menus longer than necessary in order to delay the inevitable argument about to ensue. After placing our orders, I find the courage to speak. "Why are you doing this, Daddy?" I avert eye contact, but it doesn't matter; he is averting eye contact too. "I just don't think it's about the money like you said . . . But if it is, we can fix it. Remember, I said I could transfer to UMass or maybe Fairfield or somewhere where we can save money on tuition? I just want to know why. I want to find a solution."

"Erika, what do you expect me to do?" His tone is firm. "You don't care about me. You didn't even call me on my birthday this year!"

It is November. His birthday was in February, and I did call.

"Your mother put all bad things in your head, and you don't like me anymore. I bet you told her how much money I have in stocks! Why is she involved?"

I can hardly keep up.

The waitress arrives with our meals. "Here we are! One Caesar salad and one steak tip dinner with a side of mashed potatoes. Enjoy!" For a few minutes, I'd forgotten we are in public. I stare at the waitress, blinking back tears, wishing she could somehow intervene and save the situation. My father furrows his brow. We don't speak.

I sit staring at my unappealing salad; he eats or doesn't—I don't notice.

Finally: "Erika, John MacIsaac dying started my depression, and you being a bad daughter has only added to it! And you know, your mother took you home that day just to tell you! Not because she wanted to see you! She didn't care about that—just about telling you about the house!"

I am baffled by his approach of trying to make me less mad at him and instead mad at my mom. He has to know this isn't going to work.

After more silence and an implied confirmation that there's no way he's changing his mind, we leave and head back to campus. I thank him for dinner and reluctantly kiss him goodbye. I mumble, "Tuition is due soon, okay?" This hardly feels appropriate for the moment, but I'm not sure if there is an ideal time. I swipe my ID to enter the building and climb up the stairs to my dorm room, hoping to God my roommate isn't there so I can release. She's not. I find solace in my tweezers, call my mom, and fall asleep.

21.

For the rest of the semester, I go through the motions of attending class, doing homework, spending time with Jim, and forcing myself to call my dad only to (hopefully) prevent things from getting worse. Wash, rinse, repeat.

Tuition is due in seven days, and I start to panic. He took back the house; why wouldn't he take this back too?

When I bring it up, he sighs and says, "Erika, I *know* it's due! I have to move the money to the other account. It takes time. I'm working on it!"

I gulp, swallowing the words, *I don't know whether I believe you . . . and I'm not trying to be a nag. I'm only reminding you because I know you can be forgetful.*

He pays the day before it is due, and I wonder how I'm going to find the strength to manage navigating this anxiety every semester moving forward.

In early December, I officially become an editor for the newspaper. Pete had convinced me to run for the position. I hadn't thought I was qualified, being *only a freshman* and all, but he is running, so I figured I'd might as well try. I am elected associate copy editor after a grueling two-hour competitive interview in which we are tested on proper grammar and spelling on a chalkboard as the current editorial board watches on.

New editorial board members of *The Heights* are invited to attend the paper's annual Christmas dinner at Maggiano's Little

Italy in downtown Boston. Everyone meets in one of the seniors' dorms for a pregame, and then our dressed-up, drunken selves are shuttled by charter bus to dinner. It is fun and fabulous. Free fancy dinner is always enjoyable, but when you're a broke college student used to dining hall food, it's remarkably better. I sit with the handful of other freshmen who are also joining the board and share stories and laughs over several plates of fettuccine and passed hors d'oeuvres. It's a nice change from the monotony of the day-to-day.

After dinner, the real tradition begins. We all change into comfortable clothes and head back to the seniors' dorm for a long and seemingly endless night of speeches. Every editor who is retiring from the board—because either they are seniors and their term is up or they elected to not continue as an editor—is given a bottle of champagne to drink over the course of the evening, and each says goodbye to the rest of the board members. Emotions run high during these goodbyes. Twenty-two-year-olds pour their hearts out about the experiences they've had over the past three years and how much being part of *The Heights* has formed their BC experience. They pass on words of wisdom to us newcomers, and I know I've made the right decision to be part of this community.

Night turns into morning, and we are still awake. I had been warned that the Christmas dinner is an all-nighter, but part of me didn't believe this could be possible. Around 10:00 a.m., we head out of the dorm (to the relief of our noses as forty college students who have spent the past twelve hours together in the same room after a night of drinking and emotions are not the most pleasant-smelling people) and directly to the *Heights* office. The paper comes out twice a week—one of those days is Monday, so Sunday is a production day. Hungover, exhausted novices producing their first newspaper sounds disastrous. As associate copy editor, I do not have to go into the office until the evening as I am on the editing night shift. This would be great—except I am generally incapable of napping during the day, no matter how sleep-deprived. But I know I'll be up late again tonight, so I have to at least try.

My roommate has left for the day, so I have our room to myself. I toss and turn for one hour, two hours, three hours and ultimately give up. I've already been awake for over twenty-four hours and am well aware that being on the night shift means I won't be in bed until at least 3:00 a.m. I don't know how the other sleep-deprived editors are functioning right now, knowing they won't see their pillow until after midnight. I was wrong earlier; joining the paper wasn't the right choice—and now the only thing that has made me feel like part of the BC community is the one thing I can't handle. How am I supposed to do this every week? Twice a week? I'll normally have slept the night before, but is that enough? How will I finish all my homework? How will I adjust my sleep schedule? What would happen if I quit? The thought of this group of people thinking I'm weak turns my stomach. I'm going to vomit. Pockets of air try to escape from my insides as I dry heave.

This is why I don't pull all-nighters; my brain can't handle it. My stomach is in my chest. I inhale and inhale and inhale but can't get enough air. Jim won't get it. No one gets it. Everything is crumbling. I'm no one here. I'm not at the top of my class anymore—hell, I took three AP classes last year, but here, I'm not even in the honors program. My mom is dealing with all this bullshit about the house. I don't know when we're going to move or where we're going to live. I hate what my dad is doing to us, but he's depressed and sick, so I'm a shitty daughter for being mad at him. Joining the paper made everything worse. If I hadn't joined, I wouldn't have to quit. Why am I even here?

Why am I even here?

The question echoes over and over in my mind as I stare at the ceiling for what feels like hours.

I don't want to kill myself, but I do want to die.

I want the escape. Like Melissa told the nurses when she overdosed. I want that. But I want the escape to last forever.

Fortunately, a part of me recognizes I probably shouldn't work through this by myself; and within minutes, I am talking to the on-call psychiatrist about what I'm experiencing.

The psychiatrist asks me if I've ever considered suicide in the past. "No." If I have thought about how I would hurt myself. "No." If I have access to anything dangerous, like weapons or medication. "Kind of? I have a bottle of Advil in my room?" She asks if I've hurt myself before. "No," I respond, assuming scratching my wrist with tweezers from time to time isn't what she's asking about.

Over the duration of the call, I recognize that I am safe. I know I am not going to harm myself. I just freaked out and needed some support. The psychiatrist coaches me through some deep breathing, asks what in my life is important to me, and helps me realize that it is possible this overwhelmed feeling will pass. Once she is certain I am not acutely suicidal, she schedules me an appointment with Health Services for the next day. She explains that at this appointment, a doctor will explore with me possible next steps, such as *psychopharmacological interventions*—a big concept for my tired brain.

The phone call helped to calm me down, and I take comfort in knowing I will be seen at the health center tomorrow and possibly prescribed medication, which may offer some relief. I wait until the puffiness of my face can easily be mistaken for a hangover side effect so the girls on my floor do not suspect I've just been maybe suicidal and definitely panicked. I walk myself to the communal bathroom, splash cold water on my face, color my eyelids with liner, and march down to the *Heights* office to begin my second (almost) all-nighter in a row.

22.

This isn't my first time at the infirmary, but it is my most serious (other than accompanying my friend after her overdose). I've been there for abdominal pain and an ingrown toenail—only the most glamorous of concerns!—so today feels different.

I feel vulnerable and exposed sitting in the waiting area among my classmates, as though "Psychiatric Consult" is written on my forehead, not just in my medical chart.

"Erika?" I stand up, and a petite middle-aged nurse escorts me into a private room.

"You can sit." She motions to a paper-covered exam table. "Tell me why you're here today."

"Uh, well . . . I called yesterday. I talked to the on-call doctor, the psychiatrist . . . I was feeling . . . overwhelmed, and she wanted me to come in."

"Okay, I'll be back with the doctor in a minute." She displays little empathy and shuffles out.

I wait alone for a few minutes. I think about how disappointed I feel in BC for giving me glimpses of belonging and then snatching the rug from under me. It feels easier to blame my school than to recognize how my homelife and my own brain are likely getting in the way of me having an *amazing college experience*. I wonder whether I would feel differently had I gone to a different school, but before I am able to process further, the doctor knocks twice and comes in.

"Erika, hi. I'm Dr. Weitzman. How are you doing today?" He shakes my hand.

"I'm all right . . . a little tired. I haven't slept much the past two nights because I joined the newspaper . . ."

"Oh, *The Heights*! That's great! Good for you."

"Thanks . . . I've just been feeling not so great lately, and yesterday, I started to feel kinda hopeless, so I called the support line."

His affect changes—it's obvious he didn't read my file and was not expecting this; he probably assumed I was another overwhelmed, overworked college student wanting Adderall.

He leans forward and holds his chin in his hand. "What do you mean when you say 'hopeless'?"

I freeze. Our eyes align, and his concern becomes palpable.

"I don't know . . . I wasn't sure if I wanted to live—like I *knew* I did, but the thought still freaked me out . . . It was mostly just wanting to, like, *escape* . . . But I got scared, and I was overtired, and it wasn't really a big deal."

His expression tells me it is a big deal.

"Is this the first time you've felt this way?"

"Yes, I think so. I've had a hard semester, but it never felt this bad until last night."

He cocks his head and whips out a clipboard, asking more details about my thought process and physical experience last night. I feel like I am a rare animal in a glass cage and he is studying me, observing my odd behavior, glancing at the nurse to exchange knowing looks.

He asks if I've seen a therapist, and I confirm that I am seeing someone weekly through the campus counseling center. He explains that what I experienced yesterday was a panic attack. I felt out of control for a distinct period of time and experienced shortness of breath, and also felt very alone, hopeless, and possibly at risk of harming myself.

"The latter are signs of depression," he says.

No shit, I think. But when someone else says the words out loud, it lands in a different way.

I am depressed.

I have depression.

I am depressing.

He asks me again in about five different ways if I am thinking of hurting myself. Finally, he excuses himself, and the nurse follows so they can conference in a different room. I wonder where on the spectrum of fucked-up I am—to him, to her, to my floor mates if anyone heard me hyperventilating in my room yesterday.

They come back after a few minutes with a freshly written prescription for Ativan, a benzodiazepine that will help calm me down during panic episodes. "Take one when you start to feel the symptoms and don't mix with alcohol."

At our next appointment, my on-campus therapist tells me she thinks I need to see someone off campus. I find this annoying because (1) I don't want to start over with someone new, (2) off campus means I probably have to work out transportation, and (3) I will have to pay—even if just a copayment, that's $100 a month I'll have to take from my (small) savings account. Am I too screwed up for her? Did I scare her when I felt overwhelmed last week and called the support line?

She senses my discomfort. She explains that the on-campus counseling center is designed for short-term care; and she feels I will benefit from seeing someone long term, given the extent of my social stressors, recent panic attack, and prescribed medication.

After tantruming in my head for a few days, I accept reality and call a few off-campus therapists. I settle on an older woman named Dr. Longo, and it becomes part of my weekly routine to take a bus to a train to a therapist, who offers me ongoing support and holds my dysregulated emotions in a way I so desperately need.

23.

Though several aspects of my life start to change (weeknights bleeding into weekday mornings at the paper, venturing to talk to Dr. Longo, and prepping for my first round of college final exams), Jim and I remain the same. The fights usually start over something small, like him offering unsolicited criticism about a paper I've written, and inevitably end with me crying about how he cheated on me, how he still talks to *her*, and how I can't trust him. It becomes clear that I cannot seem to forgive him, but still, I fear letting go. One day, the fight becomes so intense that I throw my claddagh ring across the room and rip up the "four-month anniversary" card the girls next door made us early in the semester. I'm not proud of the way I handle my anger, but I have no idea what to do with my emotions. I've just accepted my depression diagnosis, and I'm not quite prepared to accept the reality that I am in a dead-end relationship. The idea of not being together feels worse—better the devil you know than the devil you don't.

Fortunately or unfortunately, I can't live in my denial much longer. One afternoon, we are in his room bickering, and I say (read: project), "Sometimes I feel like you'd be happier if we just broke up." He says nothing; and this response, or lack thereof, is not the reaction I expected. The breakup happens quickly.

My breakup response is typical in that I journal about it, feel I won't ever be happy again, listen to sad music nostalgic of our sweet summer falling for each other, and cry and call my friend Julia, whose voice offers genuine comfort.

My breakup response is atypical in that I dig into my wrist with my trusty tweezers, leaving bright red throbbing marks representing my pain.

After a few days, I decide to pull myself the hell together. Rumor has it that Nikki, another girl in my dorm, recently went through a breakup with her boyfriend, so I use this as an opportunity to befriend her. We sit in the dining hall for six hours, shit-talking our now exes, drinking multiple iced coffees in a row, and feeling the excitement a burgeoning female friendship often brings. She tells me she's so glad we're becoming friends, and we plan to spend more time together next semester when we're back from winter break. I'm excited; it feels like I am forming another solid connection with someone—maybe even someone I can eventually confide in about my dad and the mess at home.

Two days later, she kisses Jim.

I walk into my room after a final exam, and Vanessa and her friend Cait greet me with "You're gonna want to sit down" looks on their faces. They break the news to me, and thank God for them because they do it in a way that elicits a response of anger, not sadness. I am not heartbroken. Jim can kiss whoever he wants, but what kind of new friend kisses the only boy in the entire school who should be off-limits given our new friendship? My roommate tells me that she heard Nikki is a mess over it, and sure enough, I hear Nikki sobbing in the hallway. I go out to confront her, and she is wailing with a group of girls around her, consoling her.

Her tears pick up as I approach her. "Erika, oh my god, I'm so sorry. I don't know what's wrong with me . . ." More wailing, more back rubs from her entourage. "I don't know why I did it. Please forgive me. I'm so, so sorry."

I take a breath and thank her for the apology. Then I surprise myself when I follow with "Nikki, I don't think our friendship is gonna work out . . ." We barely have a foundation to stand on, and now any trust I had in her is gone. Unexpectedly, this situation empowers me. I didn't break up with Jim when he violated my trust over the summer. I tried to stand up to my dad about the house, and that went nowhere. I feel as though I've uncovered some inner strength. I tackle my remaining finals, pack up my winter clothes, and head home for break.

24.

Fortunately, and inexplicably, with just a few weeks left in December, my father has decided to extend our tenancy through the end of June. I imagine this is either due to a small change of heart or, more likely, counsel from a Realtor that summer is a better time to sell. Who knows? This buys my mom an additional six months to find a place, though she's been on the hunt since the day she got the notification, not wanting to delay the inevitable. She drives from open house to open house, schedules appointments with dog-friendly apartment complexes, scours the paper for For Rent ads. She tours in-law suites, two-family homes—anything she can find. Nothing works out—sometimes because it just doesn't feel *right*, sometimes because of the timeline. She can't move our entire home all by herself and doesn't want me to have to come home midsemester to pack everything up. Movers are out of the question budgetwise, so she has to be mindful about the logistics. She reassures me she will find something, and I trust her, though I wonder if she's also reassuring herself.

I see my dad every few days while I'm home. I fake a smile to avoid the inevitable shitstorm that will come if I keep my distance. He often complains about charges related to the house, and it becomes increasingly harder for me to bite my tongue; how the hell am I supposed to respond? *Ugh, that's the worst! Home ownership sounds like it sucks! At least the charges will stop when you kick those stupid tenants out and make the sale!* There is nothing I can say, so

I say nothing; and resentment builds within me, threatening to overflow at any moment.

Other than time spent with my father, the holiday break is the perfect way to heal from my breakup and focus on things other than the impending move. I see my friends from home every other day; it's been almost a year since the Valentine's Eve internet attack, and I mostly don't think about it, instead focusing on how comforting it feels to be around the people who have been in my life for so long. We eat, laugh, and cuddle up in one another's arms, wishing the day we return to our respective colleges would move further away rather than getting closer by the minute. Whenever we're trying to decide whose house to go to, Angela offers mine; she's still the only one in the group who knows my house is being sold, and she knows I want to spend as much time there as possible before I can't anymore. I begin to move on from Jim and brace myself for a happier second semester, during which I vow to focus on making friends—and preferably not the kind who kiss your ex-boyfriend days after your breakup.

25.

Spring semester comes, and I feel like I am at a completely different school. But really, it's my mindset that has changed. *The Heights* radically improves my college experience, and I'm *so* glad I didn't quit. Although the late nights are challenging, they are 100 percent worth it—being part of the paper gives me a sense of purpose, people to talk to, and access to insane parties where we reward ourselves for our grueling nights. Four of us editors have a standing date at the Chocolate Bar, the campus cafe, every Friday afternoon. We call ourselves the Fearsome Foursome: Caroline, a junior; Lily, a sophomore; me, and one boy, my friend Pete.

From the moment we met, Pete and I have innocently flirted, which I justified because of Jim's previous infidelity. We hooked up once during the last week of the fall semester, drunkenly making out in a laundry room after a *Heights* party—very romantic, very college. I was freshly on the rebound, and he had just stopped *sort of dating, sort of not dating* another girl. We talked online occasionally over winter break, but come spring semester, our time together becomes more regular. Almost every weekend, someone in Pete's dorm pulls the fire alarm when they're drunk, so I often get a knock on my door at 3:00 a.m. when he's looking for a place to sleep.

On February 13, he calls and leaves me a voicemail, asking if I want to go out to dinner the next night.

"Do you think he knows tomorrow is Valentine's Day?" I ask my roommate, hoping for a *yes* but believing this may be a coincidence.

"Are you kidding me?" Vanessa responds. "First of all, it's the middle of the week. He obviously knows it's Valentine's Day. He's not just asking you to go to dinner in the city on a random Tuesday. Second of all, he obviously likes you. I've seen you guys together!"

I tell him *yes*, and the next night, we are off to a fancy Italian dinner in Boston's North End. It is exhilarating to be on a proper date with such a genuinely nice person. He is smart, talented, supportive, incredibly driven, charismatic, attractive, polite and has an adorable laugh.

Pete makes it clear he is interested in being exclusive; and despite my telling him I'm not ready to commit, he sticks around, confident we will end up dating. We spend weeknights and weekends together, sometimes with the rest of the Fearsome Foursome, but often just the two of us. We stumble home together after parties in an innocent way that mostly involves kissing and falling asleep, though we do visit that laundry room again from time to time.

In April, my mom invites us to Cape Cod, where she will be spending a few days with some of our family friends. My dad picks Pete and me up from school as he has offered to let us borrow his car for the weekend. It's nice to have what feels like a normal father-daughter interaction; for a moment, I forget my father is sick, that he's selling the house. He engages Pete in conversation, asking where he's from and what he's studying. I see his eyes widen as he says, "Wow, good for you!" after Pete tells him he's majoring in marketing. We drop off my father at his apartment, and Pete offers him a confident handshake as my dad flashes me an approving smile.

"He's so nice!" Pete exclaims as we get back in the car.

"Yeah, he's a good guy," I mumble, struggling to reconcile my father's behavior toward me over the past few years with the beautiful exchange I just witnessed.

We stop off at my house to get CDs for the road, and Pete comments that my house is "so big," which surprises me because he's from a private high school in New Jersey and has parents who are still married and have good jobs. I had assumed my house would pale in comparison to his. I think about my house for a bit on the drive to the Cape, explain to Pete that we're selling it, but don't say much else about the topic.

We arrive in Mashpee. Pete greets my mother with a hug, and she's immediately charmed by his charisma. "Have fun, you two," she says with a smile, handing us some of my old tennis rackets from high school. Pete and I walk to the community tennis court, where we trip over our own feet for a few rounds (and follow zero actual tennis rules). We head into town for some shopping and walk around, sipping chai lattes as we take in the crisp spring air. At night, we go to the beach. It's far too cold to swim; but we run across the sand playfully, appreciating being out of the college bubble, if only for a night. We lie in the back of my dad's Honda Accord, and Pete asks me to be his girlfriend while Ben Harper serenades us through the speakers. I say yes. My heart swells, and a palpable relief washes over my body; in a way I haven't felt in months, maybe even years, it feels like maybe *everything is going to be okay.*

The next week, Pete asks me to get coffee on a Thursday morning—at the same time as my therapy appointment. I try to skirt the issue, telling him I can't, that I have to be somewhere; and he innocently asks where I'll be. As if avoiding the anticipated sting of the bright sun, I close my eyes and scrunch my nose as I mutter, "Therapy . . ." Then I slowly open one eye to witness his reaction.

He smiles as he says, "Cool!" Then he asks if I like my therapist, how often I go, and other curious and appropriate questions.

Within weeks, I've told him everything about my dad's mental and physical decline and the real situation with our house. He holds my hand as he tells me that instead of writing in my journal, I can always come to him—a real person—for support. We fall hard and fast; and come summertime, he stays on campus for a job, so I visit often. We spend many nights wrapped in each other's arms in his little dorm room. I trace "I love you" on to his back with my finger one night; and he looks me dead in the eye and says, for the first time, "I love you too." It is unlike any relationship I've ever been in; it feels like more than young puppy love, and this softens the blow as the reality of selling the house sets in.

26.

It's a beautiful Thursday morning; the sun shines through the large window of Pete's summer dorm. We wake up slowly, wishing we could stay in bed all day. Fresh bagels and coffee summon us from the little shop across Comm Ave, and after about an hour of fighting reality, I have to tear myself away from him to get home to babysit for my neighbors across the street. My neighbors for now anyway. I blast the radio to wake me up until the caffeine fully kicks in, and after a half-hour sing-along with Top 40 songs, I pull onto my street.

It's incredible how much of an effect the combination of metal, plastic, and wood has on my heart. I've (mostly) come to a place of acceptance with the house being sold. I recognize I cannot stop it or slow it down . . . But seeing the For Sale sign standing proudly on our front lawn sends a rush of cortisol and an immediate sadness through my body. I was not prepared for this. My mom is at work. The Realtor must have put the sign up sometime this morning while my mom was deep in Excel spreadsheets at her desk, and I was snuggled up in an extra-long twin bed, sleeping too late next to the boy I love.

Blood drains from my face as any ounce of denial that was left in my body vanishes. There is no time to process; the kids I'm about to babysit run outside to greet me, their mom close behind them. She gives me a wave. I put on my happy face and step out of the car.

I fake a smile when she and her husband greet me with "Oh no! You're moving! Where? Why?" I tell them we're downsizing since I'm no longer home, that we're still "figuring out the details of where." As the days pass and other neighbors catch a glimpse of the sign, they seem to assume we're upgrading; they say, "Getting a new house? Exciting! Good for you!" To them, I nod and say, "Yeah." Meanwhile, we still haven't secured an apartment.

Now that it's impossible to hide, my friends begin to ask about the house. I say the same thing: "Just downsizing." I tell a select few the real story—that my dad has decided to sell it, so we will need to find a new place to live. When they respond with "Wow, that sucks," I instinctively become defensive of my dad, saying he needs to cover medical bills for problems I don't know the details of. Inside, though, I still doubt it has anything to do with health or money.

My doubts about my dad's financial struggles are particularly intensified when he tells me he's going to buy me a new car—his tone making it seem like a fact versus a proposal. For three years, I have been driving a 1999 Ford Escort with no air-conditioning and manual locks and windows. I started saving when I was five years old, shoving the money my mom gave me for chores and the money my dad gave me for allowance into piggy banks and, eventually, a real bank account. Before I even got my license, I bought the car for $3,200 from a neighbor.

My mom is less than thrilled when she learns that my father has shared his intention to buy me a new car. She fears that he is creating a "gotta have better" mentality in me. I have made the occasional comment lamenting the lack of AC, particularly on my long bumper-to-bumper traffic drives into the city to see Jim the summer before college, when I would arrive dripping in sweat. Still, I had never mentioned wanting a new car or even thought of it as a possibility since I'd never expected someone to just hand me the keys. I was raised to work for what I wanted; ever since I got my first job, I've been buying clothes, meals out with friends, sugary coffee drinks, and convenience store makeup with my own money.

When I started seeing Dr. Longo, I resolved to be more open about my relationship with my father, the effects of his spiraling health, and the pain of losing my home.

I tell her about the car offer and how it just *doesn't make sense*.

She squints her eyes, pauses for a moment, and says, "I wonder if it's because he knows he's dying and wants to spend money on things he enjoys and people he loves."

Dying?

A drop in my stomach.

Is he?

My brain doesn't want to go there, *can't* go there. I briefly retreat into my comfortable cave of denial. The house is not being sold. My father is not dying. Nothing is changing. Nothing is bad. No one is sick. Everything is fine.

I know my dad has always shown his love through money: the weekly Beanie Babies, my allowance, the house, the lifelong promise to pay my college tuition. But this feels weird, and my mind can't make sense of it. Does he not see how confusing it is that he's supposedly selling the house due to financial issues and is now practically demanding that I accept his offer to buy me a new car? It's possible he is doing this to ask for my forgiveness—again, he's never been straightforward with apologies.

The moment we arrive at the dealership, any confusion is put on the back burner, and all I feel is psyched. He promises the car will be in my name, not his, which my brain quickly registers to mean he can't just suddenly take it away from me. After test-driving a few models, I drive away with a brand-new silver Honda Civic and crank the AC as high as possible until I am practically shivering, basking in the glory of my brand-new icebox.

He follows me home to ask how I like it. I tell him it is great and joke about being chilly despite the high June sun. His eyes never meet mine; instead, they look around the yard. The For Sale sign stands proudly before our eyes; it almost appears bigger than before, like it is taunting us, daring us to acknowledge it. This is the first time we've seen it together.

"Erika," he says to me, "this house is going to be sold. It needs to be presentable." He points to the overgrown hedges and comments that I haven't mowed recently.

"I will," I mutter, my tone switching from sweet and thankful to resentful and angry. I feel manipulated. The mood changed so quickly, and I question whether the car was not an apology, but a trick. Leverage. *I bought you a car. Now you will do what I say and not complain.*

Despite this, my new car comes in handy all summer for frequent getaways to Pete's family's second home in the Pocono Mountains. We make the four-hour drive, leaving behind the troubles of saying goodbye to my home to move who knows where. Some nights, the pain that the change in my relationship with my father has caused me is impossible to ignore; it creeps up on me like an itch that I can't scratch but won't go away until I do. Pete's dad is incredibly kind, even-keeled, and gentle. He has a thick French accent and a playful sense of humor. He reminds me so much of my dad—or what my dad used to be. I long for those days. I wish that instead of relaxing in Pennsylvania, we were sitting around my father's dinner table, playing board games while he throws his head back in laughter, cracking jokes in his endearing Peruvian accent. I miss who he was, who he is at heart, but who he may never be again.

27.

We are down to the wire, and my mom has finally found a place for us to live—an apartment in a community neighboring the complex where I grew up. The owners had planned to sell their pet-friendly second-floor condo after they fixed it up but decided to rent it out to my mom and assured her that they no longer had any intention to sell. This was obviously a hot topic given what we're going through with my dad. As sad as I am to leave my house, part of me is looking forward to the move so that my mom can finally relax and breathe. I know she's likely been avoiding telling me how stressed she's been trying to find a place.

The downside? It's a five-minute walk from my dad's apartment. He doesn't get out much; it's unlikely we'd run into him unexpectedly, but still . . . what are the odds?

Our house is still on the market, which brings up more mixed feelings for me. I'm grateful it's still ours and not some stranger's, but I'm also confused as to why no one wants to purchase this glorious home. My happy place. My sacred space.

This allows us time to move out at our own pace, which certainly reduces stress, but in other ways feels like I am peeling off a Band-Aid very slowly and painfully. We will be living in a one-bedroom apartment due to the cost of living in what has become a highly valued town with regard to real estate. I assure my mom that it's fine. I plan to live on campus every summer after this one, so we really only need to share the small space for holiday breaks. This means we have to get rid of a lot of the things we have acquired over the past four years in the house, so our work is cut out for us.

As moving day approaches, my anger continues to build. After a long day of cleaning, packing, and hauling our donation items out of the house, the roaring fire within me becomes uncontainable. Rather than jabbing myself with tweezers, I try an outlet Dr. Longo had suggested: I write my father a letter I never intend to send.

To Whom It May Concern:

There are so many things I need to say. So many ways I need to express this feeling, this anger, this sadness, this . . . whatever it is.

I can't believe that after how you've treated me for the past two years, you still went above and beyond and made me leave the place I love.

Do you know how badly I wanted you to drive by today? While we were working . . . and working and working and working to make everything look perfect and adhere to your demands. "Oh, careful, honey. Don't scratch the wall," Mom guided me . . . you know, all I want to DO is scratch the walls and punch holes in them and ruin everything so that we can mark our territory and take it from you. And no matter how careful we are, you're bound to find some flaw, some dent, some kind of damage and take it out on me for God knows how long. It sickened me to stand over the sink and scrub and scrub and know that all I was doing was helping you. It sickened me.

I wanted you to drive by so I could scream "WOULD YOU LIKE TO HELP?" I know you hate Mom for no reason, and I know that you're living on this power high. I don't know when or why or how we became the enemies here.

I want you to listen to me confess to you all the things I do when you make me upset, all the things I do to myself when you make me hate myself, and have you sit there and look at me and NOT CARE and tell me it doesn't matter. I want you to do this because it could give me the strength to break free from you, to cut you out of my life. This isn't just about the house—this is about everything in the past two years.

But I know that if I told you I hated you or if I told you I wouldn't see you anymore or if I did anything wrong, you could ruin my life. You took my house. You could take my education—my other happy place. So I can't move. I am your little puppet.

The other day when I told you I've been in therapy, you told me that has nothing to do with you. Seriously? You don't even know. Don't tell me why I go. Don't lie to yourself about how you've treated me. Don't try to tell me you never said you might not pay for college—you DID say that! And even if you swore up and down that you would never do that, I don't think I'd believe you. Who are you? Where did you go?

Someday I'm going to be a big grown-up and have a successful job and make a lot of money and marry a man who loves me and would never even think to speak to me the way you do. And I will make enough money on my own to never worry about you and what you have to offer me. Ever. Or what my husband has. I am going to be the most independent person ever because all I've learned from depending on people is that you'll just be disappointed or hurt in the end.

Oh wait, how can I be upset with you? You do so much for me. You give me everything I ever wanted. You just bought me a goddamn car that I didn't even ask for. How can I be so mad at you? I must be so ungrateful, right? But WHY? Why do you do these things? Is it out of the goodness of your heart? Everything with you is a manipulative game, and I actually cannot do anything to escape for years. I just sit here, waiting until I graduate and do not have to be reliant on you for anything ever again. And this is the time of my life when I shouldn't be counting the days.

Nothing you can possibly do could compensate for what you've done—for the tears I've cried, for the harm I've caused myself, for the number of people who have had to deal with me, for the hours I've gotten help . . . for any of it. To think that I have to sit through a meal with you soon is almost comical to me. To think about sitting there and listening to your criticisms of me juxtaposed with you asking "How is the car running?" and "When do we pay the bill?" and I have to sit there and smile and thank you for these wonderful things you have given me and tell you I love you, and we both know it isn't real, and even that is manipulative . . . it's like you know you're manipulating me but you do it anyway.

I'm just picturing the new family when they move in. Picturing the mom and dad and son and daughter packing their things and getting in the truck and grinning and helping each other and hugging and moving into their new beautiful split-level home *and painting over the front door and going out to dinner at a cute little restaurant in town to celebrate and getting a new pet and spending weeks inside decorating and having a housewarming party . . . and then I'll drive by someday when I'm upset, and the family's dad will be out mowing the lawn and give me a little smile and a wave because he is just so friendly. But little does he know who I am, and I'll just die inside.*

So, congratulations. You have succeeded in your mission. What your exact goal was, I don't know . . . To prove that you still have an incredible power over us emotionally, financially?

My life isn't that bad. Without everything you do to me—the mind games, the emotions—everything would be a whole lot better. But I'm so goddamn dependent on you.

And you know what? After this all passes and Mom and I settle into our new place and I go back to school and have some distance from home troubles . . . I am going to feel bad about this. I am going to feel so, so guilty for writing this and thinking this way.

Thank you for making my dreams come true and then breaking my heart.

Sincerely,
Erika

While writing certainly doesn't afford me the numbing that self-harm does, I feel relief and a brief sense of pride that I didn't instinctively turn to breaking open my flesh. The letter lives safely on the hard drive of my laptop—the keeper of my most raw, unedited thoughts.

My mom's coworker Judy arrives early the next morning in a moving truck, which we fill with furniture and large boxes of dishes, clothes, and other essential items. My mom and I move the rest of our belongings each night when she gets home from work, making multiple trips in our cars to avoid covering the cost of a moving truck again. The new place is only about a mile away, so the trips are quick, but tedious.

I come to love our little apartment; the landlord is a carpenter, so the interior paint and countertops are stunning—much nicer than our first apartment's when I was a child. I can tell my mom feels badly about the limited space, so one night, I leave her a note saying "I like living here!" She holds on to this for years.

It takes a long, long time for the sting of the move to go away, though. Sometimes when I am driving home from a night spent with friends, I pass the turn to our old house and feel a strong urge to drive down, to see if the sign is gone, to see if a family with 2.5 kids and a white picket fence is moving in as predicted. I give in to this urge fairly often; it becomes a pathetic habit I share with no one. One night, I sit out front in my car for a minute—or five, the time escapes me—and my now-former neighbor startles me by knocking on my window. "Oh, it's just you!" he says, chuckling. I smile, hoping he doesn't notice that my eyes are welled with tears. "I was worried something was wrong when I saw a car just stop here in front of an empty house . . . But looks like you're just having a moment with your old home! How's the new place?" I make small talk, telling him "everything is great!" Then I drive away, not visiting again for many years.

28.

A teeny tiny part of me thought that once we were out of the house, my dad would be nicer to me. But nothing changes in our relationship—the phone calls continue to end in accusations of me being a bad daughter. One overcast Monday in July, we plan to get lunch together. I never want to anymore, but I know it's nice for him to get out rather than sit with his depression, alone in his small dark condo. I pick him up, and he is in a *mood*. These moods work like osmosis, and suddenly, I turn sour; it's not unusual for my diplomacy to fade easily these days. He is grumpy, complaining that I "never" see him. I seethe, recalling how I spent half of my first summer home from college apartment hunting with my mother and packing up my home. Even during the weeks when I felt an overwhelming resentment toward my father, I made sure to see him at least once. By the time we reach the restaurant parking lot, I can't take it anymore.

"Why do you even want to get lunch with me? You are *clearly* angry with me today. As usual." My eyes remain fixed straight ahead, and I pull into a spot.

"Erika, you manipulate me! You don't care about me! You get whatever you want—always!"

"Oh yeah, Daddy. I'm still living in my house, huh?" I'm ready to face him, and I turn toward him. Tears instantly rush as I say, "We love our place now anyway. It's beautiful, and we're happy, and it feels like home." It's like I'm willing myself to believe that last part.

Bringing up the house was not my best move; but later, I will be glad I did because what happens next gives me an uncomfortable, but definite sense of closure. He turns to me, not breaking eye contact, anger radiating out of his pupils and his brow furrowed the way he always looks when he is especially mad. His voice is raised. "Erika, I didn't buy that house for your mother. I didn't take the house from you. I took it from *her*!"

There it is. These are the words I have known were true but had not yet been spoken. I knew it was never about money. I knew it was never about the goddamn money.

I sit there speechless, unsure how I am supposed to spend the next hour eating lunch with him. But as has become second nature to me, I take a few deep breaths, get out of the car, walk to the passenger side, and extend my arms so he can reach out for my help standing up. We mosey into the restaurant, where we are greeted by a bubbly hostess with a big smile. After over an hour faking neutrality to avoid an even bigger explosion than the one we had in the car, I drive him home and say, "Bye, I love you." I repeat this several times until he finally acknowledges my words.

I'm thankful my mom isn't home when I walk in the door. I have no ability to regulate my emotions, and I don't want to talk to anyone anyway. I type furiously in my journal, the thing that keeps me sane when I fear my voice and my pain have overstayed their welcome in the ears of those I love:

> *This is a thank-you note. Thank you for—as you often remind me—everything you've done for me. Thank you for forcing us out of what we knew and loved and leaving us uncertain for eight months.*

Thank you for blaming me for everything that goes wrong in your life.

But in all honesty, thank you for letting the truth slip in your moment of anger today. You lied to me. You told me selling the house was about money. And I didn't believe you for a split second, but the point is, you lied to me flat out for eight months. Actually, more than that if you count the month before I even knew about the house, the month that I called you and you told me you loved me and how proud you were and never let it pass through your lips what was going on. Well, you know what? We're happy. We're happy here in our little place because it brought us closer by pushing you further, and we love our little community pool and our little communal laundry room, and at least now she *is free of you. I mean that.*

You make me feel like shit, bottom line. I don't know why I even bother explaining anything to you . . . I can tell you that the sky is blue, and you'll find a way to tell me I'm wrong and to criticize me and then criticize me for not wanting to be criticized. When should I give up? When?

Someday I will fix and escape this. I will. And I will be the happiest person in the world. Because as I wrote weeks ago in a letter that I wish I had the courage to give you, you are the most negative thing in my life. I wrote a letter just last night that was the complete opposite of this, a letter to my love about how much I love him and why I love him and how that makes everything else a little bit better . . . and

*thank God for that. Thank God for the good areas
of my life.*

*Maybe someday they will all be good areas, and
I will feel so free . . . I just wish I could get these
years back.*

When my mom walks in hours later, I promptly mute the
Friends rerun I'm watching to share my father's reveal. She's not
surprised. The intensity of my anger quells, and vindication
comforts me as my mom joins me on the couch to watch Ross
and Rachel fight about whether or not they were on a break.

29.

It's a sunny Saturday in early August, and my mom suggests we go to lunch. We drive to the local Kelly's and get two lobster rolls—at $17 apiece, this is an indulgence for us. We nibble our chips and discuss how quickly my second year of school is approaching.

She finishes her lobster roll, wipes the crumbs from her mouth, and says, "I have to tell you something, honey." *Jesus Christ*, I think. At this point, I'm not sure how much more I can take—the last time she started a conversation this way, she told me that my father was selling our house. We *just* finished unpacking in the new place. What else is coming?

My expression quickly indicates to her that I am expecting the worst, and she backtracks. "No, no, don't worry. It's good. But it's a long story."

She explains that earlier this year, in the spring, she received papers from my father stating that he was taking her to court for a modification of their original separation agreement. I don't totally follow—I've tried to stay out of any legal issue related to their divorce, particularly since it happened when I was a toddler and there is a lot I don't understand. Of course, I've known for a while about the "child support versus rent payment" debacle. Well, apparently, instead of *her* taking *him* to court over this, *he* decided to take *her*, hoping to come to some type of resolution.

I'm having a hard time understanding how this is "good news" and quite honestly feeling frustrated that, yet again, the legal details of my parents' divorce-related finances are being discussed with me, which I don't feel is appropriate or helpful.

She continues, "I saw this as an opportunity, honey. As you know, your entire life, your father has told you—and me—that he planned to pay for your college education. There was actually language about this in our original agreement, and I wanted so badly for this to be revisited to make sure you'd be all set."

I think I'm starting to understand what she's saying, but I'm nervous my suspicions are too good to be true.

"It's all taken care of, baby. It's in the updated modification. He is legally obligated, per the agreement, to pay for the remaining semesters of college, as well as books and other educational expenses. If he's unable to, he needs to complete the appropriate financial aid forms—which, as we both know, he never did before—with enough time for them to be processed. You're all set. You never need to worry about this again."

I'm in complete shock, and slowly, what she has said starts to sink in. I am overwhelmed with emotion—grateful to have a mom who advocated for me, relieved that I won't have to feel the constant stress of whether or not my dad will decide to back out of paying, leaving me with no possibility of remaining at BC—but mostly, I'm confused about how to proceed. I've been telling myself that ceasing contact with him is not an option regardless of how bad things get because then he would definitely not pay for school . . . But now it seems as if that may not be the case.

"Okay. So even if there is, like, a formal agreement now, I still have to talk—"

"Nope," my mom interrupts, knowing the direction in which I'm headed. "You're free. It's completely *your choice* whether you communicate with him regularly or at all."

I sit for a moment; we are both unusually quiet. *I'm free.*

"I don't even know what to say . . ." I pause again for a while. "Thank you so much, Mom. I don't know how to thank you . . . This changes everything." I move to her side of the booth, put my head on her shoulder, and wrap my arms around her tightly.

My mind wanders . . . Maybe I'll study abroad. I had wanted to but knew that he would never agree to pay for a semester where I wouldn't be able to see him for months at a time. I grow giddy at the thought of gallivanting around Australia or Italy or Greece or even Peru, of soaking in a new culture, of having a totally newfound sense of freedom and independence that living thirty minutes from home has not afforded me.

My fantasy is put on hold as I wonder what this experience must have been like for my mom—she had to see him for the first time in a while. I ask her about this.

"Honestly, it was tough. It must be so hard for you to see him like this all the time, honey. You're so strong. He looked so frail . . . so old . . . not like himself. I wish we knew more and could make sense of this . . . this *thing* that's happening to him. It was so sad. One thing that did come up, though . . . I can't remember the full context, but at one point, my lawyer asked if Daddy is seeing a psychiatrist. His lawyer confirmed that he is and said he's on 'a ton of meds.' There wasn't much more said, and honestly, I didn't want to talk to his lawyer any more than I had to . . . She's a real bitch." A surprised chuckle escapes my throat; my mom never uses this word. But as she explains further, tears fill her eyes, and mine quickly follow. "You can tell she hates discussing things with him and looks down on him. It kind of made me mad. I still have a tender place in my heart for him despite his nastiness. After talking to me for a few minutes, his lawyer actually rolled her eyes and said, 'Well, I have to go babysit now,' glancing over at your father. Terrible."

Rage fills my body. Babysit?! What an *asshole*. As badly as my dad has treated me, the idea of a person—particularly a professional who is supposed to support him—speaking of him like this, particularly so candidly, fills me with a deep sense of rage and a deeper feeling of love for him. He didn't choose what has happened to him.

We leave the restaurant, and my mind races, processing all the new information. I wonder if the thought has crossed his mind that maybe I'll stop calling altogether upon learning that college is all set. And as relieved as I feel that this is now an option, my heart breaks thinking he may be sitting in his lonely apartment in fear of losing his daughter completely.

My mom and I curl up and watch a *Gilmore Girls* marathon together before bed. My emotions are all over the place, but in this moment, I feel incredibly appreciative of her and the sacrifices she has made in order to give me some semblance of peace for the next few years. My god, she's been dealing with being kicked out of her house by my father *and* being taken to court by my father . . . No wonder it took so long to find our new cozy home.

30.

The time is approaching for me to move back to the BC dorms for my sophomore year. As each day escapes me, I grow more worried and anxious about leaving home. My mother and I have gone through a lot this summer and have grown even closer because of it. I know we will still see each other. I know we will talk every day through email or the phone or chatting online, but I feel like a little kid who just needs her mommy. I start to regret all the times I could have spent with her and didn't and all the times I was sarcastic and rude for no reason. I am grateful that she understands I am a teenager who is dealing with more than what many teenagers—at least anyone I know—typically do. She gets me a newspaper-print pillow, in honor of *The Heights*, to bring with me to school; and I carry it with me off to my second year. The pillow reminds me of her and the comfort and stability of our home—even if the home is different and little and imperfect, it is ours.

I fear going back, but I go. Even though freshman year took a turn and ended with an amazing love and sense of belonging and purpose, I fear this year won't be the same. There's just something about everything that happened this summer. Shouldn't I feel free? We have a new home, my father doesn't control us anymore, college payments are set. It doesn't make sense, but whether or not it's logical, this year feels daunting.

31.

As I'm walking through the quad to meet Brendan for lunch, taking in the crisp fall air, I get a call from my dad, which is unusual since he hasn't initiated a call in months. He tells me he's in the hospital; he was shaving and started shaking so hard that it threw him against the wall and onto the floor. He had to crawl to the phone to call a doctor and was taken by ambulance to Framingham Union, a hospital one town over from his home. He asks if I can come pick him up tomorrow. I don't have my car at school, but I want to make it work; fortunately, Pete loans me his, and I'm able to be there for my dad's discharge.

A middle-aged nurse thanks me for coming to get him. She leans down to meet my father's eye level. "José, your Life Alert device should arrive via priority mail by the end of the week. This will help keep you safe if something like this ever happens again." She places a brochure in his shaky hand. "If you have any issues setting it up, you can contact the company directly. I've highlighted the customer service line for you." He nods. The nurse steps just outside the door and reappears with a wheelchair, motioning for him to get in it.

"I can walk," he says, rising slowly.

She offers an apologetic smile. "It's just protocol."

Despite hearing what she just said, seeing him in a wheelchair sends a shiver down my spine. I accompany him outside, then pull the car around to the front of the building to take him home.

When I visit him again over the weekend, he greets me with a smile. "Erika, thank you for coming. You've made me so happy." He hugs me, and I'm grateful he can't see the confusion on my face. These tender moments are rare. It's hard to not get swept up in them, though; my mindset becomes too black-and-white. Inside, I'm jumping up and down, shrieking with glee that *everything is better! We are back to normal! He's still sick, but at least our relationship is in a good place!* It never lasts.

But for now, we spend the afternoon together, drinking coffee and chatting, the announcer of a baseball game rambling on the TV in the background. My dad tells me about Camila, his "lady friend," who he calls Camicita. Like my mom, my dad had never dated anyone (to my knowledge) since the divorce; and I'm in a place where I just want to see him happy, especially given how much of his life is slipping away. My face lights up, and I ooh and ahh as he tells me about this woman; he picks up quickly on my cues and clarifies that they are just friends. He tells me she is joining him on a trip to California to visit his sons (my much-older half brothers), and then they will go to the Carolinas to visit Camila's family.

There are holes in this story. He doesn't speak to one of his sons, so I feel confused as to why, suddenly, after over a decade of no contact, he would visit him.

The medical alert pendant hanging from his neck taunts me, a constant reminder of his fragility. He is so stiff, so shaky on his legs. I wonder if he's considered whether Camila is prepared to handle potential challenges that may arise on a cross-country flight.

I say nothing and let him go on about Camicita and their plan and smile as we have a delightful afternoon. I don't need to rain on his parade. Maybe we both know this is a fantasy, but it's all he has.

32.

One day, midway through the fall semester, I receive a call from an unknown number. I have always been someone who answers these calls that most people ignore out of a fear it may be something important, and if I miss it, who knows what could happen?

Unfortunately, I'm in class, so I can't answer. But I anxiously watch the clock until the class ends so I can listen to the voicemail this mystery person has left. A woman with a thick Hispanic accent begins to speak hurriedly, flustered. She introduces herself as Helena, Camila's sister, and says, "I don't know what's wrong with your father . . . Cami and I have known him for many years . . . I'm confused. We don't know what's going on or what to do. Please call me back."

How had I only heard of Camila three weeks ago when I visited my dad after his hospitalization? And why is this woman calling me? How did she get my number?

I call my mom, confused, not sure what to say when I call Helena back. My mom advises me not to call back since I don't know these people and shouldn't be discussing my father's health with strangers. The whole situation is bizarre. My mom instead encourages me to ask my dad about it, and when I visit him later in the week, I do.

He explains that he gave Camila and Helena my number in case anything happens to him. I am confused about whether he is referencing something like he falls in the shower, or something like . . . he dies. It becomes more and more clear how concerned he is about his health, and the absence of any medical information other than what I see with my own eyes during our visits makes it very hard for me to make sense of everything.

The last time I'd asked for more information, he'd told me I was careless and disrespectful. He is calmer today, more welcoming of my presence. I inhale deeply as anxious words leave my mouth. "Daddy, what do you mean 'if something happens'? Do your doctors know exactly what's going on?"

His sunken eyes meet mine. "I don't know, Erika. I don't know what could happen." He begins to cry. "My body has lost control, and you know my mind hasn't been working right."

I take his pale, cold hand and lean in to comfort and cry with him.

33.

Early in sophomore year, I go on two retreats—one the first weekend of the semester and another about two months in. Retreats are common at Catholic schools, and although I'm not Catholic or even religious, I enjoy these getaways because I get to escape the BC bubble and the stress at home. We're encouraged to leave our phones and watches in our rooms as a way to stay present and not hyperfocused on how much time has passed or where we *should* be and instead trust the leaders to guide us. I feel completely disconnected and, instead, fully focused on what is in front of me, not on whether I should be calling my dad because I have five minutes and *Oh no, if I don't call now, will he be mad at me because I may not have any other time today to call? And even though all I want to do is enjoy this small window of time I have between classes, I will feel insanely guilty if I do not use it as an opportunity to ask him how he is doing, only for him to likely yell at me.* Although our last few visits have been more gentle, my armor remains in place, knowing his behavior could change at any moment.

A few days after returning from a retreat, where I am feeling particularly empowered and excited to spend time with some of the people I met on the weekend getaway, I get a call from my father's friend Gerardo. My father met Gerardo through mutual friends when they were in their late twenties; they bonded over their immigration stories, Gerardo having emigrated from Honduras.

My dad and I spent many afternoons at Gerardo's home when I was growing up, his daughter and I playing with Barbies for hours as our fathers chatted downstairs, their laughter echoing through the house. They've always been two peas in a pod, both possessing a quiet, calm energy.

Gerardo and I have seen each other briefly during my father's last few hospitalizations; he's usually arriving as I'm leaving or vice versa. I'm surprised to see him calling me; we don't often speak on the phone.

"Erika? Hi, this is Gerardo. Do you have time to talk?"

"Yes," I respond, my heart thumping loudly in my chest. "Is everything okay?"

"Oh yes, yes, don't worry, Erika. But listen." Gerardo offers ample reassurance. "Your father is at Leonard Morse Hospital. He is okay, just confused. Everything will be fine, so don't worry. He is okay, but you should visit. I know he would love to see you. Listen, I have to go take my wife to an appointment, but the nurses will explain what happened, okay? Everything is okay."

While hospitalizations have become semiregular and my automatic response is no longer one of panic, Gerardo's attempt to not be an alarmist has the opposite effect he intends.

Before my thoughts spiral too far, I call my mom, who arrives forty-five minutes later to pick me up. I want to keep Pete out of this as much as possible. Despite him giving me no indication of this, I secretly fear that my neediness—both emotionally, when I need a shoulder to cry on, and logistically, when I ask to borrow his car to visit my dad—will push him away, and I will lose this rock in my life.

Shortly after my arrival to the hospital unit, I meet with a nurse, who gives me a play-by-play of what happened. This morning, my dad was trying to get into his condo, where he has lived for over two years now, but he went to the wrong door. After several unsuccessful attempts of wriggling his key into the wrong keyhole, someone called the police; and following a brief evaluation, my dad was taken to the hospital.

The staff asks me questions about him to get some understanding of the situation. They ask me about his symptoms, when they started, and where he is from. The last question catches me off guard. I don't understand why they're asking me as this isn't a question of perspective, but of fact. He is proud of his Peruvian heritage; when I was a child, he often asked Spanish-speaking waiters or store employees "De donde eres?" as he tried to guess by their accent where they were from. His eyes always beam with pride when he shares that he is Peruano. A sign hung proudly on the wall of his old garage: "Parking for Peruanos only, all others will be towed." Peruvian trinkets and various handmade pieces of furniture from his home country decorate his apartment. Of course he would have shared this with the hospital staff.

A nurse explains that, earlier, he didn't know he was from Peru.

I inhale as tears fill my eyes; the nurse gently pats my back. "I'll be honest," she says. "He's seemed pretty grumpy, so I hope he's kind to you . . ."

Me too, I think, but I don't hold my breath.

"I did overhear another nurse mention to him that you were coming, and I saw a little smile. It's the first I've seen from him since he got here." I smile in response, and she comments, "Wow, you really have his eyes and his smile! How sweet."

He's meeting with a doctor, so I have to wait a bit to see him, and the nurse stays to chat with me for a while. She asks me how old I am. I tell her I'm nineteen; and we briefly talk about where I go to school, what I'm studying, which of my classes I enjoy the most. She asks how I am coping with his dementia.

Dementia?

This is not a new word for me. I paid attention in psychology class. But I've never heard it in reference to my father. Suddenly, his confusion, his disorientation, his *neurological condition* has a name.

A million questions race through my mind: Can this explain his physical decline? His weight loss? His driving difficulties? What does treatment look like? Is there hope? Is this an expedited path to death? Does *he* know he has dementia? If he understands his diagnosis, will it change his behavior? Will understanding change mine?

The nurse senses my shock. She cocks her head to the side and squints her eyes inquisitively. She takes a breath and asks, "Have you ever heard this term before?"

I explain that this is the first time someone has used it to describe my father's condition—at least to me—and that I've never had any other explanation for the rapid changes he's experienced. She lets out a small sigh, furrows her brow, and shakes her head ever so subtly. She looks at her watch, starts to stand to presumably check on another patient, but sits back down for a moment and grabs my hand. She stares me right in the eye. "I cannot believe you have to go through this at your age. I'm dealing with the same thing with my father, but I'm fifty-two years old. God bless you."

This is a weird moment for me. I feel validated and take comfort in knowing this is an atypical situation for a college sophomore. It's no wonder I feel so alone and confused all the time—no one in my life can really relate, and the nurse acknowledging this helps. At the same time, I feel more isolated, as though no one will *ever* understand, like anyone trying to commiserate or empathize will think of their grandparent when this is my father, my daddy, my childhood hero. On move-in day, I watched as many of my floor mates' fathers lifted heavy boxes on their shoulders, taking the stairs two at a time, sweating through their shirts until their daughters were fully settled into the new space. I would bet none of these families could imagine that man forgetting his heritage or trying to get into the wrong unit in his building. In a sea of ten thousand other undergraduates, I doubt there would be enough to form even a small support group for students dealing with dementia in a parent.

I finally join my father in his hospital room, where flickering fluorescent light shines on us. I sit down on the bed, and he smiles sheepishly, as if he is thinking, *Well, this is me now.* I can feel the shame—as unwarranted as it is—seeping out of his soul.

"Hi, Mr. Vargas!" a nurse says—or yells, the way you raise your voice when speaking with someone old and presumably hard of hearing. She speaks slowly and rea-lly e-nun-ci-ates her words to be sure he understands her.

"Who is this, Mr. Vargas?" she continues. He looks at me.

"This is Erika."

"Okay, and who is Erika?"

"Erika is my daughter."

"Very good, Mr. Vargas!"

My stomach drops and my chest tightens as she speaks these words. It hadn't yet dawned on me before this moment that it is possible he could someday forget who I am. All of the negative feelings I've developed and associated with him melt away. I just want to hug him and somehow stop the dementia from destroying his brain. There is a nursing student in the room; we make eye contact, and she smiles at me. Her scrubs have the Boston College logo on them, and I realize she is one of my peers.

The nursing student conducts a mental status and memory exam, pointing out three objects in the room: a clock, the window, and the white board, where his name is written in blue dry-erase marker. After fifteen minutes, she asks him to recall the objects, and he cannot.

Thanksgiving break begins tomorrow, so after gathering some things back at school, I plan to stay in Natick with my mom for a few nights. After a good night's sleep, I call the hospital to check in on my dad; and once I'm transferred to his room, he is instantly short with me, seemingly annoyed to hear my voice. I'd thought we had a few tender moments when I visited. I held his hand and gave him hugs; he saw my eyes well with tears as he struggled, so I have a hard time understanding why he continues to harbor such animosity toward me.

He tells me he has to go because his friend Lucrecia is there, someone I have not yet met but have heard him speak of at times. I'm able to talk with the nurse for a few minutes; she has clearly overheard part of his end of our conversation and explains that his grumpiness from yesterday has ramped back up.

"Don't take it personally, okay?" she says.

Easier said than done, I think. *Please teach me how.*

"It's been a quiet day for him, no visitors. So he's probably just extra cranky."

Hmm. I ask her to double-check whether someone is with him now, and she takes a moment to peek into his room.

"Nope, no one there."

Dementia. The word reenters my mind, and I wonder how much that plays a role in all of this. Did he imagine Lucrecia? Is it like when you have a dream, but it feels real? Is she an old girlfriend from his past, but he forgets and thinks she is in the present? Does he forget all of our nice interactions and only remember the struggles? Does he *truly* forget that I call him almost daily?

I visit him again on Thanksgiving Day after Mom and I have our calm little dinner just the two of us (and Freckles, of course). I've always loved our easy holiday traditions. When people ask what I'm doing for Thanksgiving or Christmas or Easter, I respond with "My mom and I just hang out and make food!" Then I'm usually met with a frown indicating their pity. "Aw, it's just the two of you? That's so sad!" But it isn't sad—I love it. Though I loved it more when my dad used to come early on Christmas morning, hauling gifts from "Peruvian Santa" written in his own handwriting. From a young age, I giggled and rolled my eyes every time I saw this on the presents; it was *so obvious* that Peruvian Santa was a hoax. (It never crossed my mind that regular Santa might be too.) Thanksgiving is not a Peruvian holiday, so my dad never joined us for it, but I bring him leftovers every year because he loves the food, even if the story behind it isn't particularly significant to him. This year is different. I can't bring outside food into the hospital. I show up with a smile on my face to help distract from the emptiness of the unit; they are on skeletal staff since it is a holiday, and the space feels particularly unwelcoming. My dad is sleepy, and making conversation is harder than usual. After attempting small talk for about an hour, I ask if I should go since he's so tired, and he nods. I kiss him on the cheek, and on my way out, I let a nurse know he is asleep.

The day before I plan to return to school, I call him to see if it would be a good time to visit. I am immediately met with anger; he tells me I didn't see him enough while I was home. He mutters something about paying for college; his words are hard to understand as he is quite groggy, but when he finally starts to sound coherent, he says, "I'm not paying one fucking cent for college." Spring tuition is due in sixteen days. Clearly, he doesn't know I'm aware of the court order. Even though I know that him refusing to pay would put him in contempt of court, anxiety rises in my chest, knowing that, despite any legal agreement, this is going to continue to be a verbal and logistical battle semester after semester.

Just two years ago, I was feeling particularly nostalgic on Thanksgiving, and I wrote a three-page typed journal entry listing all the things I am thankful for and why. My dad's personality and physical health had just started to subtly shift, and I wrote about how grateful I felt for our relationship and how I knew that no matter what, it would never change. What a difference just two years makes.

I settle back into school and catch up with my roommate about our Thanksgiving breaks. I haven't shared much about my dad, so I sugarcoat things. I say, "Break was great! I had such a good time. It's awesome to see high school friends!" I feel like a fraud, but I enjoy the break the temporary denial affords me.

Later in the evening, I get a call from the hospital. This morning, my dad fell and severely injured his hip and may need surgery. I don't know all the details, but I do know I have seen enough TV shows to know that when an elderly person injures a major body part, death often follows. He's sixty-two, which I've never thought of as elderly. But when I see him, he looks like a feeble old man; and since he became sick, people have often assumed he is my grandfather.

The next morning, I let myself sleep in. I was tossing and turning with worry after that phone call. I don't have class until the afternoon, and after a shitty night's sleep, I need some caffeine. I swing by the Chocolate Bar for an iced coffee and am completely caught off guard. The barista looks so familiar, and within a few seconds, I realize that she is the nursing student who was at the hospital caring for my dad. She witnessed his struggle with the mental status exam and my tearful eyes when I realized there may come a time when he doesn't recognize me. For my own sanity, I have kept my school life and my homelife separate. Pete is the keeper of my secret, and a few others know bits and pieces. But no one from BC—not even my boyfriend—has seen my father in his current condition. Until now. The barista recognizes me and gives me a half smile as we acknowledge my secret with our eyes.

34.

Pete and I are past the honeymoon stage, which means fights have become part of our relationship. The arguments happen almost exclusively when we've been drinking and usually start over something that has a nugget of truth to it but is deeply exaggerated by the alcohol swirling through our systems.

After the *Heights* holiday party, Pete and I drunkenly stumble back toward my dorm on Upper Campus; and after giving him the silent treatment for the first half of the walk, I start yelling at him for spending half the party talking to his friend Kaila, who happens to be strikingly beautiful and who he happened to kiss one time early in freshman year. Though his charm is what initially drew me to him, I struggle with the number of female friends he has (especially when some of them leave messages with winky faces on his Facebook page). Jealousy rears its ugly head whenever I see him show what I feel is superfluous warmth to another girl. I want to trust him, but Jim left a scar on my heart that doesn't seem to be healing. Pete and I cut through the parking garage on middle campus, and I slouch against the frozen concrete slabs, sobbing into the sleeve of my parka.

"*Why* are you doing this?" he yells rhetorically, rolling his head back, staring at the sky.

I blubber on, and an angry sadness envelops me. My entire body tenses, desperate for relief. It's been months since I've turned to my tweezers, but I find myself wishing they were with me in this moment to provide me solace from the tornado in my brain. Instead, I do the next best thing: covertly dig my fingernails into the sides of my wrists, right on the bone. I sit there, crying and digging, praying no one will see me because even in the midst of my panic attack or meltdown or whatever the fuck this is, I have enough dignity to not want to be seen. Only Pete can see my hurt, my pain, my ugly.

35.

It's my first winter break in our new little home. Christmas Eve is always special with my mom; we manage to stick with our traditions each year—building a gingerbread house, driving around to look at the decorated houses adorned with lights and wreaths, and her tucking me in after reading "'Twas the Night before Christmas," no matter how old I am.

Just before we are about to leave to see the lights, I decide to call my dad to wish him a merry Christmas. He is still in the hospital after his most recent fall and will be staying there through the holiday. He answers groggily, his voice raspy, as if he's been asleep. His answers are short. He asks me what I'm up to, but his tone makes me wonder if he actually cares or if this is a setup. I answer honestly.

It's a setup.

As soon as I mention my mother, he explodes. "You know, Erika, your mother may not realize this, but she's not in my will. All she wants is my money, and well, she's not going to get it!"

"Daddy, she never thought she was . . . No one has mentioned that, and I can't imagine why she'd think she would be . . ."

"All you two care about is money! You always ask for money from everyone! You always have!"

Oh, this hurts. I think back to when I asked him to stop giving me an allowance as soon as I got a job. How appreciative I, as a preteen, felt when he offered me his credit card from time to

time and said, "Go buy yourself something nice. You can spend
up to $50." Then he'd wait outside American Eagle watching
families roam the mall while I tried on clothes. I think of how
I've always been so shocked by how easily the rich kids at school
plop down their parents' credit cards for weekly mani-pedis and
rooftop drinks with their fake IDs.

The anger in his voice snaps me back to the conversation. "You
even asked for money from Donna!"

This takes me a minute. Donna is my godmother, and
I genuinely cannot recall under what circumstances I would
have possibly asked her for money. I remember that my dad is
delusional at times, but I don't know how to reason with him.
Then I realize he is referencing my fundraising responsibilities
for the town drama group I participated in throughout middle
school. Every year, each member had to raise a minimum of $75
to help support the production of the play. My godparents own a
restaurant, and I asked Donna if she wanted to buy an ad in the
playbill. I cannot believe how selective his memory is and how
warped this information has become in his mind.

"Your mother manipulates you so much," he continues. "If she
told you to kill me, you probably would!"

Merry fucking Christmas.

That's it. I inform him that I will not continue this conversation.
I have defended my mother to him countless times; there is no use
getting into this spiel now. I wish him a merry Christmas once
more and hang up the phone.

My mom lets out an empathic sigh, sad for me and sad that
Christmas Eve feels so different from how it usually does, how it
"should" feel. I ask her through sobs if I have to call him when
I'm visiting Pete in early January; although she doesn't give me a
"yes" or a "no" answer, I take comfort in her response: "Honey,
I've always wanted you to try to keep a relationship with him.
And for so long, you could, and it was wonderful. But if he only

speaks to you like this? Then there's no reason you should have to. You don't need to convince him of anything. He can't be convinced. You don't need to explain things. He won't listen." She strokes the tear-soaked hair along the side of my face. At this point, I can't keep up with the number of times we've had this same conversation.

As much as I know distancing myself from my father is justifiable, I still can't do it. I imagine him in his hospital room, Christmas reruns on television featuring families going to church and opening presents while he eats bland hospital chicken and potatoes with a side of Jell-O—alone, sad, crippled, helpless.

The day after Christmas, I visit him at the hospital. It's hard to find the motivation to do so after that last call (does he really think I would *murder* him?). But I've grown so used to it that, after initial resistance and some dillydallying, I get myself there, like I always do. When I arrive, Gerardo is there with a middle-aged woman with long dark hair and a warm smile. She introduces herself as Camila, and finally, I can match a face to the name my dad has recently mentioned several times. A social worker meets with us, and my hopes are high that she will offer some intervention, some relief when she sees how he treats me. But she is paged shortly after entering and has to excuse herself.

To my surprise, my father's behavior is slightly tamer, albeit certainly not kind, than I'd anticipated. We even discuss the tuition payment, and Gerardo assures me he will help my father transfer the money to the proper account, that I need not worry about whether I'll be returning to school in four weeks.

"Erika, why are you in such a rush for the money?" he asks me, slurring his words a bit. Spittle collects in the corners of his mouth. There is no use reminding him that we are already almost three weeks late, so I say nothing. My dad goes to the bathroom; it takes him a while now as his balance is worsening and his muscles are in constant pain, so I have some time to talk with the others.

"Erika, it's so nice to meet you," Camila says, taking my hands in hers. "Your father talks about you all the time. He loves you so much and is so proud of you, especially being at BC—wow!"

"Thank you, Camila. It's nice to meet you too." I force a smile. We sit in silence for a minute or two, and I contemplate using this moment as an opportunity to express that what he says to her is very different from how he treats me. I wonder how true it is that he tells her how much he loves me or whether she's saying that in an attempt to repair our relationship. A nervous energy vibrates through my veins as I speak. "I have to be honest—it doesn't feel like he's proud of me. He's so nasty to me. He doesn't treat me like he loves me anymore, especially when we're alone . . . Most of the time, I hate being alone with him. Things have changed so much . . ." I feel tears coming, and I am sick of crying, so I stop talking. My father returns from the bathroom, much quicker than expected.

"Erika, you know your father can be grouchy sometimes," Gerardo says, flashing an apologetic smile at my dad, who seems confused as to what he just walked into. "But he loves you. Right, José?" My father nods once quickly, not making eye contact with me, with anyone.

The social worker returns and explains my father will be discharged at the end of the week. "Since the doctor has contacted the DMV to move forward with license suspension, your family will need to coordinate transportation for rides to appointments and general errands."

I glance at my father, who hangs his head, staring at the linoleum floor. The context tells me this is not the first time he's heard of this plan, but perhaps the acknowledgment of it in front of his loved ones—especially his daughter, whom he taught to drive just four years ago—elicits unbearable shame. Given how shaky and accident-prone he has become, I am relieved that someone has taken formal action to keep him, and others, safe. But my heart swells as his face falls.

Camila plans to visit on weekdays, and Gerardo on weekends. I feel ashamed for not being part of the plan, but I know he treats them more kindly, and I know I cannot be a full-time student and caretaker or even see him as frequently as he would like once I return to school in a few weeks.

I plan to visit the first day he returns home, just a few days from now. I know Gerardo and Camila will be there, so I commit to stay for a while. He's proven to be a bit less harsh toward me when they're present; unbeknownst to them, they serve as something of a buffer. I am afraid to be alone with him; although he cannot physically hurt me (he never has and is too weak to do so anyway), the emotional pain he inflicts upon me hurts in a way I'm not sure I'm capable of handling on my own.

36.

When I walk into my dad's apartment on his first day back at home, I immediately notice his black eye and a cut on his lip. Gerardo had given me a heads-up about this; apparently, he fell—again—and thankfully didn't injure himself more gravely. Attempting to hide my reaction to this visual reminder of his loss of control, I greet my dad with a big hug, and he barely hugs back. I wonder if this is because he has grown so weak, his muscles having degenerated so much and withered away to the point he cannot give me the big, strong hugs I received as a child . . . or if it's intentional and he just doesn't love me as much anymore.

The rest of the afternoon convinces me it's the latter.

We start out fine. The four of us sit and chat; small talk is hard when the only new thing in his life is having been hospitalized, but we make it work. Gerardo and Camila order dinner, and I panic as my small army exits the apartment with plans to pick up the food and return shortly.

A switch flips.

"Erika, you don't even care about me. Gerardo and Camicita have such big hearts . . . but not you."

"Daddy, what are you talking about? I'm here right now! I was there at the hospital!"

Same shit, different day. We sit in silence. I refuse to engage. Gerardo and Camila return, and every time they leave the room, he starts back up. Like clockwork, when they reenter the room, he stops. It's almost comical.

My brain reminds me that he's not completely in control of his mind, his behaviors, but I can't separate what I know rationally from what I feel emotionally. For years, I've tried to convince my mom that his illness is the only explanation for the massive change in his behavior. Sometimes it seems she has it in her mind that he's just being an asshole. After I'd cried to her following a recent battle with him, she'd said, "I know he's sick. I know dementia will change a person, but he's always been like this . . . This is how he gets when he's angry or stressed . . . Trust me, honey, I was married to him. I get it. It's unacceptable." I've grown sick of these comments over the past two years; and I'd finally barked back at her, dismissing her words, telling her she doesn't understand. I feel she's projecting some unresolved sentiments from their short marriage onto the current situation. I just need her to hear me, to understand my pain; and she tries to, but in a manner that dismisses what is going on right in front of me. By making it about his personality and past behavior, she fails to see what I see: a man who treated me like an angel my whole life, who loved me so wholeheartedly and without abandon, who now acts as if seeing me ruins his day but chastises me for not visiting more. It's as if a demon has taken over his mind and body and made him into someone so different from the man he used to be.

But today, in his living room, watching his behavior switch on and off depending on who is around, I wonder if she's right. Maybe he is just an asshole.

I twirl lo mein onto my fork as my father makes more snide comments toward me—this time in front of Gerardo and Camila. I feel a sense of relief—excitement even! How odd to feel happy when someone is treating you like shit, but I feel vindicated; someone is finally seeing what he says and does and can maybe get a tiny glimpse into why I do, at times, go days without calling or seeing him.

"Tuco, eat your meal," Gerardo interrupts, as if to say "STOP." Gerardo glances at me. I lock eyes with him and nod, grateful.

Once we stop eating, Gerardo brings up the tuition again as no moves have been made since our visit the week before when he assured me this would be fine.

This ignites a fire in my father. He shakes his head, and his eyes shoot daggers right at me. "Erika, you know, you don't even care if I drop dead as long as you have my money!"

"What?" I say. "You have to know I don't feel that way . . . and I didn't even bring up the money today!"

"Oh sure, Erika, blame Gerardo. Everything is someone else's problem, just like your mother!"

I throw my head back and groan. "I'm not blaming Gerardo! I'm just stating a fact!"

Angry spit fires out of his mouth as he yells, "Erika, you are raising my blood pressure! Is that what you want?"

He gets up to use the bathroom, and I cry to Gerardo and Camila, desperate for them to help me understand. I rhetorically question what the sense is of being here right now. Why does he treat me this way, but no one else? I am his only daughter, and he always called me his *numero uno* and would sing to me and hug me and teach me and make me laugh; and suddenly, that all disappeared.

"He loves you, Erika. He really does," they say, almost in unison.

BUT DO YOU SEE HOW HE TREATS ME? I want to scream. But I don't. I blink back tears as he returns from the bathroom and retreats to his bedroom slowly, with help from the new walker he has been using since his most recent hospitalization. I follow him in to say goodbye before ending our visit.

But he isn't done fighting. I prepare for battle.

"You don't stay longer because your mother tells you you can't!"

At this point he is lying in bed, ready to sleep, but his exhaustion only seems to intensify his anger. I stare at his wooden headboard, unsure what to say.

"Erika, if your behavior keeps up like this, you won't get one penny in my will. I will take you out completely!"

He's broken me. I have never asked about his will, nor is it something I even think about. I wonder where he gets this idea. I don't know how to stand up to this. I want to say, "Daddy, please don't die. Please don't leave me. I love you. I want you to get better, and I want to go to Peru with you and go back to Fenway Park like when I was ten years old, and I want you to come with me when I bring your future grandchildren to Canobie Lake Park."

But I am so beaten down, too worn to express any kind of love. So instead, I yell, "Why would I want to see you when you treat me this way? I don't care about your money or your will, and I don't know where you're getting that idea! Tuition has to be paid, and I hate bringing it up, but I *didn't even bring it up today*! I care about you, but you treat me like *shit*! Here I am, visiting as much as I can, only for you to yell at me and tell me I am not good enough! What else am I supposed to do?"

"Just get the hell away from me," he says.

And I do.

I tend to shy away from opening up to Gerardo and Camila. I believe that they, like my father, think of me as a shameful daughter who is too wrapped up in her own life to care about my dad. In this moment, I push that aside and sit on the couch next to Camila when she invites me by patting the spot next to her. She obviously heard the interaction, and it is no secret I am upset.

"It's just not true, Camila . . . what he says, it's just not true. I call him every other day. If it's ever less, it's only after he's really mean to me, and I just can't bring myself to do it. I don't know if he actually believes I don't call or if he just says that because he's hurt and angry and sad . . . I don't know what to do. And I don't know why he hates my mom. She doesn't want his money. She just wants him to be nice to me . . . I don't get what he's saying and why he believes these things."

"I understand," Camila says, stroking my hair. I question whether she does, whether she ever could.

But then she says something that stays with me for years: "Erika, just do enough so that tomorrow, you'll feel okay about what you did."

There is an understanding that "tomorrow" means more than just the next day on the calendar. It means when he is gone.

37.

Pete calls one day when I am visiting my father. I take the call in the dining room, just a few feet from my dad's couch—the place he spends so much of his time these days, so much so that when he gets up, there is a permanent indentation forming from holding the weight of his frame, albeit shrinking in size by the day. I speak at a low volume so as not to interrupt the Bruins game on the TV, but also to keep my business private.

"Hey, sorry I missed your calls last night," Pete says. "I ended up staying at Jared's until pretty late."

Anger and jealousy bubble up inside me. I know there had been girls at Jared's house, and it feels like Pete chose them over me.

"You don't even care about me anymore . . . then start showing it!" I hiss into the phone, blinking back tears and doing everything I can to stand my ground when I feel wronged. We hang up, and I walk back over, sitting down next to my dad.

"You shouldn't talk to people that way," my dad says, not breaking eye contact with the action on the screen.

My eyes bug out of my head. My jaw drops. The audacity! Defenses rise in my mind: *But* you *talk to* me *like that! How fucking hypocritical of you to give me advice about how to talk to the people you love!*

Oh shit. I freeze. *Am I him?* Am I a verbally aggressive girlfriend? Am I taking the anger I want to expel from my body and placing it onto my loving boyfriend? Or is it possible that my boyfriend *is* being insensitive and I have learned the language of anger from my dad? I feel confused, and terrified that I am becoming the antithesis of who I want to be. Not knowing who to blame is an uncomfortable feeling. So I just sit there, ignoring it, absentmindedly watching the B's score the winning goal while the crowd erupts with excitement.

38.

I'm thrilled to have plans with my friends for New Year's Eve. I need an escape from the mundanity of the day-to-day. Tessa is having all of our friends from Natick over to her dad's house. Angela and I blast music in her bedroom as we paint our lips red and our nails gold and try on too many tank tops before settling on our final outfits.

When we arrive, Tessa's dad takes our keys; the expectation is that we will all spend the night since we will be drinking.

And oh, do we drink.

We clench Solo cups filled with vodka mixed drinks at all times. Music erupts from the speakers, we take dozens of pictures, and I awake on the couch in my party clothes at four in the morning. I groggily reach for my phone, which is beeping intermittently. Once my spins slow, I see three missed calls from Pete and a text message saying, "I'm worried about you sweetie, but Mason called me and said you're okay. Text me when you get this."

My tongue clicks around the dryness of my mouth. I feel embarrassed and guilty for worrying Pete and grateful to Mason for letting him know I was fine, just passed out. As I feel around on the floor for my water bottle, I realize I had just lashed out at Pete a few days ago for missing my calls; and here he is, being so understanding of the same thing. Before I can give it any more thought, I fall back asleep; and a few hours later, I wake to the sound of my friends exploding with laughter about how ridiculous the night became. I join them as we toast bagels and compare the bruises on our arms from dancing and falling in the bathroom.

Last semester, my Abnormal Psychology professor had said, "Alcohol, even when used moderately, can both lead to and exacerbate anxiety and depression symptoms, particularly during and immediately after use, but also in the days that follow" as we learned about mood disorders. But I'm in college—everyone drinks excessively! It's not like I only do it when I'm feeling sad. It helps me focus on what is happening *right now* rather than what is happening at home. It's a sweet escape. I never drink alone, and my friends occasionally pass out too. But instead of taking a step back to consider how my professor's words may explain what is happening in my own body and brain, I just keep drinking.

39.

A few days into the new year, I hit the road to visit Pete in New Jersey. This holiday break is the longest we've been apart since we started dating in April, and I miss him terribly. Within hours of arriving, I call my dad to check in, knowing it will get me nowhere but feeling obligated nonetheless. He tells me he has broken his arm and leg and is in the hospital.

I gasp, "Oh my god, are you okay? I'm sorry I'm not there . . ."

He replies with a grunt, and we hang up.

I immediately call Camila to ask her for more information, and she seems confused by my call. Apparently, he sprained his arm during a recent fall, but his leg is fine.

Is he confused, or is she?

I don't know how to make sense of this; is he purposely lying because he wants me to feel guilty? Does he legitimately believe he has injured his leg when he actually hasn't? *Is* his leg injured and everyone just cannot keep up with his latest affliction?

I'd stopped going to therapy once sophomore year began to see how I would fare on my own, but in this moment, I realize I need to go back. I need to process his dementia, his change, my pain. My mom has told me over and over she is worried about how witnessing his mental and physical decline and the emotions resulting from his nastiness toward me may affect my mental state in the future. Rationally, I know I shouldn't be avoiding working through this with a professional.

Despite this realization, I don't take any actual steps to schedule a therapy appointment. Being home and facing this situation every day does not make me want to go out of my way to talk about it even more each week with a therapist. I procrastinate and procrastinate—*I'll do it after my week with Pete, I'll call once I'm back on campus*—and instead focus my energy on visiting my father as soon as I'm back from New Jersey with the hope that somehow, something will change.

Something sure does change—toward the end of my break, he is admitted to a nursing and rehabilitation center after yet another nasty fall. It's unclear whether he will be there permanently or if he is a short-term rehab patient. I am torn between praying for the former and the latter—this may be what he needs for his health and safety, but this place seems fucking miserable.

I've been seeing more of my half brother Pepe, who has been visiting here and there since my father's condition worsened. I've met him only a handful of times and am enjoying getting to know him a bit more. But damn, does it make me feel like a shitty daughter. Pepe flies in from California, where his wife and children and job are, and I struggle to muster up the energy (and courage) to drive thirty minutes on the weekends when I'm at school. My dad wasn't even a big part of his childhood, yet Pepe still manages to show up. Most of me knows it isn't fair to compare, especially given the differences in how my dad treats Pepe versus how he treats me, but I still do. I am constantly searching for evidence of whether I am a good or bad daughter, and most of the time, the evidence points to the latter.

I'm visiting my dad at the facility in Westborough, about twenty-five minutes from his condo. Thankfully, I'm not the first to arrive. Pepe is there, and shortly after I enter, Gerardo and Camila walk in.

My father is in an especially sour mood today.

"Erika, I like those shoes!" Pepe says, making small talk.

"Thank you! I just got them at Payless, only $12."

"You don't need new shoes," my father grunts.

"Erika, when do you go back to school?" Gerardo asks me.

"Next week. Classes start Tuesday."

"Yeah, and you can't find the time to visit your father," my dad fires.

"José, be nice," Gerardo says. Sitting in a room full of people who visit my father more regularly than I do, who he says have big hearts as opposed to my small Grinch-like one, is not easy; and I am grateful that Gerardo is my defenseman.

"Erika, how are your classes this year? Are you enjoying them?" Camila asks.

"Yes! I had a great first semester, and next semester, I'm starting to take courses for my major—communications."

"Are you on the honor roll?" my dad asks. My stomach drops.

The day I entered middle school, my father told me he wanted (read: expected) me to make the honor roll; and once he learned that the high honor roll was an even more accomplished distinction, the focus shifted to that instead. The town published the names of honor and high honor roll students in the newspaper, and after each term, my father would buy it and sit next to me excitedly as we scanned for my name. There was always such pride in his eyes, followed by a hug and, more often than not, a trip to Liberty Ice Cream for giant black raspberry cones as a form of congratulations.

I explain to him that there is no honor roll in college, that it's called the dean's list—a term he's never heard before. I clarify that, yes, I am on it; and for a brief moment, his eyes fill with the same pride I witnessed each term in middle school and high school during our quarterly newspaper ritual. Then as if the demon has taken over again and reminded him that he is supposed to hate me, a silence overwhelms the room until a nurse comes in to ask him about the side effects of his medications.

After another hour, I'm ready to leave. As I sit there, wondering how to tell him I'm heading home without igniting the beast, a physical therapist walks in and announces, loudly, it's TIME FOR HIS WALKING. She shoots me an inquisitive smile.

"I'm Erika," I offer. "I'm his daughter."

"Oh! Great to meet you, Erika! Okay, José, now let's get up and get moving!" She sounds like a fitness instructor from the '80s.

My dad averts eye contact with me as I walk over, give him a kiss on the cheek, hug his frail body, and tell him I will visit again soon.

I make a last-minute decision to use the bathroom before hitting the road.

As I'm making my way out of the women's room, I'm about fifteen feet behind the physical therapist, who is arm in arm with my father. She walks as he shuffles next to her.

"So that's your daughter! It's so nice of her to visit!" She speaks slowly and loudly into his ear.

"She's on the dean's list," he replies, and I can see his cheek swell, which tells me he's smiling.

I freeze in my tracks. I've never been so grateful for having to pee. Had I left, I never would have heard this. He has no idea I'm behind him and will never know how much his words mean to me.

Even though he doesn't tell me he's proud of me, he is. Even when I don't think he loves me, he does.

40.

Classes start back up at the end of January, and I just want to fast-forward to March. Pete and I have booked a trip to France for spring break. We'll be staying with his grandmother in the countryside for the first half and then will be off on our own exploring Paris while sleeping in the cheapest hotel we can find for the second half. I set a widget on my laptop to count down the days, and before I know it, the trip is two weeks away.

Unfortunately, I have to somehow muster up the courage to let my dad know I'm choosing to use my spring break to go away rather than to come home. He knows this will be my first time ever leaving the country, and I imagine this may elicit some sadness that we never went to Peru together. He visited Lima every couple of years when I was growing up, and he tried like hell to bring me when I was a toddler, but my mom put the kibosh on it. There was a notorious terrorist organization called the Shining Path going around Peru, kidnapping children, and this was a risk my mom wasn't willing to take. My father again considered taking me once I was older; but by the time we finalized everything for my passport, biology kicked in, and he began to grow ill. Clearly, this is a loaded topic; and I do not want to be the one who brings it to the forefront of his mind, even unintentionally.

The week before spring break, I attend a voluntary documentary screening about a mental health facility. I've grown more interested in psychology as I've taken classes here and there and participated in therapy for the first time. But halfway through the film, I sprint out the back door of the building and make it outside just in time to puke in the snow. Turns out I have a case of the norovirus and spend a night in the school infirmary, nasty fluids escaping my body. Still, this illness feels easier than talking to my dad about the trip.

I had gone back and forth for weeks about whether to tell him at all. I figure I have to since I won't be able to call him for a week—and if I do, it will clearly be from a long international phone number, so he will figure out I'm not just sitting in my dorm at school. I think of ways I can lie about where I will be, why I won't have phone access; but ultimately, a few days before we leave, I decide to be honest. He grunts and says "Okay." I tell him I'll call him when I'm back, and I say *au revoir*.

The week is amazing. I eat the stinkiest cheese, take the most beautiful photographs, drink wine out of baby bottles at a tiny cramped fondue restaurant in Paris, and spend my twentieth birthday atop the Eiffel Tower.

I don't call. I don't email—not that my father checks his account these days anyway. Pete and I don't argue. My sadness, anxiety, and irritability feel as though they've been lifted. It's such a nice week away—a vacation from the volatile relationship with my dad, a preview of life without the constant fear of criticism.

After a long flight back, my mom picks us up from the airport. I gift her a cute little picture frame I picked up from a souvenir shop on the Champs-Élysées. "Did you get anything for Daddy?" she asks me, and I immediately feel my defenses rise up.

"No!" I bark back. "It would just remind him that he's mad that I went."

I give myself a day, then finally pick up the phone to call him.

He is short with me, which is usually how the calls start when he is holding back some specific jab; it's like he lets it build until he can sense my discomfort through the phone. Obviously, he doesn't ask about my trip. After a minute, he says, "You know, Erika, some people are just waiting for me to die."

Hearing this would normally make me sad, but I'm desensitized to statements like this by now and know any attempt at comforting him will only lead to him using me as a punching bag. I'm feeling empowered from my time off. I don't have time for this bullshit anymore. I don't give into it and try to shift the conversation, but he doesn't like that and repeats it: "Some people are just waiting for me to die." I tell him I have to get going; we say goodbye, and I swallow a hot anger that stays in my stomach for hours.

My father's friend and former coworker, Mr. Jewell, leaves a voicemail wishing me a belated happy birthday. He calls me every year—it's his late mother's birthday as well—and sends a card with some homemade granola every Christmas. Other than that, we don't really talk. He's like a distant grandfather to me. This year, he says, "I know you don't talk much to your father these days . . ." WHAT? The hot anger rises, spreading through my bloodstream, where it remains at a constant simmer for weeks.

As I fall back into the too-familiar "Do I hate Erika today?" roulette with my dad, I grow more irritable, and the brightness I'd felt in France begins to dull. Fights with Pete resume, and so does my self-harm; through blurred vision, I tear through my makeup case to anesthetize with my tweezers whenever my emotions surge. I cry into pillows so no one can hear me, snot decorating the case, my sleeve. Sometimes I cry so hard that when I close my eyes, disturbing visuals enter my mind. Images of the top of my skull opening up like a toilet, like there is a latch on the back of my head and someone can open it and see the ugly insides of my brain. Fingers come in and pick it apart, my brains exposed—bright, electric colors surrounding it, my thoughts swirling and swirling around until I stop crying and the images go away. I don't know what it means. I never tell anyone. I don't want people to think—know?—I'm crazy.

41.

"I need to talk to you," my dad says after a minute of small talk during a phone call in late March. "Our relationship has gone downhill, Erika," he continues. I gulp, unsure what is to come while also thinking, *No shit.*

"We need to either make this better or forget it altogether."

If I'm understanding correctly, he is suggesting we either improve our relationship—a feat I feel is truly impossible at this point—or not have a relationship at all.

"I'm not quite sure what to do, Daddy," I say tentatively. "I've told you how I feel about how you talk to me, and I call and visit as much as I can . . ."

"Okay, Erika. Well, something needs to change, or we need to not have a relationship anymore."

My dad is threatening to break up with me.

It doesn't feel as bad as I would have thought.

Hmm.

42.

In early April, my mom receives a phone call from her landlord; he tells her she has two weeks to move out, or she will be evicted. Apparently, the unit has been on the market the entire time she's lived there despite the fact that they'd assured her otherwise, and they found a buyer who is looking to move in as soon as possible.

"Are you serious?" I ask her, in disbelief that this could actually happen to us, to her twice within less than two years. She is, indeed, serious.

She leaves out the details but wants me to be aware of what is happening so I'm not totally caught off guard when, once again, we have to move. I later learn that the landlord was quite nasty to her, even threatening her with physical harm when she tried to push back. Somehow, she is able to hold them off, and they agree to let her stay until the end of May. She finds a place quickly, just one street over—which, incidentally, is even closer to my father's apartment. Other than the threat of assault and battery, this is a breeze for her compared to last year's fiasco with my dad.

43.

On the weekends when there isn't a *Heights* party, Pete and I eat dinner at the dining hall or make fruit and cheese plates in his dorm room, dressing up to feel fancy even though it's just us. Some nights, we take shots out of the bottle of vanilla vodka our older friend from the paper bought us and goof around, dancing to music. In these moments, just the two of us, I feel happy, energized—the depth of our love pumping life through my veins. I hate being by myself because whenever I am, I feel overwhelmingly lonely. I need Pete. Even when we're fighting, only around him do I feel alive.

We decide to make Fridays movie night. Week 1, we toss a bag of popcorn in the microwave, trying not to set off the smoke alarm, as so many students do fairly regularly. I've heard that *I Am Sam* is a good movie with a killer soundtrack—all Beatles covers. My mom's DVD collection rivals a Blockbuster store, and she'd loaned the movie to me the last time I was home, so we pop it in.

Within minutes, it becomes clear that Sean Penn's character, Sam Dawson, has an intellectual disability, so he isn't the type of father we typically see or expect in films. I instantly think of my dad and his current presentation, albeit different from Sam's. The love Sam has for his baby girl from the moment she is placed into his arms after birth is so pure. I find myself wishing to go back to my childhood when life was simpler and the reciprocal love between a girl and her father existed without the complications of disease, depression, and finances. There is no warning for how this transference manifests in my body—everything pours out of me. Pete immediately realizes that deciding to watch this may have been a mistake; he shuts off the movie and simply holds me.

"No, no, turn it back on," I demand between sobs. He takes a deep breath and aims the remote at the tiny dorm room television, and for the next two hours, I experience a deep catharsis I didn't know I needed. Watching Sam love, raise, and, eventually, fight for custody of his daughter breaks my heart and awakens a love for my own father that explodes in my chest and courses through my body. I want to call him, but it's 11:00 p.m., and I know—or hope anyway—that he is sound asleep. I want to tell him how much I love him, how I know he is struggling, how I miss being his little girl and him being my big, strong daddy. But I doze off next to a pile of crumpled tissues next to Pete's bed, feeling a bit lighter than I did a few hours ago.

I call my dad the next day, feeling inspired to change our relationship, but still unsure how. He initiates an unusual conversation, perhaps with the same thing in mind.

"Erika, I would like to pay you to take care of me," he says with the same businesslike seriousness he used to exhibit when calling to inquire about real estate.

Oh, my heart swells up. I am still fragile from the emotions the movie elicited the night before, but the rational part of me knows I cannot allow myself to do this. I've been through the ups and downs with him enough at this point that I know I cannot subject myself to this—for our relationship, for my own mental health, for my independence. I need to be a caretaker for me too. Even logistically, I don't know how I would manage—my mom has a one-bedroom condo, and so does he . . . Where would I live? Plus I'm in school, and I imagine he's seeking regular care. I can hardly cook and have no experience providing medical care, save for helping stop the bloody noses of the kids I babysat back in high school. I cannot bring myself to do what a nursing aide would do—help my father bathe and assist him on the toilet if he's having a hard time balancing.

"I'll even give you a day off," he continues, and this breaks me. He is bargaining before I can even process the information. I cannot imagine the humility it must take for him to ask me this.

It's hard to find the words to tell him that I can't do it. I cannot leave school. I cannot live with him in a sad tiny condo with little sunlight—when my own depression is only deepening, not resolving—to be his nurse, a job I'm not qualified for, neither professionally nor emotionally.

"I'm not sure I can do that, Daddy . . . ," I mumble, the awkwardness of the moment sending pangs of guilt through my chest. Turning down any job is awkward, but turning down a job to help your sick, helpless father is unthinkably excruciating.

This conflict tortures me; and later, as exhaustion overwhelms me, I scratch my inner wrist raw. The ritual feels normal to me, like something I should do when I feel low. To me, it is not a problem, but a means of survival.

A part-time home health aide visits daily to care for him. She is often late, and I try to explain to her that she needs to be on time and answer the phone when he calls her. I speak in broken Spanish and hope the message gets through, but not much changes. I want to call her agency to complain but don't want to play a role in her being deported, which my father explains is a risk as she is undocumented. She talks on her cell phone all day while he sits there watching the news or sports games or whatever else is on TV, his eyes glazed over, resigned to the monotony.

44.

I leave the cool, sunny spring day to enter the O'Neill Library basement for my three-hour shift affixing security tags inside new books. I started this job earlier in the semester; it's boring as hell, but it pays. I don't mind going. Adrian, my crunchy yoga-loving boss, is awesome, always wearing an ear-to-ear grin and cracking jokes.

"Well, hello, Ms. Erika," he greets me. "You're extra smiley today! Do you have any fun weekend plans?"

I blush. "Actually, yes. My boyfriend and I are leaving for the Cape later this afternoon. It's our one-year anniversary."

"Oh wow! That's so great! And what a day for it!" Adrian leans in and lowers his voice. "You know what? Leave early. Enjoy the sunshine. Mark your time sheet as if you worked your full shift, but leave here in an hour or so." He winks.

"Oh my gosh, really? Thank you, Adrian! That'd be really great, but I'll just enter my time as an hour—"

"Don't be silly," he interrupts. "You work hard. It's not a problem."

I smile and reach for the tower of books in front of me so I can get to work. My sleeve retracts and reveals slow-to-heal self-inflicted scratch marks.

Adrian's smile falls. "Hey . . . you okay?"

My heart stops. I've never been caught.

My brain gets to work generating an excuse. "Oh . . . yeah." I stumble over my words. "My friend's cat got me. It was so annoying . . . Yeah, honestly, I've never really been a cat person."

He looks me dead in the eye. "Okay," he says, and I know he knows I'm lying. He starts to walk away, then turns around, wearing a sympathetic smile, and says, "Be careful with yourself."

It takes almost the full hour for my racing heart to stabilize. But this sensation is eventually replaced by happy butterflies as I exit the dark library, my mood as bright as the sun, and meet Pete in the Lower Campus parking lot.

Thanks to Adrian, we beat the traffic and have time for some extra adventures. We drive past the house where we stayed one year ago with my mom, take silly photographs and run along the beach where we officially started dating, and shop around Mashpee Commons. We fill our bellies with penne alla vodka and chocolate lava cake and head to the Town and Country Motor Lodge in West Yarmouth for the night.

I had called my dad earlier today, and he informed me he was in the hospital again. It seemed like one of the more benign matters, something about high blood pressure, something where he would be home the next day.

I call him again later in the evening to see how he's doing. He knows I'm away for the weekend because I mentioned it when he told me he'd been admitted, and I want him to know that I care enough to call.

To my surprise and relief, he isn't angry. He says he is feeling all right, and we have a quick conversation. After we hang up, Pete and I flip through the channels of the dingy two-star hotel's television; and suddenly, he turns to find me silently crying. Clips from *I Am Sam* run through my head like a film reel. Pete hugs me, kisses my head over and over, and tells me it will be okay, that I'm doing so much. I tell him, "No, no I'm not," expressing my discontent with how little I have done for my father, lamenting that it simply isn't fair, that he doesn't deserve this.

I share stories from my childhood, reminiscing about the afternoons when my dad and I would play "goalie" in the side yard of his Ashland town house. The time I scored the winning goal in the soccer game and he cheered like hell on the sidelines. The time on Christmas, when after giving me all my gifts, he asked me to get something for him from upstairs; and I found close to fifty Beanie Babies on my bed, completing my collection. The time his car doors were so frozen from the cold snow that they wouldn't open, yet he still managed to get me to my morning drama rehearsal on time. I reminisce about the song "Erika Baby" that he wrote for me as a toddler and how he would sing it to bring a smile to my face whenever I was sad.

Then I fast-forward a few years to the day he signed the paperwork for the house, how proud he was every report card day, how excited both of us would get the mornings when we decided to go to Mel's Cafe for breakfast. Images of him as a healthy younger man with a gut—certainly not from beer, but likely from all the sugary food we would eat together—swim around in my mind, countering the images of his now-sickly figure, with his walker and cane and too-big polo shirts.

I eventually settle down to sleep, and as always when I have a breakdown, I feel better in the morning. Pete and I go out for banana-chocolate-walnut pancakes at the same place we went last year. We return to the beach; it's chilly, so we exchange gifts in the car. I give him a poem I wrote and an engraved watch that contains a photograph of us inside; he gives me a customized version of Monopoly featuring photos of us and locations significant to our relationship. He also gives me an adorable music box with magnetic ladybugs that dance as the song plays. He says to play it whenever I miss him, but I can't help but think back to a memory of my father—something I am trying to avoid after last night's breakdown. When I was eight years old, my dad bought me a music box at the mall. There was a ballerina inside who danced beautifully to the song that played when you twisted the gold knob on the back. I am flooded with nostalgia as the music box from Pete plays the same melody.

We enjoy a butternut squash ravioli dinner at the Yarmouth House, a rustic restaurant with exposed brick and glowing string lights. We eat too much but still follow the meal with giant ice cream cones and head back to the hotel. Pete does everything he can to make sure I am happy for the rest of the night, forcing me to watch silly Animal Planet shows. We open a cheap bottle of red wine. Pete proceeds to spill it all over the bed; and though we are never quite drunk, we both fall into an easy alcohol-assisted slumber early on, stopping me from having any time to think about the world outside our budget hotel room.

45.

Final exams are over, and after what has been a particularly challenging year both personally and academically, I'm excited for the freedom summertime affords me. I move into a beautiful brand-new building on Lower Campus, where I will be living and working all summer. I work a few four-hour shifts each week at the BC Welcome Center, conveniently located in the lobby of my new home. I greet guests arriving for reunions and conferences, handing them the keys to their weekend dorm rooms. I share a giant four-bedroom suite with three of my new coworkers; we each have our own bedroom, and it's the first time I have my own space since my mom and I moved out of the house. I push the two extra-long twin beds together, forming what feels like a king-sized bed. I am ecstatic to be living just one dorm over from Pete, who is a freshman orientation leader for the second summer in a row. He spends most nights in my air-conditioned room with me. The on-campus summer community is small—a big change from the school year, where I can get lost in a sea of strangers. While I don't have any close friends on campus (other than Pete, of course), the other orientation leaders working alongside him often shoot me a smile when we pass each other in the dining hall, offering high-fives as they ask, "How ya doin', Mrs. Pete?"

I have my car on campus, which makes traveling home to see my dad quite easy. Every time I strap on my seat belt, my heartbeat quickens, anxious to find out which mood I'll be greeted with upon my arrival. I often find myself exaggerating my lifestyle and saying I work more than I actually do so he's less likely to reprimand me for not visiting more frequently. It makes me feel both guilty and safe.

During a Monday evening chat, out of nowhere, he says, "I don't know how much longer I'll be here, Erika. I think I should give your mom my car since I don't use it. I know her minivan's falling apart anyway." I don't know how he knows about the condition of her car, but I don't ask.

He continues, "I could maybe even buy her a new one."

I don't understand.

As quickly as they enter my mind, the words slip out of my mouth. "Daddy, you've made it clear that you hate Mom … why would you want to help her and buy her expensive things?"

"I never said I don't like your mom," he says, and it's as if my brain flashes DOES NOT COMPUTE. I say nothing. I want to laugh at how ridiculous this statement is, but I don't.

The silence makes me uncomfortable, so after a few seconds, I ask what he is doing today. I hate asking this; I already know the answer, but I don't know what else to say.

"Erika, the house has sold," he says.

My heart sinks. It's not like I thought he would change his mind and we'd move back, but the finality of it hits me hard. The news also gives me some insight into why he's suggesting buying my mom a car. Just like when I drove off in my new Honda Civic last year, perhaps buying her something will alleviate the guilt he feels for taking away her home and maybe for putting me through so much distress that, in his rational mind, he must realize my mom bears the brunt of.

In the same breath, he tells me he will pay for my car insurance like he used to. There is no *fucking* way I am allowing that to happen. I refuse to put myself in another position where he has power that he will inevitably only use against me later. I thank him sweetly but tell him I am all set. But god, that $80 I pay to Liberty Mutual each month could go so far. I know I need to go back to therapy, but I continue to put it off, partially because the copay just feels like too much. With no summer meal plan, I am paying for my own groceries for the first time in my life; and naturally, mental health is easier to put on the back burner than daily nourishment.

When I tell my mom about the house, I imagine it hits her in a similar way it hit me, perhaps only slightly less emotionally loaded. She is hopeful, though, that with an improved financial situation (I learn from an internet search that he turned a pretty profit on the house), his mood and behavior toward me may improve as well.

A few weeks into the summer, Pete's uncle dies. He had been sick with cancer and suffering for a while. The night after, my dad calls *me* for the first time in a while, and I am caught off guard by his face smiling back at me from my cell phone screen—the photo I took in May 2005, when I received my first camera phone. I remember that when I took the photo, I'd thought he looked sick. Looking at it now, the picture version of him looks so healthy—he still had color and some fullness to his face.

When I answer, he's crying; he fell again—he's okay, just shaken. He so rarely opens up about how sad and scared he is in his illness. We cry together into the phone; with the news of my boyfriend's uncle's death fresh in my mind, I imagine losing my father. It would be my first major death; the only other losses I've faced have been grandparents, with whom I was not particularly close. My mom's parents both died before I was in elementary school, so I was young and blissfully naive about what death was, what it meant. Growing up is great in so many ways, but sometimes it means knowing and feeling too much.

46.

I find that I am not as nervous to see him on Father's Day as I am on any other ordinary day. Maybe it's because of our recent conversation; maybe it's because today is a celebration of fathers.

I try to look nice because even though it's just my dad and me, it's a special day. I swing by the campus bookstore to buy the BC mouse pad he'd requested, but they don't have it in stock. *You're not doing enough. You're letting him down again.* I shake my head, as if to shake the thoughts away too. After a quick traffic-free drive, I stop at CVS.

In the greeting card aisle, a man in his late twenties perusing the "Father's Day – Humor" section turns to me. "Last minute too, huh?"

"Yeah . . . and I'm about forty minutes late. Whoops," I say.

"Join the club. I was supposed to be at my dad's hours ago!"

I offer a small laugh and peek inside a card.

"Aww, how sweet and sentimental of you," he says, playfully mocking me. "Little different from what I'm going with." He shows me his selection—a crude-humored card about boobs.

To ease the feeling of awkwardness, I force a giggle and say "Heh . . . My dad would never go for that."

I wonder how different his father must be from my own.

Picking out a card for my dad, for any occasion, has not been an easy task for me since the sickness took over his personality. I have to put back the cards that read "You're the best, Dad!" with a

179

smiling cartoon character; it feels too insincere. All the cute cards with jokes about asking for money are also taboo . . . obviously. Cards that read "Dada" are out of the question because we would probably both break down right on the spot, nostalgic for the sweet name I called him as a toddler when life felt much simpler. This leaves me with a very small selection, but I eventually find a nice, safe card and make my way to his apartment.

Upon greeting me, he is kind. We hug. I give him the card, and he says he will open it later.

"What's on your eyes?" he asks, squinting.

"Oh . . . just eyeliner," I reply, realizing he doesn't often see me with makeup.

"It looks nice," he says, flashing a quick smile.

We sit and talk for a few minutes. I help him get his shoes on, and we decide to go to the Olive Garden, his favorite restaurant. On the way out, he stops suddenly and says, "Can you bring my card?" Tears fill my eyes before the words even finish rolling off his tongue. He doesn't realize he just made my day. He acknowledged something I did, something so small, and it means something to him. What I wouldn't give for this moment to last.

When we arrive, he waits in the car while I run in to see how long the wait is. We decide to wait the twenty minutes; and as we walk inside, people immediately give up their seats, noticing that he is using a walker. After a short while, our table is ready; and the hostess walks too fast for my dad, not realizing he's lagging behind. I have to stop her. My father and I sit and have a nice conversation about my responsibilities at the Welcome Center.

Between our salad and entrée, I remember the card and pull it out of my purse. Upon opening the envelope, his reaction reminds me of his past playful demeanor; he opens his eyes really big and curls his lips into an "Oooh" and says, "You got a fancy one . . . expensive!" At this point in our relationship, it's still okay when *he* makes a joke about money. We both smile. I tell him it was the best card I saw, and that's what mattered.

"Happy Father's Day" is written in gold script on the front. The paper is glossy and opaque, decorated with purple and yellow flowers. I wrote a simple message on the inside: "Thank you so much for everything you do. I love you, Erika"—because just as finding a card is tricky, so is finding the right words to say.

As he reads the card, his facial expression warms me in a way I hadn't anticipated. He smiles; it's subtle, but palpable even though we do not make any eye contact, and he keeps his focus on the card. Time slows down; waiters bustling across the restaurant carrying dishes of pasta become blurred in the background. I can feel the warmth in my father's veins and can see the happiness he feels in this moment. I wish I had a photograph of this calm expression of love or a short video recording from beginning to end, though it's not necessary because it will remain forever embedded in my memory. He does not expose his teeth but simply lets the sides of his lips curl up in a smile that silently says, "I appreciate you, Erika. I love you." And for the first time in a long, long time, I know he means it. He does not speak until the end, when he says, "Thank you." But his two-second smile had said it all. I melt and wonder if he feels as connected in this moment as I do.

47.

In between shifts at the Welcome Center, I spend about eight hours a week as an education and outreach intern at a local agency that treats and spreads awareness about eating disorders. I spent the spring semester interviewing for various internship opportunities, all unfortunately unpaid and most of which focused on advertising and business. On a whim, I found this agency and applied. I walked out of my interview feeling the nervous and excited energy you get when you really want something. Serendipitously, this is the only offer I received, and I happily accepted. I spend most of my time there designing PowerPoint presentations about eating disorder statistics and body image in the college population or hanging up flyers around town announcing events for the nonprofit.

It's another Wednesday at the office, and it starts out fine. I had a good night's sleep, my morning coffee was perfect, I have plans with Pete later. But something just isn't right, and I can't shake it. Halfway through the afternoon, I start to feel numb—numb internally, externally. I'm just sitting in front of the computer screen, completely unmotivated. Being a typically hardworking, driven person, it's clear something is wrong . . . But I find myself not wanting to fix it. I take a strange, inexplicable comfort in this state. For once, I let myself sit with what I'm feeling. A throbbing headache thunders through my skull; and I sit with my eyes glazed over, staring, waiting for an answer from the desktop computer.

Time passes slowly, and after what feels like days, my shift is over. I get in my car and start to drive, and the feeling remains. I am numb, and I don't care. The only way I know I am alive is through occasional blinks.

I genuinely feel like I could die and be okay with it.

There is no specific reason. There is no "I want to die because . . ." I just do. I try to make sense of this, but in doing so, guilt and shame rise in my body. *You have a great boyfriend. The last time you saw your dad, things were fine. You're fortunate to have summer housing and a job. It doesn't make sense to feel this way. What's wrong with you?* I pull up to the intersection at Newton Centre and turn left and wish a car would hit mine because then maybe I would feel something. Or die. And either would be fine.

The extremity of this thought is sobering, and I have the foresight to pull over and call for help. Ever since my panic attack freshman year, I've kept the number for campus counseling in my phone. I select it and press 1 for the psychiatrist on call. A woman answers, her voice warm, curious. I tell her I was driving and pulled over on the side of the road because I didn't care if I lived or died and still don't but mostly want to live—I think? And that I'm scared because I've had thoughts kind of like this, but not *like this*—not while in a car. I tell her about my work, my internship, my relationship, and, finally, the constant ups and downs with my dad and realize that this is the topic I continue to procrastinate addressing, the topic that is largely the source of my numbness in this moment. We talk until she knows I'm safe. I realize that my gut reaction to pull over probably means I'm actually terrified to die, terrified of my own thoughts, and that something inside me is trying to shake me and say, "Erika, you are having a *really fucking hard time*, and you need to *do something about it*."

I schedule an appointment with a therapist at the campus counseling center for later in the week. We hang up, and I'm on my own again.

48.

Freshman year repeats itself. I meet with a therapist on campus, who, after an intake meeting, quickly refers me off campus to a psychiatrist (a.k.a. someone who can prescribe me pills) who also provides talk therapy. The familiar feeling resurfaces: *I am too much for them. My emotions cannot be handled. My problems are too big for short-term therapy, too big for this school. I don't belong.*

Fortunately, I am motivated to find someone quickly, so I call a few names from the printout of local referrals the counseling center gave me. Dr. Sally Rose is the only one who returns my call. Dr. Rose's office is on Sunny Lane, about fifteen minutes from campus. Sunny Lane feels like an ironic location for a therapy office; it's like a little joke the universe is playing, so it at least amuses me.

I parallel park on the street and walk inside. The house smells old, musty, and I sit on a lumpy chair in Dr. Rose's waiting area. Within a few minutes, a tall, thin woman in her early seventies opens the door. "Did you park on the street?" she greets me.

"Um, I did . . . ?" I answer, confused if this is my new therapist, a receptionist, or the patient before me.

"You can't park there. Please move to the driveway."

I do as instructed and quickly learn that she is, in fact, Dr. Rose. I'm unsure whether I am going to like her.

When we begin our meeting, she asks the typical questions: what my symptoms are, what my family is like, if I can perform my "activities of daily living." Despite my initial impression of her, honest and unedited words pour out of me. I am desperate for someone—anyone—to listen and to hold my emotions. While explaining my family, I mention that my father has depression and dementia and that has been a big source of my own sadness, anger, hopelessness. She blinks, scratching away at her yellow legal pad of paper with a pen.

I walk out and don't feel happy per se, but I feel a bit lighter. I see her again the next week, and we discuss medication. I don't ponder the potential side effects or explore various options. I walk right into the Newton Centre CVS, fill my brand-new Celexa prescription, and pop a pill in hopes that something will change.

Dr. Rose had said it could take up to eight weeks to feel a shift. I don't know if I can wait that long.

49.

Pete and I manage to align a week off from our summer jobs, and it's time for another trip to the Poconos. After picking up some road snacks from Campus Convenience, we arrive at my mom's for the summertime BBQ she's been itching to have with us. We stuff ourselves with corn on the cob and potato salad and play a quick round of Lie Detector before it's time to head to Pennsylvania. But first, I decide I should stop by to see my dad.

The decision to visit my father takes courage. I am leaving one happy place (home) and going to another (the mountains). I'd rather not taint it with stress and guilt; before one of our Poconos trips last summer, my dad had barked, "Oh, so you have time for Pete, but not your father?"

When I call him to tell him I'm stopping by, he says, "You don't have to come by. You can just say goodbye on the phone." But I push for it. I know he has an underlying desire to see me, and part of me really wants to see him too.

I walk in, and Gerardo and Ynes are there. I say a little prayer inside my head, thanking the universe for its timing.

My dad seems happy, and it makes me happy. At the same time, though, I wonder why I can't make him as happy as he is in this moment with his friends. He smiles the weak, hopeful smile that breaks my heart in two. He fervently chats with Ynes and Gerardo in Spanish while I sit there, an observer. Ynes, having noticed my silence, asks me when I am leaving for my trip; and I reveal that Pete is waiting outside in the car. Everyone encourages me to invite him in, so I do.

This is nerve-racking because Pete has not seen my dad for over a year; the only other time he saw him, he could drive and was much healthier—or rather, less unhealthy. I'm a little nervous about whether Pete might feel uncomfortable, but mostly, I'm nervous for my dad, who I know feels a deep sense of humiliation and shame about his current physical state. This is why I never bring Pete around; it is a way to protect my father, for him to maintain the belief that in Pete's mind, he is still the strong(er), able-bodied man of 2006.

Pete walks in and greets my dad with the warm, charming smile that drew me to him in the first place, shaking my father's hand as he says, "Great to see you again, Mr. Vargas!" I introduce him to Gerardo and Ynes, and we sit there while my dad continues to talk mostly to his friends and not to us.

Somehow, the conversation turns into a discussion of restaurants. My dad turns to me and says something about the time we went to the Naked Fish. We didn't.

"Daddy, I think you're thinking of a different restaurant. Bertucci's maybe? I've never been to the Naked Fish."

For some reason, he seems very confident about this memory. "Yes, Erika, remember? We went there—recently!" he keeps saying.

This feels different from other times I've given in to what he says; this time, saying "yes" is actually a lie. I am unsure of how to handle the situation. Am I supposed to enable his delusions? How do I clarify his memory without starting a fight or embarrassing him? I look at Gerardo, and he looks back, and we silently conclude to drop it. The room remains quiet. Everyone seems uncomfortable, fidgeting in their chairs and mentally searching for a new topic.

Ynes begins telling a story about her children, and I tune everything out. I'm too in my head, trying to process yet another example of the severity of my father's brainsickness. His brain forgets things that do happen and invents things that don't. Seeing him like this is always heartbreaking, and it tends to hit harder on the days that don't end in a fight.

After a few more minutes of small talk, Pete and I offer hugs goodbye and have a lovely drive to the mountains. I feel grateful and relieved that the visit, albeit sad, went fairly smoothly. Unlike walking away from so many of our visits over the past three years, this time, I can breathe.

50.

This day has potential. I'm back from the most relaxing week in the Poconos, feeling refreshed. The sky is clear, and I look forward to spending some time outside this afternoon, soaking up the warm summer sun. I head to my doctor's office for an early-morning cystoscopy—a painful intrusive gynecological medical examination—and top it all off with a monster shot in my arm to prevent any infections that could arise from the god-awful procedure. Somehow, despite the fact that I cannot feel my left arm and have to stop to pee every five minutes, I am still smiling. I head to Natick because I am meeting up with Julia at our usual Starbucks, then having dinner with my dad. I have a few hours before these plans, so I pop into my mom's to take Freckles for a short walk and go through some boxes of old stuff. This always cheers me up because I live in the past, and finding little middle school notes and silly pictures from summer camp can brighten my day more than anything else.

After I finally tear myself away from reading the myriad of since-forgotten inside jokes scribbled on the inside cover of my eighth-grade yearbook, I call my father to remind him about dinner. He doesn't answer. I wonder where he is because he always has his cell phone, so I try his home line. No answer. I will try again soon; he may be in the bathroom or on the other line.

After carefully organizing everything into boxes marked "Sell," "Keep," "Take to School," and "Recycle," I head to Starbucks to meet Julia to catch up. On the way, I call my father again—cell and home—and am surprised when, again, there is no answer. I park. I see Julia, and we sip iced tea outside because the sun is at its highest. We have a beautifully reinvigorating talk, discussing our love lives and petty jealousy and our college weekends and our summer jobs. I carefully avoid mentioning my dad; this moment is too good. We shop Old Navy sales for some new clothes even though we know we shouldn't spend the money, and it's the best girls' day out I've had in a while.

At this point, I have called my dad at least four or five times over the course of several hours and tried both of his phone numbers. Panic sets in as I leave Julia, and I wonder if something has happened. I immediately call Camila—no answer. I call Gerardo—home and cell—to no avail. For a split second, I wonder if this is some kind of sick joke and then realize they are adults and are probably busy with their own families and careers.

This has happened once before, where I was worried sick that he was not okay, and he ended up being fine. I know he has his Life Alert necklace. I know he has the part-time aide. But still, something feels off. As I pull up to my father's building, I mentally prepare myself to see his dead body—or at least a very injured version of him—lying on the ground, helpless. I find my strength and step out of my car. I push his apartment buzzer—nothing. I'm not totally surprised. It can take him a while to get up from the couch and get over to buzz guests in, but concern and fear continue to build in my gut. I buzz again, again, again—allowing as much time between buzzes as I can tolerate without drowning in cortisol. I walk around the side of the building and peer in his bedroom window, thankful the blinds are open, and clear a circle of pollen with my fingers so I can see inside. Adrenaline courses through my body, traveling from my legs to my wrists, through my chest and to my neck.

I see him. He sees me. He is sitting on his bed, staring at nothing. I am angry and simultaneously relieved he is there. This is the only eye contact we will share all day. Large tears start to pour down my cheeks—a mix of relief, anger, fear, and confusion. Why didn't he answer? As I walk back around the building and up the steps to ring the buzzer once again, I suspect he must be angry about something I've done, though I have no idea what. He buzzes me in, which surprises me slightly; and I nervously enter, pondering potential explanations for his not answering any of my phone calls. When I enter his apartment, he is standing by the dining room table, facing away from me. I say hello, and he doesn't reply. I try to hug him, and his body involuntarily jerks at my touch. But otherwise, he does not move. I ask why he didn't answer his phone.

Finally, he speaks. "Because I didn't want to talk to you." It hits so hard that my heart skips a beat. We haven't fought in a while—and still, even when he's angry, he always answers.

I ask why.

"You're a *liar*," he says.

As soon as the words leave his mouth, I know what he must be referencing. It is Monday. Last week, I had told him I was coming home over the weekend to see him "probably on Sunday." On Saturday, I realized it made much more sense to come home Monday because I would not have to rush back for work like I would on Sunday evening. I called him early Saturday afternoon—he'd been sleeping so was therefore groggy—and told him I would be coming Monday instead. On Sunday, I'd woken up to a missed call from him; and when I called back, he'd asked when I was coming. I'd explained that I had told him I was going to come Monday instead. He'd told me he did not have food, and I'd asked if he needed my help ordering something. He'd said, "I don't know *what* I am going to do, Erika." Him using my name means he is angry.

I'd known he was mad on Sunday, but I'd figured it would pass. I'd felt a bit guilty for not coming home but remembered there was a reason I'd called Saturday—to prevent this issue. It was a simple justifiable change in plans, and I'd offered to help him order food to solve the problem. Still, I'd had a feeling this decision would come back to haunt me.

Standing in his apartment on Monday, I ask him why I am a liar, just to verify my suspicions. Sure enough, he says, "You *know* why." I try to calmly explain that I'd called him to tell him about the change in plans, but he just won't have it, which is something I intuitively knew would happen but struggle to accept. Part of me still holds out hope that someday, after an argument or misunderstanding, he will say, "You know, you're right. I'm sorry I overreacted. I love you. Let's get dinner."

But there is no such dinner invitation. Instead of "I love you," it's "I'm ashamed"—a phrase that has become much more commonplace than the former. He refuses to acknowledge the tears streaming down my face as I tell him I was looking forward to seeing him and getting dinner. He grunts and says, "Well, I don't want to."

"But it sounds like you need food, and we planned for this, remember? We can go to the grocery store afterward to get you—"

"You have absolutely no respect for your father, Erika," he interrupts. "You don't worry about me. You don't even care about me!"

"What? If I didn't care, why would I be standing here in your kitchen? Why would I have been worried sick when you didn't answer my calls?"

I know I am right. He doesn't let it sink in.

The argument escalates further, culminating in me saying something I'm not proud of—something that my overwhelming frustration pulls out of me before any impulse control kicks in to stop the words: "You make me want to die! You make me want to kill myself!"

"Then we'll bury you," he says without skipping a beat.

My heart implodes. I try to form words, but nothing comes out of my mouth. I storm out of his apartment, feeling as though I might vomit. As bad as the needle hurt this morning, I would take ten more to avoid the five minutes I stood in my father's tiny kitchen—helpless, hated.

I rush over to my mom's in a stupor, the buildings and trees a blur. Through the slider, I see her cozy in her recliner, eyes focused on her laptop. As I place my hand on the door handle, she sees me and immediately hoists herself up, shaking her head sadly, knowingly. She pulls me into her and holds me in her arms, letting me cry like a toddler who just lost their favorite teddy bear.

I tell her I don't want to talk yet. I'm not ready to repeat what was just said to me—the words still cutting at my heart. I dig a notebook out of the trunk of my car so I can take five minutes to purge my emotions. I curl up on her bed and scribble sentences like "I seemingly can't do anything right even when I think I do . . . I cry myself to sleep thinking about how sad you are . . . But you are not my father to me. Not anymore. You aren't the wonderful man who taught me soccer and how to drive stick shift . . . He is long gone. You taught me how to stand up to bullies, but not the emotional bullies, the ones who beat you down, picking your vulnerabilities inside out until you have nothing left to give. That's what I needed today, what I've needed for years. But even if you had taught me that, I never expected the bully to be my own father."

I wipe my eyes, blow my nose, rest my hand for a moment, and then write, "This may be the hardest thing I ever do, but I think I have to cut you out of my life. I don't want to, but I need to. I can't ride this roller coaster anymore."

I end it with "You are my unhappiness."

My mom and I discuss what happened and consider my options. I'm not ready to make a decision and need to focus my mind elsewhere, so we pick up where I left off earlier, sorting through my old stuff. We stumble upon the board book *Daddy & Me*, which he used to read to me as a toddler. She tries to push it away so I won't see it, but I do and place it into the "Keep" pile. I can't let the memory of my dad and our glory days go.

We also come across an old stuffed animal that I remember but am not sure why I want to keep. I tell my mom to save it. She laughs, playfully rolls her eyes, and comments about how I want to keep everything. I cry. I apologize for not being good enough at clearing everything out and for not doing a good job. Tears fill my mom's eyes as she hugs me again and firmly, lovingly holds my shoulders to meet me dead in the eye, saying, "Honey, you are always, always good enough. Do not let him make you feel otherwise."

I wash my face, then leave to head back to school, and my mom walks me out. I call Julia on the way and leave her a jumbled three-and-a-half-minute voicemail about what happened today. She calls back ten minutes later, apologizing for not answering.

"Talk," she instructs. She knows only bits and pieces of what's been going on, so it takes me the entire drive back to school to catch her up on the past few months and how, even among the ups and downs, I never thought he'd say anything as horrifying as he did today.

"Erika, why haven't you told me any of this? Jesus, I'm always here, okay? I had no idea that it was *this* bad—that he's been so abusive."

Abusive.

Is that what this is?

The narrative shift from "My dad is really mean to me" to "My father has become verbally abusive" is significant. Maybe he doesn't mean what he says, but I still feel the pain. A car accident is not intentional, but it still hurts. We reflect on everything I've tried: I have called daily. I have not called daily. I have visited once a week. I have set limits on how often I visit. I have been so sickeningly sweet at times that I made myself nauseous. I have stood my ground. But through it all, I have only sunk deeper into depression. We agree that it really may be time to stop contact.

"Nothing's permanent," she assures me. "You can always change your mind."

The problem is I can't stop thinking about the worst-case scenario. What if not talking to him makes it worse? What if my guilt, my anxiety, my depression increase? What if this makes me feel like I'm drowning even more?

But most of all, *what if he dies?* How will I ever forgive myself?

As I enter my building, I flash a smile at my suitemate, who's working the front desk of the Welcome Center. I keep my sunglasses on and pretend I'm on the phone to avoid stopping to chat. I don't have it in me, not now. As I unlock the door to my suite, I realize all my roommates are out, thank God. I toss a veggie burger into the microwave and splash water on my face, then eat mindlessly while my thoughts race. I decide to write everything out, not knowing where it will lead me. I read through journal entries from last summer and find some clarity. I needed help then and just thought it would pass. I wrote about how I would never get these years back, how I've started to believe that I really am *a selfish, bad daughter*, and how I thought that when I got back to school, things wouldn't seem as bad. I was wrong. I call my mom to talk it out again, and she tells me how badly she wishes there was a law against emotional abuse.

I feel like a sick child—helpless, tearful, in and out of awareness. I am alone in my suite; it's been a few hours since my call with Julia, and she calls me to check in (which I think is her way of making sure I'm not *actually* going to kill myself).

I make my decision. I am going to stop contacting my father. I have to. I feel a brief sense of relief, take a breath, and feel empowered. I have no idea how long it will last—maybe a day, maybe a week, maybe forever. But I will take it one day at a time until I start to feel like myself again . . . until his words—"Then we'll bury you"—stop echoing in my brain.

And despite all this, despite the pain and revelations and tears, despite assurance from one of my most trusted friends and from my mother that I can't afford to put up with this any longer, I cry myself to sleep, picturing my father alone in his sunless living room, flipping through the channels and crying helplessly, wondering where the hell he is going to find the energy to make it to his bedroom tonight.

DURING: PART II

51.

I wake up puffy-eyed.
I don't call my father, and he doesn't call me.
This pattern goes on for days, weeks.
I am liberated.
I'm free from the prison. Every time I feel like total shit for not contacting my sick, depressed father, I remember how depressed I've become; and that keeps me in check. *It's just a break*, I tell myself when I struggle. I try to remind myself that this break means I won't spend each day trying so hard but feeling like it's never enough. It is my only hope of staying sane, even with weekly therapy, which is still so new that it's hard to tell how much it's helping.

It feels easier to get up in the morning, and I drift off to sleep more quickly at night. It has been weeks since I've dug into my flesh.

Angela and Tessa visit often; we take shots of cheap vodka in my dorm and go out for sushi and crash on my makeshift king-sized bed. Weekends are spent at the beach, weeknights wrapped up in my boyfriend's arms; we are fighting less and less. By no means is it my happiest summer, but the shift is significant. I feel lighter, brighter.

Summer vacation ends earlier than usual as I'll be a resident assistant (RA) this year, and training begins mid-August. Pete will also be an RA—just one building over from me! After moving all my belongings from my air-conditioned suite on Lower Campus to the tiny single I will call home for the next year, I walk into the Duchesne Hall common area for the first meeting with my new staff: three other girls, four guys, and a director, Jocelyn.

Jocelyn greets me with a warm handshake. "You're Pete's girlfriend, right? Lisa mentioned you'd be on my staff."

I wonder for a moment what else she already knows about me, if Pete's boss shared anything besides my relationship status.

"Erika," I say, smiling. "Nice to meet you. I'm excited to be here!"

While most people roll their eyes at the schmaltzy getting-to-know-you activities, I'm all about them. We eat Starburst while sharing fun facts based on the colors we choose: Orange means share your most embarrassing moment. Pink means tell your childhood nickname and where it originates. We order a pasta dinner on the Office of ResLife's tab, and on my first night in my new room, I sleep well and wake up refreshed the next day.

The early mornings and eight-hour days spent out of the sun and inside lecture halls learning about diversity, housing policies, and how to write incident reports are intense. But I feel a renewed sense of purpose. If I can't be enough for my father right now, maybe I can be enough for these kids as they transition into their freshman year of college.

Some activities are more emotionally loaded than others. For all the candy-themed icebreakers, we also watch sexual harassment videos and role-play challenging situations we may encounter with our residents: assault, eating disorders, substance abuse—the unfortunate college trifecta.

I am *on fire* with the role-plays. I've always been praised for my empathic nature and sensitivity when discussing hard topics. In preschool, my teachers nicknamed me the Protector because of my proclivity for checking in when others were hurt or crying. I feel helpful, empowered, alive.

One day, our final activity is called "Step into the Circle." It's as simple as it sounds; we all form a large circle, and if you identify with the statement that's read, you take a step into an inner circle. It's like a PC, less-risqué version of "Never Have I Ever." I like learning about people's hobbies and interests and what we have in common.

Step into the circle if you played a sport in high school.

Step into the circle if you have a pet at home.

Step into the circle if you like sushi.

So far, so good. This activity is right up my alley.

Step into the circle if you identify as a person of color.

The statements are starting to get less frivolous and more personal. Everyone still seems comfortable.

Step into the circle if both of your parents attended college.

Step into the circle if your family owns your home.

I don't know whether to step inside. My dad owns his home, which is not mine, and he *used to* own my mom's home. Where do I fit regarding this statement? Is there a "sort of" option? An "it's complicated" way to respond? I feel a flutter of shame in my stomach, though am relieved when a handful of others don't step forward. I choose to stay back.

Step into the circle if you have ever felt judged because of the size or shape of your body.

Step into the circle if you can walk down the street holding your partner's hand without fearing judgment.

Step into the circle if someone close to you struggles with mental illness.

With a disability.

With dementia.

A drop in my stomach. A previously familiar word, I haven't heard or thought of *dementia* in weeks. This training is forcing me to face the realities in my life I prefer to ignore when with others and pretend are *just fine, thank you.* As I slowly step into the circle, I make eye contact with Pete, who remains on the outside. Privilege takes on a new meaning to me. He hasn't had to experience the pain of watching a loved one fade away in this way. Pete has been my rock for the past year and a half, and in this moment, we are worlds apart. I've never felt so distant from him.

RA training comes to an end. It was an interesting two weeks, and I met a lot of great people, but I can't shake the feeling the "Step into the Circle" activity brought up for me. I wonder if the others who stepped in because someone close to them has dementia were all thinking of their eighty-year-old grandparents or if others have a parent with similar circumstances as my dad.

Move-in day arrives; and I have a floor of thirty-five girls who are fun, eager to start a new chapter of their lives, and actually willing to talk to their RA. I start planning potluck dinners, late-night ice cream socials, and group yoga classes in the dormitory lounge. One weeknight evening, I arrive home and find that the girls have organized their own fashion show—in protest of the synchronous Victoria's Secret fashion show—in the third-floor hallway, clad in leggings, tank tops, and silly hats. They beg me to join in, so I change into the required attire, grab a Santa hat, and strut down the "catwalk" with them while will.i.am's "I Got It from My Mama" blasts from a set of speakers.

I find joy again. The experience of mentoring these young women changes my life, offering me relief from the hell that was sophomore year. Girls show up at my door to talk out dating problems, express worry that they've chosen the wrong major, and share concerns about roommates who drink too much or eat too little. This role offers me insight into what I want to do with my future, what I want to be when I "grow up."

I feel like a completely new person. With the help of my psychiatrist, I have changed up my medication (Goodbye, birth control! Hello, Celexa increase!), giving my brain a healthy dose of much-needed serotonin. I'm drinking less often. When I'm not studying, I'm at the *Heights* office, attending RA staff meetings, or working as a manager at the tiny Newton Campus gym. I start working out for the first time in college, my headphones blasting music as I sprint on the treadmill. Pete and I go to hot yoga classes up the street whenever we can afford it. Sometimes, I even meet up with some friends from the paper for lunch on Main Campus. On weekend nights when Pete is busy, I can tolerate being alone and even come to enjoy this independence. I am excited about . . . everything. This is a feeling I hadn't remembered being capable of having.

52.

A gentle September breeze streams in through my open window, slowly waking me. I'm instantly in a great mood because, for the first time in three weeks, I am not sweating in the sauna that is my third-floor dorm room. The first home football game of the year kicks off at 3:30 p.m., and Pete and I will be heading to a *Heights* tailgate a few hours beforehand. I savor the comfort of my bed for a few more minutes, then roll out to check my email and get ready for the day.

While brushing my teeth, my cell phone rings. I run over to it, see that it's Gerardo, and consider not answering since I have a mouth full of toothpaste.

I haven't spoken to my dad in two months. The last time I saw or even spoke to Gerardo was in July. I wonder why he could possibly be calling me, and my first thought is that my father is dead.

In the time it takes for me to process all of this and to rinse out my mouth, the phone is still ringing; and I answer, my stomach vibrating, my face warming the way it always does when I anticipate awful news.

"Hi, Erika. It's Gerardo. How are you?" His thick Honduran accent has always been comforting to me; still, I panic. He continues, "How is school? How is RA business going?"

I try to give quick answers to expedite the conversation. It works.

"Erika, I just wanted to let you know that your father was recently in the hospital again, but he's home now. He has an aide with him twenty-four hours a day who cooks for him." My eyes well with tears—relieved he is alive, safe, and with consistent care. It's clear Gerardo knows we haven't spoken, and I wonder if he is going to address it.

"He is doing much better," Gerardo continues. "He's eating. He's taking some new medicines, and when he talks, he makes a lot more sense—you know before, sometimes he didn't make sense. But that's getting better. So when do classes begin?"

Gerardo has always had a way of changing the subject right after sharing difficult information. I appreciate this because it gives me the opportunity to ask more about what he just said or to choose to continue with the subject change. This time, I ask.

"Thank you for telling me, Gerardo." And then words I've been too afraid to speak for fear of answers I've been too afraid to know flow out of me without warning. "I-I've been wanting to ask you . . . Have the doctors said any more about what they think this is? I mean, a nurse told me he has dementia, but I don't know . . . I always wonder if there's more to it, and I've been kind of scared to ask and no one has really shared too much with me . . . Is there any new, like, *official* diagnosis?" I stutter a bit and am rambling, delaying the inevitability of his response. This is something I have been avoiding for far too long, something my current therapist had encouraged me to investigate during one of our very first meetings back in June. It's weird to think that in a matter of seconds, I could potentially know the answer.

"It's Alzheimer's . . ." His words trail off, and my heart skips a beat as I pick at a hole in my dorm room couch, tugging at white clumps of stuffing through trembling hands.

Tears streak my cheeks; it's as though my body responds before my brain can fully process the information. First, depression. Then neurological condition. Then dementia. Now Alzheimer's. I'm a bit stunned; part of me expected Gerardo to beat around the bush, to say that the doctors are running tests, that they're not completely sure what's going on, but that he has good care—something that would reassure me that he's *okay enough* while also protecting me from the grief a diagnosis carries. But he didn't. He answered quickly, plain and simple.

I take a breath. "Is it definitely Alzheimer's, or is that their suspicion . . . ? Has it actually been diagnosed, or do the doctors just see some Alzheimer's symptoms . . . ?" I ask a series of questions that have the same meaning, but I want to be sure Gerardo understands that I am seeking assurance, not speculation.

"They're saying it's Alzheimer's based on his symptoms . . . To be honest, things are going to get worse, Erika. But right now, they're a little better because he's having care all the time."

This time, Gerardo does not change the subject. He knows it's sinking in. The cause of my dad's—and my own—three-year pain has a definitive name.

Gerardo explains that he has been appointed my father's health-care proxy, meaning he makes medical decisions in the absence of my father's ability to do so. I feel an overwhelming mix of appreciation and vulnerability. I pleadingly say into the phone, "I would really like to see him sometime, Gerardo. I'm not sure when . . . But I can't do it alone."

I am unsure of where that courage came from, where that honesty was hidden inside me, but I know I mean it. Gerardo says to call him anytime and he will meet me for a visit.

I skip the tailgate and football game. Being around a bunch of drunk kids laughing and thrusting girls decorated in school colors into the air every time BC scores a touchdown does not sound like something I want to do today. Even though I've known for a long time that my father has been sick, this new name, this new information has a sense of finality to it. I want to be alone with my thoughts and try to find a place of accepting that what I've known deep down, what I've feared for years is true: my once sweet, loving, strong father—with whom I am currently not speaking—will never *ever* be the same.

53.

I want to believe that having a name for the illness means the problem is solved, that I can face him now. Just as *dementia* helped me make sense of his confusion, perhaps *Alzheimer's* will help me make sense of the rest of his symptoms and accept his prognosis. Knowing is a powerful thing. But although I can now name the beast, I don't know that I can handle the abuse, and I have no reason to believe his animosity toward me will change. I spend nights tossing and turning, rationalizing my decision to continue to not call him, then undoing the logic over and over until my eyes finally close and my brain shuts down for a few hours.

One particularly hard night, I grab my laptop and bring it into bed with me. I frantically type out my emotions and my struggles to my mom in hopes of lightening my mental load and no longer being alone with this, at least for tonight. "Hi mom," I type, tears blurring the screen in front of me. "I'm going to bed but just wanted to let you know I really, really miss Daddy. I had a bad dream about him last night and woke up and missed him all day, and I just cried about it for a while with Pete. I want to see him, and I don't know what to do because if I do (with Gerardo, for sure), I don't want to play with my own or Daddy's emotions. I really miss him and want to make him smile and make him feel better even if it's only for a little while, but at the same time, I wonder if that's really a good idea." I was hoping that writing the

211

email would help me make sense of what the right decision is, but it only highlights my apprehension and confusion.

My mom is coming to visit in a few days for the Parents' Weekend football game and Pops on the Heights concert. Even though I usually see her every few weeks anyway, she still celebrates Parents' Weekend annually, and we both look forward to it each year. But I've seen her a bit less than usual these past few weeks since I'm not going home to see my dad anymore, and my heart has been aching for a mom hug.

54.

The weekend arrives, and Mom and I cheer on BC in the stands of Alumni Stadium, order a pizza to eat in my tiny dorm room, then sit in the nosebleeds at the evening concert at Conte Forum. I get many, many mom hugs, and Parents' Weekend goes as fast as it came. We don't end up discussing how to handle the situation with my father. It's much easier to avoid, so I continue about my day-to-day life without contacting him. Despite the occasional surge of guilt, I continue to feel good.

One weekend, I don't have any RA responsibilities or big exams coming up, so I shake things up and plan to visit Colin, whose school is just a few towns over. It's been a while since I've spent time with my Natick friends, and he had called me earlier in the week saying he needed to talk to me and wanted it to be in person and as soon as possible. Though he is always a pleasure to see, this conversation scares me. *What if he's sick?* is my first thought—possibly due to my frame of reference with my dad, possibly due to me being a world-class worrywart.

Saturday comes, and I pack my bag. Angela, Kyle, and Colin all go to college together at Bentley University, so I plan to make a night of it. Pete loans me his car, and I hit the road for the twenty-minute drive.

Colin greets me in the parking lot with a big hug, and his anxiety is palpable. "Let's go to my room," he says, taking my bag for me. We make the walk across campus and get cozy (as cozy as you can get on a dorm room futon). He makes us each a coffee; and when he sits back down, I notice he's tapping his hand on his leg, which he's bouncing up and down.

"I've been wanting to talk to you . . . I've been thinking about some things and realizing some things . . ."

Okay, so he isn't sick . . . hopefully. I'm so anxious wondering, wanting him to take his time and be comfortable while also wanting him to spit it out.

"Hey, man . . . Oh, hey, Erika! How are you?" His roommate walks in, and the blood drains from Colin's face. It is clear that whatever he wants to tell me is not something he'd planned to discuss with his roommate present.

We make small talk, and Colin stammers out a lie about how we were just heading out. He takes me to the library; it's a Saturday night, so it's pretty empty.

"Okay, so I'm so glad we can finally talk . . ." He's blinking back tears. "I'm just gonna say it . . . So I'm . . . I'm gay."

Relief washes over my body. I smile and give him a huge hug. I tell him that we sort of knew since every girl in our high school had a crush on him at some point (myself included), but he'd never dated anyone. I try my best to be supportive. This is the first time someone has come out to me.

We talk for a while. He shares his fears: that he won't be accepted, that his roommate will feel weird around him once he knows, that he won't have the traditional family he had imagined as a child. His tears start to flow.

My phone rings.

It's my dad.

My body goes numb.

Colin is in the middle of crying, questioning his entire future. Normally, I would never ever answer a phone call under these circumstances. Epithets Colin had fired at me during that

Valentine's Eve chat three years prior immediately flash through my mind: *You're melodramatic. You're so self-centered.* If I answer the phone, am I proving him right?

Tears fill my eyes as I trip over my words. "I am so, so sorry, but I haven't talked to my dad in four months. I-I think I have to take it, and I'll be short. And again, I'm so sorry."

Colin smiles and says, "It's okay. Take it." He touches my hand. I answer.

"Erika, it's your father."

"Hi." I gulp. I struggle to form words. "H-how are you?"

"I'm good. I would like to see you. Can you come by tomorrow?" *What?*

"Sure. Okay, yeah. I can do that. What time?"

"What time works for you?"

"Uhh, afternoon, like one?"

"Okay. I'll see you then."

I flip the phone shut.

Now Colin and I are both crying. He tells me he's crying for me; he had no idea I hadn't talked to my dad in so long. I've kept that to myself with very few exceptions for fear of judgment (who refuses to speak to their sick father?) and not wanting to get into the whole story. I'm crying because of the adrenaline surge from seeing my dad's face on my phone, from hearing his voice. For Colin and his sadness and for relief that he has come out and is taking a step toward living a life in which he feels comfortable. And for fear of seeing my dad tomorrow and not knowing what to expect. Colin and I sit, crying, talking, hugging for another hour, processing his news and my phone call.

I call my mom on our walk back to Colin's dorm and explain to her what happened. It's clear she's concerned, and within an hour, I have an email from her with tips for fair fighting.

Colin and I meet up with Angela and Kyle for dinner and have a fun night playing games in Kyle's dorm room. Always a fan of a good game, I stay mostly in the moment; and Colin flashes me a warm knowing smile whenever he can see that I'm starting to appear a bit checked out, too in my head. I return the smile, a way of thanking him for being there for me and for allowing me to be part of his deeply vulnerable moment.

After a few hours, I get a phone call from one of the residents on my floor. She and her friends were partying after the football game; and one friend, another resident of mine, got so drunk that she passed out and shit her pants. They are worried and want to get her help but are afraid of getting in trouble since they are freshmen. I talk her through it and help direct them to Health Services so they can be sure their friend is safe and can be monitored for alcohol poisoning.

I like the helper role, being the Protector. I chose to become an RA. I feel proud that I am among the first few friends to whom Colin felt comfortable coming out. When Melissa overdosed two months into freshman year, I was scared for her, and also touched that she felt safe speaking to me. Julia calls me from time to time so I can talk her down when she's having a strong urge to purge; her eating disorder is mostly in remission, but the thoughts resurface during times of stress. I have a unique ability to stay calm in times of crisis—at least when it's not my own. I'm the first to be there when a friend or a resident needs me—even a stranger, for God's sake. But when it's my own father, it feels harder. Maybe it's because of the role reversal. It makes sense that I help my sick or troubled freshmen. It makes sense that a friend who needs support reaches out to their same-aged peer. But being twenty years old and feeling I must check on my father daily or else be guilted by him (or myself), helping him walk, eat, dress, and use the bathroom . . . it's too much. I know it's not his fault—he is facing horrifying circumstances. But I'm twenty. I shouldn't be visiting my father in geriatric hospital wards. Dementia isn't supposed to be part of my life yet. I can't shake this feeling of how unfair it is—and not just for him, but for me. I feel sorry for myself. And then I judge myself for feeling sorry for myself. Perhaps I pour so much energy into helping other people as a way to compensate for not being as willing to or accepting of helping my dad.

55.

Late the next morning, Colin walks me to the car. I feel rested and so relieved I'm not hungover. We didn't drink last night and I'm grateful for my clear head today—I'm going to need it. Colin offers me the most comforting hug.

"Good luck, Vargas," he says, my head nuzzled into his shoulder. "You're so strong. You've got this. Call me later if you want to talk about it. And"—he squeezes me tighter—"thank you for listening last night."

We pull back, but my hands make their way into his warm palms; and we look at each other, tears welling in both our eyes, not wanting to let go. I feel closer to him than ever before, though there is a nagging voice in the back of my head: *Way to usurp Colin's moment, Erika . . . Maybe you really are selfish.* I shake my head, willing the thoughts away. As soon as I turn the key in the ignition, these thoughts are replaced with new racing questions and fears: What is my dad going to say? What is he going to do? Is he angry? Does he remember we haven't spoken in four months—since July 9?

The drive from Bentley to Natick is about twenty-five minutes, but it feels like hours. I park the car in front of my mom's for a little pep talk, where I am greeted with another warm hug. It's like my brain and body can relax in her arms, and I don't want the feeling to end. I try to procrastinate leaving the comfort of her apartment for the unknown of the rest of my afternoon, but she pushes me to go.

I walk over to my father's apartment with my stomach in my throat. My finger hovers for a couple seconds, but I force myself to ring the buzzer. Memories from the last time I stood here, when I was moments away from "Then we'll bury you," flash through my mind but are interrupted by a buzz back. It's quicker than usual, and I remember that since I last saw him, he has full-time help.

I walk inside and am taken aback when my father, sitting at his dining room table in boxers and a white tank top, greets me with a smile. I force myself to mirror this, trying to maintain a poker face as my mind rushes to register his paler skin, his weight loss. I tentatively lean down to offer him a hug, which he reciprocates.

"It's nice to see you," he says, and it's as if nothing ever happened. "This is Manuela." He motions to a woman in her thirties, who I presume is his new home health aide. "Manuela, te presento a Erika, mi hija." We exchange smiles and handshakes. I wonder what she already knows and thinks about me.

My father asks if we can go get some groceries, and I'm fine with that—I can't imagine he will berate me too much in a public place.

"Would you help me get changed?" he asks me as he starts the slow walk to his bedroom.

I glance over at Manuela, who is texting on the couch. *Oh god*, I think, *is she going to be more focused on her phone than on my father, like his last aide?* I imagine dressing him is typically her job, but I oblige without asking for her support. I must tread lightly. I fear he'll snap if I make the wrong move.

He lowers himself onto the bed and points his cane toward a pair of khaki pants folded across the back of his desk chair. I grab them and put each of his feet through each pant leg, noting that the muscle tone in his legs seems to have deteriorated quite a bit and he is left with a bundle of bone, tendon, and flesh. His feet shake as I slide the pants up his leg. He winces as he uses all of his strength to lift himself up so I can slide the back of his pants over his bottom. He begins to zip up and fasten the button; it takes him a few seconds, his shaky hands struggling to get a good grip. I hand him his belt, which he loops through and finally clasps into a makeshift hole someone must have poked for him when they realized the smallest setting was still too big. It appears adult pants, or belts, soon won't fit his waist.

I grab his keys and pull his car around to the sidewalk behind his unit, with the passenger side about twenty feet from his living room slider. People in neighboring buildings stare. This is where their children play, and I imagine they are about to yell "You can't drive there!" . . . until they see what happens next and understand why I am violating the rules of the road.

I lean over him as he grasps my shoulders, shaking and trying to find balance until, eventually, I am holding him up. Manuela looks up from her phone and retrieves my father's walker, which helps him take small calculated steps with a bit more ease. Still, the walk to the car—even with my twenty-year-old arms helping to support his sixty-three-year-old 115-pound frame—takes a few minutes. He has grown more fragile, more afraid.

We walk around the grocery store. I think it feels good for him to move, even if we have to go slow, because even after everything on his shopping list is in the basket, he insists we go down each aisle. I link my arm in his to offer extra support. Passersby shoot us sweet smiles, as if we look like we're on a cute little father-daughter (or grandfather-granddaughter) outing. We stop into Dunkin' Donuts for his large coffee; it continues to give me pause every time I see him ingest caffeine as I have to imagine this only exacerbates his already-worsening tremor. He asks if we can get something to eat. We request a table for two at Barber's, a local lunch spot, and slowly, steadily take our seats.

"Erika," he says, clearing his throat. "You have not been very nice to your daddy."

Here it is.

But it's different this time. His voice is calm. It sounds like how a parent would talk to their small child about some small transgression: "I didn't like the way you called your sister 'stupid,' Noah. It wasn't very nice." He seems less angry than in the past, but still firm.

"I haven't called, Daddy . . . You know I've told you that sometimes the things you say make me really upset. A lot of the time, actually—"

"Erika, I called your mother last month to ask why you weren't talking to me."

He did?

"What? I had no idea . . ."

"This is very hard for your father. I'm sick. I have Parkinson's disease. You don't care about me. You don't want to help your daddy . . ."

His voice trails off.

Parkinson's? I thought he had Alzheimer's? Had Brendan been right all those years ago when he noticed my father's trembling hands? There's no time to process this. I want to stay strong. Maybe somehow, after four months apart, he will hear me.

I tune back in to him. "Erika, you haven't talked to me, and you have upset me very much. Gerardo doesn't like you either. Everyone is always asking, 'Where is Erika? Why doesn't she come to help?'"

I stir my spoon around in my chowder. I knew this was a mistake. With tears dripping down my cheeks, I calmly reiterate that I needed some space because of the way he treats me, the things he has said to me, the way he makes me feel. I tell him I will visit him in a few weeks at Thanksgiving, when I am home for the break.

Silence.

The check comes—and thank God because this is going nowhere fast. While he pays, I pull the car up to the curb and help him out to it; and it hits me that it must feel so incredibly humbling to need your daughter, with whom you are currently quite angry, to help you walk fifteen feet to the car to drive you home. We drive without speaking; fortunately, his apartment is right around the corner from the restaurant. Once I get him inside, he returns to his spot on the couch; it has become yellowed from what I imagine are likely occasional urine spills when he cannot get up in time to make it to the bathroom. Coffee stains decorate the cushion next to his spot, the result of trembling hands. I kiss him on the cheek, say goodbye to Manuela, and head home.

My mom has been waiting. Her worry is palpable. She greets me with a hug and asks how it went. "It was fine," I mutter. I furrow my brow. I can't keep it in. "Did Daddy call you a month or so ago?"

She nods her head and doesn't seem to pick up on why I'm upset. I blink back the hot tears that are trying to escape, but she catches on.

"What's wrong, Erika? I know today must have been so hard . . ."

"That's not what this is about, Mom! Why didn't you tell me that? Why didn't you fucking tell me?"

"Tell you what?" She seems genuinely confused.

"That he called you! That he was thinking of me!" I'm shrieking now.

"Erika, calm down. Take a breath. What do you want to know? How will this be helpful for you?"

I *hate* being told to calm down, but I know she's right. I take a few breaths until my racing heart slows a bit. "I want to know everything. I want to know why he called and what he said. I'm sorry, I just haven't told you how sad I've been thinking that he just, like . . . stopped caring about me."

"Okay." She pauses. "Give me a minute." She gets up, walks to her room, and returns with her laptop. "You know how I've been keeping track of everything with him? I wrote it all down right after the call. If you really want to know everything, why don't I walk you through it? I want to warn you, though, he says some pretty hurtful things, honey."

I nod. "I do. I'll be okay . . . I mean, I've made it this long with him, haven't I?" We both half smile as she opens the computer.

Apparently, he called her four times over eight days; she didn't answer because she assumed it was unintentional, accidental. She figured if it was someone calling on his behalf (a caretaker, Gerardo, a hospital), they would leave her a voicemail. But a voicemail never came.

She tells me that part of her had hoped it was him and he was calling to make amends. She'd become stuck in the mind game that I've found myself in over the past three years—wishing he would change, wishing he could be himself again, stuck in the denial of that impossibility.

A week passed. She and I chatted one night to coordinate my trip home to attend the funeral of a family friend. My cell service was terrible. I was in the *Heights* basement office. Our call dropped, and within a minute, an unknown number was calling her. She assumed it was me calling from the office line.

It wasn't me. It was my father, borrowing his aide's phone. She suspected who it was based on his voice but asked to make sure because he sounded so different from the last time they had spoken years prior. His voice was garbled, weak, scratchy. There was no small talk.

"She's a bad daughter, Nancy. She hasn't called me in *weeks*," he'd grumbled into the phone.

"Why's that, Tuco?" she'd asked. Silence. She repeated herself. Finally, "Because I told her I'm ashamed of her!"

She reminded him of his words on that day back in July: "Then we'll bury you." She told him she knows he couldn't have meant it and asked him if it was worth getting to where we are now.

"She only thinks about herself!" he'd responded, avoiding the question.

"Jesus, Tuco . . . See, you can't talk to her like that. I know you do, that you have been. She's *had it* with being treated badly. You used to treat me this way too when we were married. But she's your daughter, and she can't divorce you. So this is what she had to do. I know this is hard for you. We're both so sad for you. We feel so badly about your illness . . . But she's a *wonderful* girl, and you can't keep treating her this way. Tuco, she loves you very much. But almost *every* time she called you or visited you, she came out of it crying."

Any anger I'd had toward my mother subsides; she truly has always had my back. I have a glimmer of hope that the next thing she shares will be that he had a breakthrough in which he realized, even for a moment, how much his words and actions have played a role in my pain.

"So it's always my fault? She never comes over!" he'd replied.

My heart sinks. He doesn't understand; he never will. I think of one of my psychology classes where we recently learned how to write up a mental status exam. *Patient presents with limited insight, rigid, ruminative thinking, irritability. Speech is garbled.*

"Tuco, I'm not going to talk to you anymore," she'd said firmly.

He'd paused. "Okay," he'd finally responded. My mom interpreted his tone as shameful with a tiny hint of remorse.

I wonder why he never reached out to me directly. I wonder what his goal was in going to her. Was he trying to get me in trouble? Did he think he could turn her against me? Was he sad and begging for her to get through to me, albeit ineffectively? I ponder this aloud, and my mom says she was just as confused.

She'd tried to be nice to him. The recent news of his Alzheimer's (which I explain to her that, according to him, is apparently Parkinson's) was weighing on her. She tells me she'd choked back tears as she spoke, and it took everything in her to not offer more sympathy. She'd feared that if she wasn't firm, though, he would walk away thinking he was in the right and could continue to blame me for everything.

She tells me she was *so hoping* he would understand why I had stopped calling, but she knows he didn't.

"Honey, I half wanted to hug him and half wanted to smack him—even through the phone. It made me feel crazy. This must be how you feel with him all the time. I wanted to tell you about this call over Parents' Weekend. But I was so, so worried it would set you back," she says, stroking my hair as tears fill her eyes.

It's like she's so afraid of what my response will be that she continues to justify that she did not want to tell me in order to protect me from guilt, from feeling like I *had* to go see him. If I decided to make a call or go to see him, she wanted it to be of my own volition—because I truly felt ready, not because I knew he was sad. I apologize for being so mad at her earlier. Now that I've calmed a bit, I realize that although she's been by my side through this journey, she can't read my mind and doesn't realize how often I'd been thinking he didn't give a shit about me, wondering if he didn't care that I went months without calling him. And she is absolutely right. Had she told me he'd called, I would have gone crawling back, my guilt driving the bus.

Once I've stopped sniffling, I call Gerardo and confirm that, sure enough, the doctors are now calling it "Parkinson's disease dementia."

"I apologize for not calling you about this sooner, Erika. I'm dealing with some illness in my own family. But . . . you saw your father today? That's great. Remember, you can always call me to meet you there, okay?"

What an incredibly selfless man. I wonder why I didn't think to call him to meet me today.

I am hesitant to attach to a diagnosis given the mixed information I've received over the past few months. But part of me takes comfort in the fact that, suddenly, it feels slightly less serious than if it were Alzheimer's, whether or not this is actually accurate. A memory pops into my head: *Alzheimer's is a death sentence.* My AP Psych teacher had said this during a neuropsychology lesson during my senior year of high school. It's funny how information like this remains stored in the brain. Somehow, it had stayed repressed when Gerardo first said "Alzheimer's" through the phone two months ago; but it now rises to the surface of my mind, offering relief. All I know about Parkinson's disease is that Michael J. Fox developed it at a very young age. My mom had been a big fan of *Spin City*, and I remember her telling me he retired from the show after sharing that he was struggling with a movement disorder. Since then, whenever I've seen him in interviews, he seems lucid enough to maintain his status as a public figure and spokesperson. I will myself to stay optimistic, focusing on the relief I feel that *Alzheimer's* no longer needs to take up real estate in my brain.

Later, I drive back to school, and it all sinks in. He and I are in contact again. He expects me to call. He expects me to see him. I feel badly for the pain he has felt, for the emptiness in his life, for the way Parkinson's disease is destroying him. But I am not sorry for taking a stand and taking care of myself.

Although today truly wasn't as terrible as I'd anticipated, I fear that all of the work I've put in over the past four months is out the window. It's been months since I've had even a fleeting thought of self-harm, and I don't want my tweezers to sneak their way back into my routine. I am so goddamn scared that I will sink back into the depression I felt over the summer, that I will be driving and suddenly not care if I live or die and want a car to hit me so I can be free from the pain.

56.

Having more information about my father's diagnosis makes therapy much more helpful. I'd never unpacked the Alzheimer's diagnosis with Dr. Rose; she'd been on vacation for a week, had a conference on our usual meeting day, and I'd canceled a few appointments on weeks when I had big exams. By the time I did see her again, the diagnosis was no longer at the forefront of my mind . . . Or maybe I was just avoiding it. Now that my father and I are in contact again, I know I owe it to myself and to him to learn more.

Since Dr. Rose is a psychiatrist, this means she went to medical school, so she has an understanding of Parkinson's—certainly much more than I do.

"I'd wondered about Parkinson's, actually," she tells me. "But I didn't want to plant any suspicions in your head and confuse or stress you out even more." For a brief moment, a warmth fills the room as she offers a gentle smile. "It must feel a bit better to have some answers."

She notes how much Parkinson's can change a person, that it is a progressive disease. I think about the word "progressive" and how it's often used as a positive thing. "You're really progressing!" is what you hear when someone is doing well with some form of accomplishment. How could this same word possibly fit this debilitating illness?

"Would it be helpful for me to explain more about the disease?" she asks, peering to her right at a library of books. I nod, and she retrieves a large gray textbook from the mahogany shelf by her chair. She opens to the index, navigates to the *P* section, and licks her finger. Then she turns to a page about two-thirds of the way through the giant text.

She explains that Parkinson's affects motor function due to insufficient *dopamine* levels, leading to slowed movement (*bradykinesia*). He may have trouble balancing, low blood pressure leading to dizziness, shaky body parts (*tremor*), and difficulty with writing. He may experience changes to his posture and take short shuffling steps (*impairment of gait*). The motor difficulties may give way to poor self-care, including compromised personal hygiene skills.

She says he may sometimes appear sad or angry—even when he is not—or simply blank. This is the *Parkinsonian stare*, or a *masked face*. He may speak quietly and with a hoarse voice, making it difficult to understand or hear him (*hypophonia*). He may experience random and involuntary muscle spasms (*dyskinesia*) as a side effect of his medications. He may struggle with fatigue, feel full more quickly despite not taking in sufficient calories, and become depressed, anxious, irritable, apathetic.

Most of this, of course, I already know. Most of this I have been watching unfold—first slowly, then at lightning speed—for years. It explains why he uses a shoehorn to help get his shoes on when he dresses himself, though this is becoming less frequent now that he has an aide to assist him. This explains his drastic weight loss. It explains the wobbly small signature I used to watch him put on my mom's check back before I had any idea how serious or chronic his condition was. It explains his irritability. I'd be irritable too if all of this *shit* was happening to my body and I couldn't keep up with the changes.

Everything seems crystal clear. He matches the symptoms she has listed to a tee. I can't help but ask myself, *How the hell did no one know what this was sooner?*

She clarifies that some people develop Parkinson's disease without also developing dementia. I shift in my chair, wondering why, *how* my father faced such misfortune. She goes on to matter-of-factly explain that his dementia *will* worsen—that *yes, it is possible that he will forget people* . . . like me.

I let out a deep exhale, unsure how to express everything going through my head. She waits, holding space.

"It just keeps hitting me over and over . . . I feel like I've completely lost him," I say, plucking a tissue from the box beside me and feeling tongue-tied by my new Parkinson's disease vocabulary words.

"You *are* losing him. He is different from the dad you knew. It's so hard for the brain to process the fact that you're grieving the loss of someone who is still there," she says empathically, pausing for a moment to let this sink in. "Okay, our time is up!" She switches affect quickly. "See you next week," she says, showing me to the door.

I don't love her, I'm not sure I even like her—she doesn't have the best bedside manner and is often quite brash, but I feel fortunate to have someone who is helping me understand this *thing* that has taken over our lives for the past three years.

As I walk out to my car, I repeat what she said—"You are grieving the loss of someone who is still there"—over and over in my mind. This phrase offers me a new perspective that is incredibly helpful. He hasn't died; but he is dying every day in new and different ways, constantly in conflict with his body and brain. I want to let myself grieve, but I don't know how. My head can't keep up. I'm not sure how this conceptualization is going to help me, but I trust it will.

57.

To my complete surprise, the calls and visits that have followed our reunion have been . . . fine. Good, even. There are no accusations. No fights. No running out of his apartment in a blind rage. No crying myself to sleep.

I chew the inside of my lip, trying to predict how long this will last.

As the weather gets colder, I finish up my final exams, host a cheesy holiday party for the girls on my floor, and, finally, head home for winter break after what has been the busiest semester of my college experience. Within a few days of being home, my father is admitted to a nursing and rehabilitation center in Framingham following a fall and subsequent injury to his hip—thankfully, not the same one he'd hurt years prior. I visit him a few times a week and wheel him around in his wheelchair—which, moving forward, will be a necessity, not an option. I can feel the shame pumping through his veins as staff members give him the same sweet smiles you give a small child you pass in the supermarket.

One day, the topic of our conversation is the special socks hospitals and nursing homes give their patients—the nonslip ones that have treads on the bottom, preventing already-compromised patients from further injuring themselves. He spends most of his days lying in bed or being wheeled around, but he still loves the socks. They give him a pair of bright orange ones, and his face lights up when he jokes about how *exciting* they are—a nice break from all the boring gray ones he's been given previously. We call them "pumpkin socks" and joke that maybe the center bought them for Halloween to boost morale and are giving new patients the leftovers. I kiss him on the cheek and head home, relieved that we had another nice visit and I got to see him laugh. I imagine he must have recently started some type of antidepressant as his mood certainly seems brighter, especially considering his current circumstances.

The next day, when I call him, he says, "Erika, I have to tell you something . . . I got you the pumpkin socks!" With his memory fading fast, it warms my heart that he remembered our tender moment. He gives them to me at our next visit, and I wear those hideous orange nonslip socks to bed and fall asleep quickly.

During an evening chat, he tells me that earlier in the day, he drove his car and got lost in a parking lot somewhere. It's been about a year since he lost his license, and I know for a fact he is still in the rehabilitation center. I visited just yesterday, and the staff informed me that he has at least another week left until discharge.

"Are you sure that was today?" I ask, not sure how to respond.

"Yes, Erika! I just got back! It took forever to find the car!" I know he isn't intentionally lying, but I wonder if he is making this story up in his head to pass the time and has convinced himself it is true or whether his delusions are becoming more vivid and regular.

58.

There are moments when it hits me.

The once-beautiful white-walled, white-carpeted home with cathedral ceilings and floral furniture is now a tiny dark apartment with stains on the couch.

The potpourri-scented powder he'd put on the carpet before he vacuumed to enhance the aroma of his home will forever remind me of Saturday mornings at my daddy's house. Now his home smells of sour coffee, spoiled food that has been in the refrigerator for days, and human waste.

There are grab bars in the bathroom to support him using the toilet and shower, a walker always within reach to help him travel from point A to point B in even the tiniest of rooms.

The same couch we used to sit on all night watching Nickelodeon or *The Three Little Pigs* on VHS is no longer for a little girl eating too much junk food, but for my sixty-three-year-old father's full-time home health aide who lives with him in his one-bedroom apartment.

That image I held as a child—him shoveling through mounds of snow to get to me, "Erika, I'm coming for you!" erupting from his mouth, his declaration of love echoing for miles—is now not only an image, but also an impossibility. He can barely walk. He certainly cannot lift a shovel.

There are moments when it hits me. He's here, but he's gone.

59.

My dad is discharged after another week and a half, and we go to Mel's for breakfast. It's just the two of us. He orders his usual western omelet with home fries while I await the delivery of my Belgian waffle with strawberries and whipped cream. As the waiter approaches our table balancing the tray of food, my father tells me he has to go to the bathroom.

This is the first time we've been out together in a while; usually, I've been visiting him at home or the rehab center, where Manuela or a nurse takes care of these types of needs. I realize I'm going to need to be the one to help him. His wheelchair is folded up next to our booth. I unfold it, hoping I'm doing it right since this is my first time.

I walk over toward his side of the table; he shuffles his butt and thighs over toward the end of the booth. I lift him up under his armpits, my muscles flexing. Even though he weighs less than I do, he is still heavy to me—someone who has never lifted a weight in her life. "I've got you," I reassure him, though, secretly, I need the reassurance just as much.

His knees are bent, and he winces as he stands for a moment, long enough to take the three steps over to his wheelchair. He hovers over it, clearly in pain by the look on his face, and gently releases the tension in his thighs so gravity allows him to settle into the chair.

Phew, that was tough, I think and then realize we will have to do it again in just a few minutes.

I wheel him over to the bathroom and am unsure if it's weirder for me to be a woman with him in the men's room or for him to be a man with me in the women's room. I peek into the women's room, and no one is in there, so I wheel him in. I lock eyes with a waitress, who takes it upon herself to stand guard at the door—to offer my father some privacy, I imagine. As we make our way in, I overhear a patron ask what is going on; the waitress explains, "There's a *man* in there."

The woman responds, "Oh . . . oh my . . . Never mind, I'll wait." Then she walks away. It seems silly that someone might feel this way; comfort is such a spectrum, and the pain and discomfort my dad is in feels like it should trump any slight discomfort a woman may have emptying her bladder one stall over from a handicapped old man.

We're one-third of the way through the journey. We enter the handicapped stall, and I position the chair where I think it will be easiest for him to get from point A to point B: the toilet. I forget to lock the brakes, and when he stands, the chair moves from beneath him. His eyes grow large, and I feel his panic. Fortunately, I am able to hold him while kicking the chair and the brake into a proper position, offering him more peace of mind that if he falls, he won't end up back in the ER, but instead back in the safety of his chair. We shuffle over to the toilet, facing each other, his hands on my shoulders and mine on his; and I position him above the porcelain bowl. He unhooks his belt, and his pants slide down immediately; there is no need to unbutton or unzip them. He removes his left hand from my shoulder so he can slide down his boxers, and I keep my eyes focused on the wall behind him. I begin lowering him slowly, slowly, afraid his weak bones will crack if he lands with anything but the most gentle contact.

He has no body fat to protect him; and I imagine the toilet seat feels cold, hard, cruel.

I hear more women outside asking why the door is blocked, how long it will be. Only in this moment, I pray that compromised hearing is among the side effects my dad is experiencing; but unfortunately, it seems he does hear. He looks at me and shrugs, and I feel a sense of acceptance coming from him. It's clear this isn't the first time he's been in this situation, and it makes me wonder what I missed during our four-month hiatus.

I ask if he wants me to stay in the stall with him, and he says it is up to me—an answer I hate since I feel like I always make the wrong decision in his eyes. I stand right outside the stall with the door cracked since, obviously, there is no one to lock it from the inside.

I hear him start to grunt, and the sounds of passing gas follow. It is clear he is having diarrhea, and I wonder if this is a daily thing for him. Between a weakened immune system, compromised muscle function, and a rainbow collection of pills with a wide array of side effects, I imagine gastrointestinal upset must be inevitable.

After a few minutes, the noises stop, and the smell takes over the small space. I want to get out of there, but I can't, and I know he wants to too.

"Erika?" he calls me. I come back in. He is holding on to the handicap bar on the side wall, hovering six inches above the toilet. His penis dangles between his legs. Urine drips from the tip. I immediately avert my eyes, but I saw it, and it feels like it will be implanted in my memory forever.

He knows I saw him. "I bet you never thought you'd see your father like this," he says, shaking his head sheepishly.

He is trying to wipe himself. I reluctantly ask if he needs help. I don't know my role here.

Our eyes meet as he says, "No." Then I wonder if he really means it or if he just can't go there with me. I shudder at the idea of him sitting around like this all day—unclean, ashamed.

I help him pull up his boxers and pants and tighten his belt as he grips on to the bar, hoping and praying his grip won't give out. In this moment, it dawns on me that he continues to wear nice slacks, a belt, and a tucked-in polo shirt every day even though sweats and an old T-shirt would likely be easier and more comfortable. He's always been a man of class. Even if it makes things harder at times, I imagine dressing like his old self allows him to keep his dignity.

I support him on our short walk back to the wheelchair, unlock the brake, and wheel him to the sink, where he washes his hands. This leg of the journey has been rough.

As we make our way out of the bathroom, everyone averts their eyes. But it's clear they were staring, wondering what was necessitating a "guard" outside the women's room. I feel as though everyone has been let in on our secret, and their pity is obvious.

Leg 3 of the bathroom journey is a piece of cake now that I've completed legs 1 and 2. I lock the brake, lift him from the chair, and lower him back into the booth. He flashes me a quick humble smile, as if to say "Thank you." Then we eat our breakfast, feeling a bit closer to each other than we did earlier this morning.

60.

While I'm visiting him at his apartment one cold, snowy afternoon, a nurse from the rehab center comes to check in on him. She speaks to him like an adult—not a child, as many other medical personnel tend to do. She checks his eyes, ears, nose, mouth, and vital signs and performs what she explains is a brief neuro exam—assessing if he can feel hot versus cold and asking if he knows what day it is. "You're doing great, José, healthy as a horse!" she says.

"I don't need much more time," he says with a confidence I haven't heard from him in years. I don't quite know what he means—it seems like the nurse is wrapping up momentarily.

"What?" she inquires, sharing my confusion. "I'm heading out. You'll have plenty of time with your daughter, don't worry!"

"No, no, I don't need much more time," he repeats. "I just need two more years."

"Daddy, what do you mean?" I am shaken by this announcement; it seemingly came out of nowhere, but I am also interested to know how he came to this seemingly random number.

"Well," he says, "I just need to see Erika graduate and get married."

The heaviness of his comment is put on hold as I can't help but erupt in laughter. "Um . . . Sorry, but I'm *not* going to be married in two years!"

He isn't laughing and seems confused. "But you're in a serious relationship?" he contends.

The nurse smiles at me, and I explain to him that I am not planning to marry that young. Pete and I have been together for just over a year and a half, and things are different here and now as compared to when my dad was growing up.

"José, you have a long life ahead," the nurse says, patting him on his leg reassuringly. I wonder if she knows that or if it's just something she feels she should say.

61.

As the second semester of my junior year kicks off, my improved mood remains. I have added a second major, human development, with the hopes of entering some type of career in psychology after graduation rather than entering the communications field as I had originally planned. As my course load shifts from Public Relations and Journalistic Writing to Developmental Psychology and Applied Adolescent Development, I feel a shift in myself as well.

The renewed energy I've felt this year motivates me to audition for and land a role in the taboo and controversial (at least on a Catholic university campus) *The Vagina Monologues*. On the way out of the first rehearsal, a sophomore castmate mentions that she recently became vegetarian. I share with her that I'm also vegetarian, and this is enough to initiate a conversation that lasts until we part ways at the library, where she introduces herself as Megan. At the next week's rehearsal, I plant myself next to her, and she tells me about her experience transferring to BC from Santa Clara University. We become fast friends, meeting for vanilla lattes and off-campus dinners regularly. Meg is in a long-term relationship too, and we gush over each other's cute couple photos. I'm bummed when she reveals that she will be studying abroad in Nepal for all of next year, meaning she won't return to campus until I've already graduated. Still, we spend a lot of time together over the course of the semester. I continue to feel myself coming back to life—a new major, a new extracurricular, and a newfound peace in my relationship with my dad. My guard is constantly up, of course. I don't know when things might change.

Things don't change, though . . . at least not for a while. Sophomore year was such a shit show, and I actually feel like I made the right decision by choosing not to talk to him for those four months. Perhaps he's learned he could lose me if he continues to treat me the way he had been . . . Or perhaps he's feeling better from a new medication regimen. The demon of his illness pops up here and there, like on Easter, when I call him from Pete's family's home in New Jersey to say hello, and he berates me for not being with him instead. I cry, and Pete's mom comforts me, unaware of the depth of the situation. But I bounce back quicker than I have in a while, enlightened by my new understanding of the biological and psychological basis of my father's thoughts and behavior.

Maybe the diagnosis is helping him too. Maybe with a name and a better understanding of what is happening to him, he can move from anger to acceptance—or at least anger toward the illness, not toward the people in his life.

62.

I visit once, sometimes twice a month throughout the spring—no more than I have in the past. Sometimes Pete comes with me, and we sit on my father's couch, struggling to make conversation.

"Don't ever get sick," my dad usually says to start.

For being a twenty-year-old college kid, Pete handles this like a champ, making an empathic sound accompanied by a subtle shaking of his head, as if to say, "I see your pain, and I wouldn't wish it on anyone."

"I never did drugs. I never abused alcohol. I used to smoke cigarettes, but I quit . . . I don't know what I did to deserve this," my dad continues.

We sit there awkwardly, wanting to offer him solace but not knowing how.

Things may feel better between my father and me, but that doesn't mean the effects of the past three years have reversed. Having a parent with Parkinson's disease dementia should come with a list of side effects: *Children of the ill may experience chronic anxiety and/or depression, catastrophic thinking, poor confidence, second-guessing of interpersonal exchanges, excessive and compulsive apologizing.* Although I no longer dread seeing him, the narratives "You aren't doing enough" and "You don't have a big heart" run through my subconscious, dictating my self-worth.

I go on my first-ever service trip over spring break, loving every second of the twenty-seven-hour drive to Natchez, Mississippi, in a van with twelve other students. We all grow close by the end of the week, having spent every waking moment together reading to elementary school children, rebuilding and painting their playground, eating every meal as a group, and sleeping on the floor of one large empty room in the school.

John, the dean of the education school at BC who oversees the trip, pulls me aside one day.

"Erika, you have got to stop apologizing all the time."

"I'm sorry," I say instinctively, only noticing the irony after I've already spoken.

"It's annoying, and it's going to make you sound insincere when an apology is actually warranted."

John has a way of being simultaneously loving and bitingly straightforward. He reminds me a lot of my dad pre-illness—he's quiet and calm, down-to-earth, and has a contagious sense of humor. I take what he says to heart and try to change, but man, is it hard when I'd been made to feel like I've constantly been screwing up for years.

63.

The end of junior year is the end of an era.

In December, I resigned from *The Heights* to allow time for other interests, like *The Vagina Monologues* and the trip to Natchez. As the leadership of the editorial board changed, I noticed myself enjoying it less; one of the head editors was constantly talking shit about board members behind their backs, making misogynistic comments, and was just generally cranky. If I learned anything from the four months in which I didn't speak to my father, it's that setting limits and taking breaks from things that don't make you feel good are okay. Just two years prior, I'd sat on the floor among strangers, watching board members cry into their champagne bottles as they said goodbye to their fellow *Heights* editors. The next day, I'd called the psychiatrist on call after suffering my first panic attack. The contrast strikes me; at this year's Christmas dinner, I'd just begun to feel like myself again for the first time since walking onto campus in September 2005.

In January, I began babysitting two awesome little girls who live in Newton; and when I'm there, playing Monopoly Junior on their living room floor, I am transported to the carefree nature of being little—before you start to worry about your parents and money and health and life and death.

In March, I participated in—and ultimately won!—a public speaking contest on campus, delivering a speech about cyberbullying.

In April, Pete and I celebrated our two-year anniversary.

Now it is May. I move out of my small single in Duchesne Hall and stare back at the building where I found my passion on this campus, in this world. Although I've already made arrangements to live with a friend from *The Heights* and two others in an on-campus apartment next year, I could have stayed an RA for these girls forever.

64.

Summer 2008. I am selected, along with almost forty of my soon-to-be closest friends, to be an orientation leader (OL) for incoming freshmen. My head explodes with arrogance—and how could it not? Our boss's office features framed photos of former groups of OLs with the caption "The few, the proud, the Orientation Leaders!" below their smiling faces.

Pete is living just outside San Francisco for the summer, having landed an internship with a fancy company in Silicon Valley. I'm used to seeing him almost every day, even in the summers, and a part of me feels abandoned by him. He has been my rock for two years, and I would never have chosen to be so far away from him. Whether or not this is rational or fair, it is how I feel, and I find myself starting to mentally slip away—texting him less, focusing on my new friends more.

The OLs spend three long weeks in our own orientation, getting to know the nuts and bolts of what we will be doing for the seven freshmen orientation weekends this summer. We spend the first two nights at a retreat center, eating delicious food, sleeping in beds much more comfortable than the dorm mattresses our bodies have tolerated for years now, and forming connections with one another through the same cheesy icebreaker activities I loved during RA training.

After dinner on the second night, my eyes meet those of a familiar face—a boy named Michael, who had also participated in the public speaking contest last semester. While a few of the other OLs gather in a rec room to play board games, Michael and I start chatting in the hallway—small talk, like where we call home and what we're studying. After twenty minutes, we realize the conversation isn't ending anytime soon, and we find our way to the computer room, where we can sit. He recently visited Peru, and he describes trekking to Machu Picchu in such beautiful detail I feel like I'm there. I tell him my father is Peruvian, and naturally, he asks if I speak Spanish. I feel my cheeks flush when I admit that I know very little. I wait for the inevitable judgment and questioning—*What? That's crazy! Why didn't your dad teach you?*—that I've grown used to over the course of my twenty-one years.

"Oh, that's gonna change," he announces, his eyes brightening with excitement. "I'll teach you some this summer. I mean, no pressure of course—only if you want to learn. I'm pretty much fluent!"

I already feel quite comfortable in—and comforted by—this new friendship. Our conversation, decorated with laughter, continues to flow without skipping a beat. He tells me what it was like growing up in the Midwest and how much of a culture shock Boston was when he first arrived. I admit that I sometimes regret staying so close to home, that as much as I love BC, it would have been nice to get a change of scenery. We race through our sentences because there is so much we want to share.

The board gamers walk past us on their way upstairs. "We were wondering where you guys went! How long have you been in here?" one asks, laughing awkwardly as he offers side-eyes to the girl next to him. The ticking clock on the wall informs me that it is ten o'clock. Three hours have passed. I can't remember the last time I felt so engrossed in something that time had escaped me quite like this.

"Guess we should get to bed," I say. "Thanks for the 'life chat'!" Michael and I hug and follow the others upstairs. I fall asleep feeling grateful for what seems like the start of another meaningful friendship. I isolated myself so much the first few years of college, and it feels like I've been making up for lost time.

In the morning, we all take the bus back to campus to continue with our training. At our first meeting of the day, the directors give us an assignment to prepare a ten- to fifteen-minute narrative about a time we've been resilient in the face of adversity. We will then share this with the group, which includes all forty OLs and the three program directors. We exchange uncomfortable grins and wide eyes with one another as we pass around a vase filled with crumpled-up papers to determine speaking order. I luck out with number thirty-two, so I don't have to speak until the final week of training.

I already know I will share the story of my father's physical and cognitive decline, the years of no clear diagnosis, and the effects all of this has had on our relationship, including the period of time in which I did not speak to him for four months. I've always been confident in my public speaking abilities, and since I'll be preparing and rehearsing for this, it shouldn't catch me off guard to discuss something so painful. It will feel like I'm simply telling a story.

But this initial confidence crumbles as soon as I sit down to begin my outline, and second thoughts begin to babble in my brain. A protective armor envelops me. If I don't share the story of my father's illness and the subsequent emotional turmoil I've experienced, people won't have the opportunity to confirm my father's belief that I am *bad, ungrateful,* my friends' belief that I am *dramatic.* For years, I have protected myself from this potential judgment by sharing the details of my father's illness and our relationship with only a select trusted few. This is the first time I've considered opening up about it to a group of people.

But I don't know what else I'd discuss. This exercise feels weirdly competitive. There is an underlying vibe that your story better be good enough; if you get up there and talk about how much pressure you put on yourself to get a 4.0 GPA in high school, get in line because all of the other overachieving BC students have dealt with that same struggle. You need to have something that will require tissues for the audience or at least lead to some serious blinking back of tears. In the first week, people talk about near-death experiences, living in New York during 9/11, eating disorders . . . It feels like my story can't compare. But I still have time to prepare, so I breathe.

Not only do I breathe, but I drink. My new group is heavily focused on alcohol on the nights we aren't working—so basically Tuesday through Friday. Someone throws a party to celebrate the end of week 1 of training. It is OLs only, and since we are a small army, we are sardines packed into a cramped off-campus apartment. Within the first hour, Michael takes a few shots of Bacardi, puts his hand on my hip, and whispers in my ear, "You're the prettiest girl here." A few hours and even more drinks later, I'm kissing this boy—who is definitely not my boyfriend—in a room as another OL looks on in shock. I'm in a committed relationship. I'm not single. This is not allowed.

On the first night of the training retreat, I had been in the bathroom with another OL, Emily. We hadn't gotten to know each other yet; and somehow, while washing our hands, it came up that she had just ended a five-year relationship. "Oh my god, I'm so sorry!" I blurted out sympathetically.

The cool confidence in her response shocked me. "Oh, it's fine—it was my idea. I love him and want to be with him. It's just not the right time—maybe in the future. I want to be single right now."

I had thought of this conversation each day that followed as it resonated with me so deeply in the moment. I've been so scared of what life without Pete would look like that I've been ignoring the fact that maybe part of me wants to not be tied down to someone—even someone I love so profoundly. I think back to times I ran into his residents on the school shuttle, and they waved, yelling, "Hey, it's Pete's girlfriend!" . . . to the first day of RA training, when my own new boss greeted me in the same way . . . to the times last summer, when his coworkers playfully called me "Mrs. Pete" . . . But now I wonder if they even knew my name. Do people know anything about me other than who I am in the context of someone else? Do *I* even know me other than who I am in the context of someone else? Of course, this isn't Pete's fault; it doesn't feel like a fair reason to break up with him, but I don't want my identity to be defined by someone else's name. I want to be *Erika*. Not "Pete's girlfriend," but me.

And now here I am, kissing someone else—being unfaithful, hurting someone I love. I just spent junior year coming back to life, and now I'm losing myself.

Still drunk, I leave the party around 2:00 a.m. and head back to my dorm. I wake up to the sobering memory of kissing someone who isn't Pete for the first time in over two years. All of it feels bad, but not bad enough to stop. A few nights later, at another party, I'm doing the same thing, with the same guy.

During an evening phone call with Pete the next week, I tell him I think we need to take a break. I feel his heartbreak through the phone—his immediate silence speaks volumes—though I think both of us saw this coming. We haven't been talking as much as usual, and while we have attributed that to the demanding training schedules of our respective new jobs, I think we both secretly know that the distance has been really challenging for our relationship. Neither of us is ready to commit to a full breakup (although, really, what *is* the difference between a break and a breakup?). We continue on in limbo; we're *still involved* and *still in love*, but not *exclusive*. At least that's how I interpret it. Suddenly,

I have the freedom to continue doing what I've been doing, but without the guilt. But the guilt lingers; it's always there, even if I push it deep, deep down, buried beneath my busy schedule and lots of alcohol.

I kiss Michael whenever we can slip away from a party into stairwells or study rooms, our heads spinning with liquor. We are great friends by day, clandestine makeout buddies by night. Many of the other OLs suspect it. I hear rumors and whispers and can read their judging faces at parties. I try to read the face of the OL who was at the scene of the crime but can't tell if he's shared our secret. I don't say a word and know that if confronted, I will deny, deny, deny. To them, to myself. Kissing, like alcohol, keeps me so present that I forget everything going on outside of that moment: my on-hold boyfriend living across the country, my degenerating father, the depression I'm trying to keep in remission. Not like any of that justifies it. I have hurt Pete, even if he doesn't know it, and it is easier to keep kissing than to stop and feel the pain of having earned myself a scarlet letter.

Even though Pete and I aren't *technically* together anymore, the guilt overwhelms me one night; and I eventually confess that I've been kissing someone else, though leave out the important detail that this started a week or so before our break began. He is understandably hurt, but given that we are already on our break, it's not like anything really changes with us. We continue to talk pretty regularly, and I continue to slip away into my new group and new life.

A few weeks after the first offense, I finally tell Dr. Rose, who dismisses it with a literal wave of the hand, pompously stating, "Clearly, you're not ready to be in a relationship right now."

Obviously. This is why I initiated the break from Pete. While I don't expect her to support or encourage my infidelity, I expect her to help me work through it. All her statement does is make me not want to talk about it with her anymore. So I don't.

Despite feeling unheard, I recognize that I tend to feel better when I'm actively in therapy versus not, so I keep going week after week. I've opened up more to Dr. Rose than to anyone else I currently see on a regular basis. As much as I've tried to convince myself that *I don't need him!* without Pete here, I have no one who gets it, no one who has seen me through the constant ups and downs over the past few years.

I tell Dr. Rose about the upcoming narrative exercise for which I'm preparing. "I'm going to talk about my dad," I explain. "It seems like the appropriate thing to share given the assignment, and maybe it will help me feel more supported this summer."

"I don't like this at all," she says, shaking her head and wincing. *Of course* she winces.

"No, it's really great!" I become instantly defensive. "It helps us all connect! I think it'll be really good! We were all in tears over one girl's story about how she almost lost her mom in a tragic boating accident."

"It creates a false atmosphere of trust," she explains. "It's too soon in your relationship with these people to share something so deeply personal in such a candid setting. The directors are forcing you to be vulnerable with each other—it's not organic."

I'm fuming in my head. It is well known that each summer, the orientation leaders form an unshakeable bond, and I'll be damned if Dr. Rose is going to try to take that from me. *These are my friends. They care about me. They're amazing. She's just a bitter old lady. She'll never get it.*

I refuse to change my plan about what to share . . . except for a fleeting moment, when I actually consider confessing my original kissing sin to the group, with the goal of explaining that I fear I may have already ruined my summer before it truly began, knowing the effect it could have on my friendships and reputation among the OLs if my indiscretion comes out without me getting ahead of it. Fortunately, I quickly recognize this as a horrible idea.

Ultimately, the day arrives, and I stick with the original story about my dad and his decline into Parkinson's disease. I see a tear shed, and I get my kudos and support in the moments following my speech. One kid who generally seems chronically annoyed by me at worst, indifferent to me at best offers what feels like an inauthentic hug; and for a moment, my therapist's words—"It creates a false atmosphere of trust"—run through my head. It is the only time this kid will ever show any affection toward me all summer, and I realize that us sharing our sob stories does jack shit to change anyone's raw opinions of us as people. He hugged me because he felt it was the right move, the socially appropriate follow-up—not because he actually cared.

Even when I start to share with others that Pete and I are on a break, there is a massive palpable judgment of the quickness with which I moved on, everyone seemingly still (rightfully) suspicious of my dynamic with Michael. Many of the OLs worked with Pete last summer, and I imagine their allegiance is to him. It is clear that I am still in love with Pete; I talk about him often, people overhear us on the phone from time to time, and I still have a photo of us on my desk. The murmurs and judging glances continue whenever Michael and I drunkenly interact. I know what I am doing is hurtful to Pete, break or not; and while I certainly don't expect a pat on the back, part of me wants someone to stop me, someone to figuratively (or possibly literally) slap me across the face and ask me *what the fuck I'm doing* and where I think it's going to get me.

Another OL, Mateo, asks if I'm up for a walk around the city reservoir one afternoon when training ends early. As we walk in the sun, iced coffees in hand, I mention an upcoming beach trip I've planned with a few others, including Michael, and ask Mateo if he wants to join. He stops walking and looks me right in the eyes.

"Erika, I know you've been fooling around with him. A lot of us know. People are talking about it a lot and—"

"What? Oh my god, no, no, we're just friends."

The intensity of his stare deepens. "Cut the bullshit. You're an awesome girl. You don't have to lie to me. I'm not gonna tell anyone you admitted it."

No one has ever spoken to me this way before, and the tough love feels oddly comforting. Before I have time to decide how I want to handle this, I feel a tear running down my cheek.

"Okay," I say, wiping my eye. I don't need to say more; my reaction confirms his words. All the emotions I've been pushing down rise to the surface, and Mateo leads me to a bench, rubbing my back while I finally let myself release.

"I know things are hard for you right now, Erika. I feel for what you're going through with your family. Just be careful not to lose yourself."

We sit for a while, watching the sun begin to set. This is the type of genuine friendship I've been wanting. I'm used to overhearing gossip, but not actually being called on my shit from a perspective of concern. Mateo becomes the "What the fuck are you doing?" friend, and even though my antics continue, he at least helps me realize that kissing doesn't actually make anything better.

Michael becomes less of a security blanket and more of a friend I kiss sometimes. My focus shifts to forming solid friendships with a few girls, Kara and Annie. We drive around the city blasting music, eat cartons of ice cream until our stomachs hurt, snuggle up and have movie marathons on rainy summer days, and dance until two in the morning at countless Boston bars. Mateo remains the only friend who knows the truth about Michael. Behind my smile in all the photographs of road trips to Canada, dinners out in Harvard Square, and kayaking along the Charles, I remain riddled with shame.

65.

After over a month apart, I visit Pete across the country in Berkeley, California, for the Fourth of July weekend.

The night before, I lay on the floor of Kara's dorm room; she gave me a French manicure and asked me to tell her *all about my plans for the week with Pete!* Hearts basically shot out of her eyes. I wasn't feeling happy. I wasn't ready to leave the community that had quickly become my sacred space. I'd been struggling with the fact that seeing Pete will make me have to face the conflicting feelings I've had about wanting independence but still being in love with him . . . and of course, the guilt about Michael. I feign enthusiasm, and as soon as my nails dry, I head up to my room and go to bed in hopes of getting some rest before my early-morning flight.

It isn't until about an hour before my plane lands that it finally hits me—I am about to be in the arms of the boy I love so much. A switch flips—excitement overwhelms me, and I take a photo of myself in that moment with an ear-to-ear grin to show Pete when I land. My therapist would probably say I'm compensating, going above and beyond, as if to say "Look! I *am* excited! See? I can prove it with this photo I took!" But really, I take it to capture the freeing moment where any internal conflict escapes me, and I again feel like the girl who fell madly in love with him two years ago.

Pete picks me up at the airport, greeting me with a bouquet of fresh flowers, which, unbeknownst to him, I don't deserve.

He gives me a tour of his office, we eat lunch at an Italian bistro downtown, and we get ready to go out to some grungy club in the city. Pete just turned twenty-one last week, so we can finally go out to the bars together. Drinking has become an Olympic sport for me this summer, but that doesn't mean I'm particularly good at it—Pete and I both end the night with our heads over trash cans, sick until the next day.

After spending the day recovering in bed, Pete and I have some wine and cheese on the rooftop of his summer sublet. My hangover exacerbates the guilt that has been swirling within me for weeks, and before I know it, I'm telling Pete the truth about Michael—that the first few times I kissed him were before we started our "break." Pete is understandably upset and tells me it feels like I came to California just to tell him I cheated on him. We both cry. He paces. I apologize and beg for forgiveness.

We go to bed, and in the morning, we head out for a day of horseback riding. But on the way, we both end up in tears again. Subconsciously, we both know this may be the end of our relationship, but we don't want to admit it—we just want to have a nice last week together.

But we don't break up.

Our "break" continues.

And I don't change a thing.

I return to Boston, somehow confident in our relationship—knowing I want to be with Pete, but not entirely convinced I'm done playing kissing roulette either. This makes me feel like a sack of shit, and instead of taking another good look in the mirror and reevaluating my morals, I just continue doing what has (kind of) worked for me all summer. Despite how many times I tell Michael that we have to be done, every time we get drunk, we end up making out in some secret spot in whatever building we're partying in.

I go home one night, needing my mom, needing a break from the highs and lows of living on campus. I cry to her about my original indiscretion, the ongoing makeouts that only confuse me further, and she rubs my back. When my tears subside, she holds my shoulders and looks me in the eye.

"Honey, you've got to stop doing this—not only for Pete, but for you."

I return to school, empowered. It felt really good that my mom expressed concern for *me*, recognizing the effect that my own poor choices were having on my mood and self-esteem. Her words echo in my head whenever I go to a party, and I stop kissing so I can start getting my shit together.

Pete visits me in early August. He receives a warm welcome from the OLs he'd worked with the summer before. Michael is thankfully out of town, and I breathe a sigh of relief that we will avoid that awkwardness.

After grabbing pizza across the street from the dorms, Pete confesses to me that, earlier in the summer, he kissed a girl he met through his internship. He says he had suspected I had been unfaithful to him, which, of course, turned out to be true. Although it feels unfair to be hurt by this given all I have done, I can't help but feel betrayed by this person who has loved me so deeply for so long. I also feel a small sense of relief in knowing he is capable of fucking up too—his indiscretion makes me feel like less of an asshole.

Just like in Berkeley, we go out to a bar—this time, with a few other OLs—and drink Midori sours, Jäger bombs, and Red Bull vodkas until we take a cab home and puke all over my room. I have to wonder if we went extra hard because of the conversation we'd just had or because we knew what was coming.

We spend a day with the worst hangover of our lives, lying around, cleaning up vomit, and somehow dragging ourselves to my mom's apartment for dinner, where our stomachs turn with every bite of the meal she has prepared. The next day, I drive Pete to the airport, and it finally happens. We acknowledge that, clearly, neither of us is happy; and while sitting in my little car in Terminal B at Logan Airport, we decide to actually break up. It's unclear how this is any different from our "break," and we both know this probably isn't the end, but it's what needs to happen right now.

The timing is terrible. The OLs are all going home for three weeks for our August break, and I've been so immersed in my new little community that I haven't talked to my friends from home in months. I need support more than ever, and I just let my biggest supporter go. I've visited my dad every few weeks since May; and witnessing his ongoing physical and cognitive decline has been painful but mitigated by the guarantee of constant fun and distraction back on campus—until now. I feel a click in my brain as if my depression has been turned back on.

66.

The three weeks at home are hard, but I keep busy with babysitting jobs and going out to bars with home friends and getting lots of sleep so I never have time to think or feel. Within a month, I am *totally fine*! I have moved into my senior dorm early in order to run the final orientation session right before the start of the academic year. I live in an incredible two-story town house, and I'm going to parties with the other OLs all the time. We pack into the malodorous Mary Ann's (the unofficial BC dive bar) on Tuesdays, dance all night at the Harvard Ave bars on Thursdays, and party on campus Fridays and Saturdays. Newly *truly* single, I dance and flirt with guys and feel only a *teensy* bit guilty.

But on the nights when I'm not out at the bars or a party, a familiar feeling of dread kicks in; my stomach knots, and the deep, pervasive loneliness I'd felt that first semester of freshman year and all of sophomore year returns. Being alone with my own mind is painful and feels inescapable without a party to distract myself. Thoughts race through my brain—second-guessing whether I should have broken up with Pete, hating myself for cheating on him, questioning if I'm even capable of being single, shaming myself for not having made more girlfriends over the years, and guilting myself for not being a better daughter.

The sense of purpose and community I'd felt since the start of junior year and into the OL summer begins to fade. I no longer have a floor of mentees depending on me. When we aren't out drinking together, the other OLs spend their time with the friend groups they've had since freshman year. Kara and Annie, my closest friends from the summer, are in Barcelona for the semester. I'm no longer involved in any extracurricular activities. A pit forms in my stomach every time I hear groups of girls shrieking with laughter as they trot down the hill outside my window, headed to dinner or the library to study together. Although I'm being more social, I feel less whole.

While I don't have the large group of forever girlfriends I'd imagined, I begin to grow closer with my roommates, Pia and Courtney. Other than them, most of the people I spend time with are more of "drinking buddies"—peripheral friends, people to party with. Brendan and I get lunch every few weeks, but he's always asking me why I'm not back with Pete if I'm still *so in love* with him, if I *totally see myself marrying him*, so I find myself initiating fewer and fewer lunch dates, not wanting to acknowledge to myself that I don't have a good answer to this question. Angela visits most weekends, so much so that my new drinking buddies just assume she goes to BC. On the walk home from a party one night, I finally confess to her that I'd cheated on Pete prior to our breakup. Just like when I told her about my dad's depression, she hugs me, and it is understood I will bring it up again as needed.

As much as I miss the comfort of my relationship with Pete, I've realized—with the help of my therapists over the past few years—how beginning college with a boyfriend, then going all in on another relationship shortly thereafter prevented me from connecting with other potential lifelong friends. Maybe there's still hope for this year. I want to prove to myself *how okay I can be* when single and that I can branch out. Easier said than done, though. Pete lives down the hall from me (something we'd planned junior year), which makes it hard to act broken up; it was easier to act single when he was three thousand miles away. My roommates are friends with his roommates, so we end up spending a lot of time together. We cram into Pete's car to take a road trip to Maine to photograph the red, orange, and yellow trees; meet in the study lounge to hold one another accountable when we just can't bring ourselves to focus; and pregame with drinks mixed at the minibar the guys built.

A few weeks into the school year, a boy I met my first weekend of college, Tim, passes away. He had been close friends with Vanessa and was always hanging out in our room freshman year. He'd been diagnosed with leukemia as a sophomore, left school for a while, and now he's just . . . gone. Although I was not particularly close with him, he had never been anything but nice to me, always yelling "Vargy!" and smiling when he saw me walking across the quad. I write his memorial piece for *The Heights*, interviewing his loved ones for quotes as they pat their faces with tissues. I attend his funeral, which is standing room only. Like when Pete's uncle passed away last year, death again feels more real to me.

I head to Natick every other week or so to visit my dad. My father's body continues to appear more shriveled, his face more ashen. One October Sunday, I drag my hungover self to lunch with him, and he asks me about Pete. I haven't told him we've broken up, mostly because I don't want to explain why—it doesn't even quite make sense to me. My dad loves Pete, and I know he will make me question everything, making it harder for me to ignore the brewing realization that I am less—not more—happy without him. I blink back tears as I shove an avocado club sandwich into my mouth, each bite offering me sweet relief from the hangover.

"He's fine," I say, forever in denial.

Although I can drown my feelings in alcohol on the weekends (and some weeknights), weekdays make it harder to run from reality. In one of my psychology classes, we discuss the impact of cultural background on human development, and I start to reflect on how little I know about my Peruvian roots. Things have been so much calmer with my dad since last year, and I consider taking a trip to Peru with him.

I am eager to tell him about this plan the next time I see him; it will help him see I *do* care about him, I *do* want to spend time with him, I *do* care about my Peruvian culture and family.

But when I tell him, he hangs his head.

"Erika, I don't think it's a good idea . . ." He doesn't look up. "I can't do that in my condition . . ."

"But, Daddy, I'll take care of you! I know the plane ride might be hard, but I've seen Manuela. I can help you get around, use the bathroom, eat . . . Or maybe she could come with us for help?" I see his expression has not changed.

Regret fills me—not only for not going to Peru with him sooner, but for telling him about this plan, which I fear has made him feel more hopeless as he has to face the reality that he will never ever get on a plane to go to his homeland again. Every time he has to acknowledge the things he cannot do anymore, a piece of his spirit is crushed.

I am angry. Angry with my mom for nixing the Peru trip when I was a little kid. Angry with myself for not expressing more interest in going before it became too late. Angry that his illness has made it so his connection to his country, his family, his heritage—the things that define him and give him confidence and pride—is *gone*.

67.

After slipping in the shower, my dad is admitted to another rehabilitation center in December. I finish up the week's classes and head that way to see him.

Walking into a nursing and rehabilitation center is never a pleasant experience. The smell hits you as soon as you open the door—a stale mixture of soiled adult diapers, Ensure, and bodies in desperate need of a bath. My father shouldn't belong here. He's only sixty-four.

A staff member walks me to my dad's room without making conversation. Actually, I've never met a staff member who greets me with any degree of warmth; the only conversations are practical, instructing me where to sign in and asking me which patient I am here to see.

My father is lying in bed and greets me with his warm half smile, as if to say, "Hello, my love. Here I am . . . again . . . in a place I never dreamed I'd be." I hug him, and he wraps his fragile arms around me, giving me the tiniest squeeze; he doesn't have much strength left.

"My TV doesn't work," he complains. I notice that three beds down, past the curtain divider, there is a working television that belongs to a man who is sleeping.

"Seems that guy got lucky, huh?" I respond.

"He's always sleeping. He sleeps *all day*. He never watches."

I tell him I'll go ask the staff if they can switch his television with Sleeping Beauty's. But before I stand, my father leans in closely and whispers, "One of the nurses here has a knife."

Well, that knocks the wind out of me.

"What?" I ask, confused, hoping I misheard.

"One of the nurses has a knife," he repeats, his scratchy voice lowering in volume with each sentence. "She showed me. Don't say anything to anyone."

I don't know how to respond to this. I'm sure he's misunderstood something. Maybe there is another explanation.

"Are you sure? Maybe it was left over from the dining room?"

"No, Erika. She has a knife, and she showed it to me. She could hurt someone. Or me." He looks genuinely concerned, with the same expression on his face and sternness in his voice that he would have had in a serious situation before his illness took over.

I'm frozen. I'm sure he's wrong. Is this because I'm in denial? Shit like this is all over the news—elder abuse, medical crimes. But I just can't bring myself to believe it. I have a very, very sick father whose entire existence has changed over the past four years . . . The possibility that he is confused feels more likely. It's not that I don't believe him. I believe that *he thinks* the nurse has a knife.

Does he have psychosis? I wonder, remembering that unit from my Psychobiology of Mental Disorders class. If so, shit just got way more real.

I have no idea how to proceed. He asked me not to report it . . . But should I be listening to that? The sad reality is that if I share what he's told me with a staff member, they will probably try to keep him here even longer or just chalk it up to my dad being loony . . . But am I doing the same thing?

I look him dead in the eye. "You tell me if she shows it to you again, okay? I have to make sure you're safe."

"Okay, mi amor. I will. Thank you."

We chat for another half hour or so, and then it's time for me to go. I stop at the nurses' station on the way out to inform them of the TV situation, but I know nothing will change. And I hope to God I've made the right decision not to report the knife.

68.

The Vagina Monologues auditions are the first week of second
semester. I stand in the bathroom of McGuinn Hall, practicing
my audition monologue in the mirror when, to my surprise, Meg
walks in.

"What?" I drop my sheet of paper and wrap her in a hug. "I
thought you were in Nepal?"

"I was, but I decided to come back. I missed Boston . . .
It's like, I just got here last year, you know? I was hoping you'd
be auditioning again! I got a new phone, so I don't have your
number . . . It's so good to see you!"

We spend four hours in the dining hall the next night and
plan to make this a weekly ritual, even if our dinner dates won't
always last longer than *Titanic*.

I haven't been to therapy since before winter break, and I
don't plan to return. Appointments with Dr. Rose were helpful
in understanding the Parkinson's diagnosis, but since things have
been better in my relationship with my dad, therapy has felt less
necessary to me. I'm not interested in someone challenging me
about my recent hookups or my feelings regarding my relationship
status. On the walk back to my dorm after a coffee date with Meg,
Dr. Rose's name appears on my cell phone, and I decide I should
answer. I owe it to her to tell her I don't plan to schedule another
appointment.

"Hi, Dr. Rose," I start.

"Hi there. It's been a long time, and we need to schedule another appointment." Her tone is just so . . . formal, cold.

"Oh, yeah, I actually have been meaning to call you . . . I think I'm all set for now, so—"

"Ms. Vargas," she interrupts. Oh boy, this suddenly feels serious, like I'm in trouble. "You are on medication. I will need to see you, even if less frequently, to continue prescribing . . ."

"Oh, I actually stopped taking the meds last week! I've been feeling a lot better."

She sighs; her disapproval palpable.

"You just . . . took yourself off? Cold turkey? That's quite dangerous—there are many side effects you could experience, both mental and physical."

. . . So that explains the hammering in my temples and overwhelming nausea I fought whenever I glanced at the fluorescent light in my American Sign Language class last week.

"Okay . . . Thank you for everything, though. I'll reach back out if anything changes. I've really appreciated your help," I say, and I mean it.

She asks a few questions about my current symptoms, like whether I've had thoughts of suicide, and I'm relieved to be able to tell her *no*. Despite ebbs and flows to my mood these past few months, I've never not wanted to live.

69.

Over the first few weeks of the semester, something clicks, and I finally start to accept the fact that I'm kidding myself with this "Pete and I aren't together" thing. I've tried being single. I've had my fun, finding validation in the sexy glances from cute boys across the room at parties, waking up in the same guy's bed over and over for a few weeks when our nights always seem to end up with a drunken makeout. For three years, I've watched girls teeter back to their dorm rooms on Sunday mornings, still clad in their dresses from the night before. It feels like I've been making up for lost time, never having truly participated in hookup culture, and basking in as much of the excitement as I can before Pete and I inevitably get back together and marry each other someday, which I feel certain will happen—even when I'm kissing someone else at the bar.

But whenever I wake up from these nights, whenever the alcohol leaves my body, my heart aches for Pete. We made a rule back in the fall that even though we still act couasey sometimes, we can't go out on dates with each other since we aren't *together*. It crosses a boundary that feels reserved for real couples. It doesn't matter that we get the occasional dining hall dinner together and spend weeknights lying in one of our beds, studying; dates out feel like too much.

This changes on Valentine's Day 2009, when we decide to say "fuck it" and go to a nice Italian restaurant in Beacon Hill. Since our first date was on Valentine's Day three years ago, it just feels right. By the end of dinner, we are officially back together; and in this moment, lovey-dovey eyes staring at each other across a candlelit table, it feels wonderful.

We arrive back to campus just in time for the Valentine's party my roommates and I are hosting. I help Pia hang the cheesy Brach's Conversation Heart decorations we'd picked up at Party City, and I share the news—we're finally back together!

"Oh, that's great!" she says. "You two are the cutest. You must be so happy."

"Yeah." I smile, but my stomach flops, telling me I'm not so sure. Although my heart feels healed, I know our relationship is not.

This thought is quickly interrupted as Angela arrives, a bottle of Smirnoff in each hand. We mix together passion fruit vodka, raspberry vodka, Crystal Light, and seltzer water to create a pitcher of our own concoction: VIP Drink—the beverage we always make and reserve in the back of our fridge for only our favorite people. I don't end up drinking much of it, though. Some of my OL friends show up and feed me shots that I just can't turn down, and within a few hours, I'm facedown in the toilet.

I wake up less hungover than I'd anticipated, probably because much of the alcohol I consumed found its way to the sewer before it could completely soak into my bloodstream.

I roll over, bumping Angela awake.

"Hey," she yawns. "How are you feeling?"

"Ehh, it sucks that I couldn't make it to the end of the party. I was having fun," I admit.

"Girl . . . ," she starts as she sits up against the window. "You've been getting sick a lot lately, like, a lot of the weekends I'm here."

I feel my defenses rise. *It's college! And just a few weeks ago, she ended a night with her hair held back over the toilet! Who is she to judge?* But somehow, my brain cuts itself off, knowing she's right.

While I'm certainly not sick *every* weekend, I've been drinking since I was seventeen and have thrown up more over the past eight months than I have in the past five years.

I don't know what to say.

"The next time you throw up from drinking, you have to donate money to a charity of my choosing, okay?" Her face softens, and I know she means well, even if her tough love humbles me and makes me want to hide in a closet where no one can judge me. I make a commitment to her, and to myself, to reel it in—not to stop drinking, but to take fewer shots, to take more breaks between drinks, to take better care of myself.

Pete and I continue to fight over the same shit we used to argue about before we broke up in the first place—jealousy of time he spends with female friends and feeling like I'm not a priority. I become a broken record: *You don't care about me! You make time for everyone else but me!* I hear myself saying the words—or regurgitating them, really; the language in these accusations is all too familiar. But it's become cellular; and the thing about learned behavior is it's really, really hard to change, even when you know exactly where it's coming from and how hurtful it is.

There's a shift in Pete since round 1 of our relationship; he starts walking out when we fight, telling me I'm "not worth it." He begins to treat me more condescendingly; after a dinner out with his older brother, he looks at me with stern eyes and says, "Did you thank him for paying?" *Yes, I did, thank you. I have common courtesy and I don't need you to parent me.*

Surprisingly, we don't really fight about anything specifically related to last summer, though it's not lost on me that it likely plays some role. We find a way to be a couple while spending much of our time with our friends separately—something unique to senior year as every year prior, we'd been attached at the hip. We rarely attend parties together; sometimes we unintentionally end up at the same bar. We go on dates here and there, but mostly, we just find each other snuggling into the other's bed after a night out. It's nice to have some independence, but it doesn't feel like *us*. I know we have grown apart and our relationship has suffered what may be irreparable damage, but we do our best to keep on keeping on for the last few months of our college years.

70.

Not much changes with my father's health during my spring semester, which certainly isn't to say anything gets better—just not worse. I visit every few weeks and call daily between classes, and he always ends the calls with "I'll see you soon, my love." What a contrast from my freshman and sophomore years. I wish this meant I felt healed, but the collateral damage from those challenging years is significant, and I live with a constant longing for a college do-over.

But a second chance at college is, of course, impossible; and before I know it, it's the night before graduation. My roommates and our boyfriends hang around our dorm, listening to music nostalgic of the past four years and making mixed drinks before heading to the all-night parties. Around four in the morning, we make our way to the Beacon Street parking garage to watch the sun rise over Boston; this has been a BC senior tradition for decades. As I watch my classmates console one another—drunk, but genuine tears streaking girls' mascara and leaving guys puffy-eyed—I don't cry. While I certainly have some good friends—Meg, Pia, Courtney, and a handful of OLs—it has not been the best four years of my life.

After a few hours atop the garage, we head back to our dorms to freshen up. I, along with 2,500 other seniors, arrive at the graduation ceremony after not having slept for over twenty-four hours. I freeze in my little white dress and black gown on the football field while a mist of rain falls and the wind blows enough for all the girls to be shaking. I wave and smile at my mom, my aunt who flew up from Florida, and my uncle who flew in from Nevada, sitting in the bleachers behind me. After hours of speeches, handshakes, and battling my eyelids to stay open, I am officially a college graduate.

As I marched up onto the stage to receive my diploma from the dean, my peripheral vision latched on to the accessible seating section with hopes of seeing my father sitting there with Manuela. But I didn't see him, and although I was disappointed, I was not surprised. In the weeks prior, he asked over and over when my *graduación* was, but he kept forgetting the date. I reminded him daily during the two weeks leading up to the ceremony. Of all the people in the world who I wanted to be there, it was him. His years of encouragement pushed me to set my sights on Boston College, and his hard work and determination made it financially possible for me to attend. He deserved to see me graduate. I know the sight of him would have absolutely melted my heart and caused me to weep involuntarily right there onstage in front of the entire education school and their families, but it would have been worth it. I know he is as sad to have missed it as I was to not see his smiling face in the crowd.

There's no time to process any feelings as the rest of the day is focused on moving out of my dorm and into my new apartment. Immediately following the commencement ceremony, my uncle catches a flight back to Vegas, leaving my mom with a bad foot and aunt with a broken toe to help me. Of course, neither of these problems is their own fault. But with every step I take down the stairs of my fifth-floor dormitory and every step I take up the unstable brick stairs to my summer sublet a mile from campus, I feel a twinge of resentment. Mature or not, I have always been bitter that every time I have moved in the past four years, I have done most of it completely alone, aside from a brief hand here and there from a friend who was bored. The same is true today. I do the heavy lifting while my mom and aunt hold open the doors. We finally beg my new roommate and her boyfriend to give us a hand. Once I've made the last trip from the car, my legs turning to jelly, I thank my mom and aunt for their help and collapse onto my bed. Within minutes, the tears I didn't cry last night finally escape from my eyes.

One of the people who has been unable to help me move, of course, is my father. He has never set foot inside any place I have lived over the past four years. In this moment, I'm not upset that the lack of his help meant I had to do more work. I am upset because I know that deep down, whether or not he would ever admit it, it kills him that he can't help. During move-in and move-out weeks, fathers are scattered about the dorms, often helping people they have never met lift giant duffle bags, heavy futons, and big-screen televisions. Every time I have moved since my father became sick, I have avoided mentioning the move to him. He'd prided himself on his skill in hands-on labor his entire life: the odd jobs at John MacIsaac's apartment building, surprising us by mowing the lawn at our dream house, coming over early on winter mornings to snow-blow so my mom wouldn't have to—even thirteen years postdivorce. As I lie in my new room surrounded by boxes, I cry not because I have left behind my past and started a new chapter in my life, but because my father can't.

71.

Three days after graduation, I wake up, and the sun is shining—a beautiful day to walk around downtown Boston with an iced coffee and a good friend. I quickly shake this fantasy as I've committed to visiting my father.

Within minutes of my arrival, my dad questions why I haven't been home for so long, and I can't find a way to explain what "senior week" is.

He wants to get food. He also needs to go to the bathroom, so he empties his bladder into the new portable plastic urinal he keeps next to his bed so he won't have to get up and go to the actual bathroom. I wonder whose idea this was—his, or Manuela's because she did not want to deal with helping him up every time he needed to go. If the latter, I can't decide whether I'd blame her.

Manuela grabs an adult diaper from a Depends box next to his bed—a precaution in case he can't make it to the restroom while we're out. We help him to put on pants, change his shirt, wiggle into shoes, and straighten his collar. I drive the car onto the sidewalk behind his apartment. The neighborhood kids playing ball move aside to make room; they now know the drill.

Manuela helps my father into the passenger seat and tells us, "No puedo ir." I wonder why she won't be joining. Even if I've grown more confident in my basic caretaking capabilities, it bothers me a bit that the assumption is that I'll adopt this role while we are out. No one has ever really asked me how I feel about this, what it's like for me taking on caretaking responsibilities at age twenty-two.

We fold up and position his wheelchair into the back seat and are en route to Applebee's, my stomach growling the closer we get to the restaurant. He asks why I didn't wait for Manuela, and I remind him that she told us she wasn't coming. He furrows his brow, seemingly confused and disappointed. I wonder if he prefers a caretaker to be there too, especially after that bathroom trip last year.

As we are nearing Applebee's, he states that he wants to go to the bank first. He tells me this in Spanish. I understand some of the words, enough to get the gist. I took Spanish for three years in high school, but certainly not enough to fully follow. This, combined with his garbled speech, means that if he continues, I am going to be lost in the conversation—and fast. I gently ask him to please speak English with me since I don't speak Spanish. I know it's tough for him because even though he's an incredible English speaker for it being his second language, he's often around Spanish speakers these days. When he uses the phone, he calls his family in Peru and Pepe, who is a native speaker. Gerardo and Camila speak Spanish with him. Manuela speaks Spanish exclusively. It's completely understandable that he might slip into his native tongue; this has happened here and there since he became sick; and usually, once I acknowledge it, he continues the conversation in English.

But today is different; the demon is quickly activated. "Erika, I *know*!" he yells, and I calmly tell him I was only reminding him. He then begins speaking Spanish again.

"Please, Daddy, English," I say again gently so as not to anger him more.

The cycle repeats.

"Erika, I *know*! Why do you say that? I don't want you to say that."

The exact same situation occurs twice more until I finally ask what an appropriate alternative would be to me asking him to speak in English. He tells me to just say, "Please speak English." I bite my tongue; and the next time he speaks Spanish—which is the next time he speaks—I use the same words and tone that he used, following his directions exactly.

He is not satisfied.

"Erika, I do *not* like the way you're speaking to me!"

I can't comprehend how for a fleeting moment he remembers to speak English and how quickly this passes.

I try to hold in my sigh, but it slips out. "I don't know what to say . . . I'm using the exact words you suggested."

He huffs and shakes his head.

My father shaking his head always hurts my heart. It is his way of expressing utter disappointment. Sometimes this is because of something I've done, like in this situation. More often, it is because of his illness. Headshakes follow memory lapses, physical difficulties getting up, admittance to yet another rehabilitation center, et cetera, et cetera. It is an expression of pure helplessness and hopelessness.

The difficulty of this particular situation is that if I bite my tongue and let him speak, it will still cause a problem because he will become angry when I do not—cannot—respond to what he says.

"Okay . . ." I know I'm grasping at straws. "If it'll make you happy, I'll stop asking you to speak English. But that means I won't understand, and I want to be able to understand so we can—"

"Erika," he interrupts. "You never learned Spanish because when you were little, you didn't like when I spoke it to you! You should have learned it—the language of my country!" This is not the first time he's said this to me and, healthy or ill, he never seems to accept "I was a child" as a valid response. I know this is a pointless argument, so I change the subject. He speaks Spanish. I feel helpless. It does not get better.

As the minutes pass and we get closer to the bank, I find myself taking slower, deeper breaths. I reassure myself that even though it stings every time he yells at me for reminding him to speak English, it is not an unreasonable request. I'm not a bad daughter; he's not a bad father. He is sick, and his illness makes the situation complicated. Despite the fact that he interprets my request as an insult, I know what I am asking for is simply to rectify a communication barrier. I also know this is unlikely to change anytime soon.

Ever since he became sick, my father has begun yelling directions at me, whereas he used to be so calm and even-keeled. It's as though his brain is now hardwired to think that if things do not go exactly the way he'd like, then he will lose total control—of which he already has so little. When I pull up to the bank and insert his card into the drive-up ATM, he yells directions at me (in English—progress!) like I am a soldier.

BALANCE INQUIRY!

NO, PUT IN THE CODE! ("It did not ask me for the code yet, Daddy.")

MAKE SURE YOU GET A RECEIPT! A RECEIPT!

This could have been a smooth transaction, even in spite of his commands, but the machine informs us there is an ERROR. We reenter his PIN over and over; he tells me I am going too fast, but despite the number of times I enter the same exact number sequence (the same PIN he has had since I was a little girl), the machine rejects it.

I park and walk into the bank to investigate. The bank is of no help; they need to speak with my father directly. I suspected this would happen given that I am not the cardholder, but I'm pretty drained at this point because I have been with my dad for under an hour and he has already yelled at me multiple times in two languages. Rationally, I know the bank is protecting identity theft. Still, somehow, I expect that they should *just know* my father has a debilitating illness. I just want someone to do me a favor, someone to understand. I calmly explain to the bank teller that my father has trouble walking and it would be much easier if he did not have to come inside; then I ask if there is any alternative. Another teller, presumably a supervisor, overhears and calls me over, his face twisted up in a scowl. I feel like I've been sent to the principal's office. He coldly states that my father is going to have to come in so the woman in charge of PIN changes can assist him, and that is the only option. My eyes well with tears as I bitterly (read: immaturely) say, "Okay, I guess I'll try to get him in." Then I turn around and march out to the car.

We begin the slow ordeal of getting out of the car, into the wheelchair, and into the bank. As it turns out, we were using an expired card. The teller helps us renew it, we leave to get our lunch, my father resumes speaking Spanish to me. When I drop him off at his apartment, Manuela meets us at the back slider to help him inside.

As I drive back to the city, although I recognize that our interaction today certainly could have been worse, I reflect on just how much has changed over the past five years and wonder how much might change over the next five.

HERE AND GONE

72.

Shortly after I've received my diploma, real-world life kicks in, and I begin taking summer graduate classes at BC. I'm working toward a master's degree in counseling psychology, on the path to becoming a licensed mental health counselor. I've landed an assistantship in the Student Services department within the graduate school of education. It's only been a few weeks; but my bosses and coworkers are super nice, and the job itself is easy. I'll be there twenty hours a week for the entirety of my graduate school career; and although I'm making only a cool $16K a year to support myself with rent, groceries, car insurance, my cell phone, and other bills, the job pays for almost 100 percent of my tuition, which is amazing. I am beyond grateful to have my undergraduate and graduate degrees covered.

As a necessary supplement to this income, I'm spending afternoons working at a day camp on the BC campus. The job is very convenient (a five-minute walk from the office where I spend my mornings), and the kids are absolutely adorable. Surrounding myself with three- and four-year-olds each day is a way to give myself the mental break I need. Not that working with kids is easy—they're wild, crazy, and almost always covered in snot. But it reminds me of the days when the worst thing in the world was Mommy or Daddy being late for pickup.

It's the first really hot summer day, so when it's time to leave, I'm excited to sit in my air-conditioned car for the drive. I'm even more excited because a Realtor I had been contacting finally got back to me and said he could schedule viewings of a bunch of apartments right after camp. Starting in September, I'll be living with Meg. For the summer, she is living in an apartment that's just a five-minute walk from mine. Pete is living with a friend in a high-rise downtown, so we see each other when we can, but he is working around the clock starting a new business. Often when I call, he doesn't answer. Often when I visit, he has to work—sometimes leaving to run a business errand while I sit and chat with his roommate, watch TV, or fall asleep in his bed. I've started to rely less on him, more on Meg.

There is an energy Meg gives off that makes me feel safe—she reminds me of Julia in that way. At age thirteen, Meg lost her mom to cancer. Although our experiences are quite different, she understands what it's like to watch a family member deteriorate in their illness. She is fiercely compassionate and empathic and looks you right in the eye when you're talking, as if she's tuning out the whole world around her to listen to only you. When I open up about my dad, she reaches for my hand and says, "God, you are so strong." When I share with her that I'd cheated on Pete last summer, she asks how that experience affected me, how I feel about it. She is constantly checking in on me. Our serious talks are balanced by fits of laughter. With Meg, I don't bemoan the fact that I never got the large group of college girlfriends I'd hoped for; having a friend who offers such unconditional love and support is enough. I can't wait to have her as a roommate.

I bask in the air-conditioning for a few minutes, then rush to pick up Meg. We waltz into the Realtor's office and are *so excited*—we might find our first *real* grown-up apartment today! Not just a temporary summer sublet, but an apartment with a real lease and everything!

The Realtor greets us, quickly giving off a weird vibe. "I'm not here to scam you girls," he starts. "I'll show you some absolute *steals*! I'm not gonna lie to you, though. It's tough—there are only a handful of places available for the first of September, so you'll want to jump on it . . . But truthfully, renting is basically throwing away money, in my opinion. Let's get going!" Despite his odd flow of thoughts, we are eager to begin our search.

The Realtor drives like a maniac. The first apartment, frankly, sucks and is not in the best location for commuting. We fear for our lives en route to the second place. He says he used to be a cop, and he drives like we are chasing the most-wanted felon in town. We arrive, and he takes a ten-minute call, covering the phone with his hand at times and telling us, "So sorry, girls. This is a huge deal I'm about to make. I'll get you drinks later, I'll get you drinks!"

We just sit.

Once we finally go inside, we fall in love with the place. It's beautiful; the hardwood floors glisten in the sunlight streaming through the large windows, and the walls boast a fresh coat of stark white paint. It's a bit more than we want to spend, but it's gorgeous. The girls who currently live there are home, high, and dogsitting a little puppy who humps everything it sees. Drugs, a horny dog, and a cop-turned-Realtor promising us a round . . . this has been quite the adventure.

We are pumped for the third apartment. It's a bit farther from campus than we wanted, but it has free designated parking and is the cheapest we have seen so far. Our hearts are racing as we walk up to the front door.

The Realtor doesn't have the goddamn keys. We are locked out. We laugh. "It's fine," we say. "We're just hungry. Hahaha!" We force uncomfortable, ungenuine laughter, and he calls the tenant to figure something out. My phone rings.

I look down to see an unknown number. I don't really feel like being asked to participate in a quick survey about my health insurance plan or being (falsely) informed I've "won a cruise!" But

I'm a prospective tenant locked out of an apartment. I guess I don't have anything else to do, so I answer.

"Is this Ms. Erika Vargas?"

"Yes? Who's calling?" Solicitors, am I right? Tell me what you're selling, and we'll get this over with.

"Hi, Erika. My name is Cathy. I'm a nurse at Leonard Morse Hospital in Natick. Your father has been admitted. I need you to get here."

He has been hospitalized so many times that my brain no longer sounds the alarm when I get calls like this. I feel like an asshole, but I know it's unlikely that it is actually urgent. I'll get more information and visit him this weekend, as planned.

"What's going on? What happened?"

"Your father had a seizure. He's in the intensive care unit. Erika, you really need to get here. He's currently unconscious, and he isn't doing well."

What?

How?

He was fine last week. Not *fine* fine, but fine enough that he wasn't about to have a goddamn seizure. He's never had a seizure. This makes no sense. My mind races: *What if Manuela forgot to give him his meds, and this is some rare terrible side effect from missing a dose?* I don't know how logical this is or if I'm just looking for someone or something to blame; either way, I can't let myself go there right now.

"Ms. Vargas?"

"Sorry, I'll be there as soon as I can."

"Erika, he's very sick . . . You really need to come home . . ."

Why is she being so pushy? Like reminding me several times I need to get there. I GET IT. I need to be there. I said I'm coming! I'm sorry I wasn't there enough. I'm sorry I didn't take his illness as seriously as I could have because it's been too hard for me to face alone. I'm sorry!

It feels like she is yet another person who thinks I'm doing it wrong. If I didn't know my dad was unconscious, I would have assumed he already gave her the old "Erika is a terrible daughter who doesn't care about her father" speech based on how much she is pushing this right now.

After a moment, I stop being defensive, and I let it sink in that this is more serious than the usual "He's been admitted" calls. It feels like he could die. Like he might die. Like maybe he's already dead, and this is their way of getting me to the hospital to tell me in person. Is that legal? My head can't stop spinning. It feels like my stomach has flipped over and my heart is beating out of my chest—*ba boom, ba boom*, there it goes.

"I can be there in forty-five minutes," I say, a response the nurse seems to accept.

I start crying in front of the Realtor. I feel bad for *him*, as though I must be making him uncomfortable. My voice is quivering. I tell him my dad's in the hospital, that he had a seizure, that he's been sick for a while . . . Why am I opening up to this man? We hop back in his car and he drives like a fucking maniac to get me back to mine.

With a little uncontrollable sass in my voice, I say, "Just get us there in one piece." I force a giggle, not wanting to make the situation awkward.

Bless her heart, Meg quickly clarifies, "Listen, your driving is scaring us."

The Realtor slows down a bit and very kindly offers to arrange a police escort to help get us to Natick faster. Because so many other thoughts are racing through my head, I say, "No, I'll be okay, but thank you." Meg and I get out of the car as the Realtor tosses us two of his business cards and tells us "good luck" and to "be in touch!"

"E, I'm coming with you."

Megan is the best.

I tell her she doesn't have to come. I know she has a phone date with her long-distance boyfriend later tonight.

"Stop," she says firmly, but with a look I know means *I love you, and you need to let me help you.* She adds, "Unless you *truly* prefer to go alone, I'm coming."

I confess to her that I do want her there, I really do. This might be it—my dad is going to die today. I can feel it. She offers to drive, but I drive anyway and thankfully get us there safely despite my shaking hands. I talk the whole way, discussing the apartments and interrupting myself with worries about what is to come in the next few hours, then going back to discussing how crazy the Realtor was, then crying about my poor, sick father, sedated in a hospital bed. It's a bizarre sensation I couldn't have prepared for, couldn't have predicted. I feel like I'm losing my mind.

My phone battery has been dying since the end of camp, and I probably should have grabbed my charger before rushing off to Natick. Megan takes down Gerardo's number. I know everyone else's by heart. We get to the hospital and rush to the ICU. Meg sits in the waiting room, assuring me again that *she's fine*, and grabs last month's *Us Weekly* from the table.

The sight of my father forces tears down my cheeks and chokes me up. Anxiety and fear mask the hunger I've felt since two this afternoon.

He is lying in his hospital bed, motionless save for the rising and falling of his chest, which is only possible due to a ventilator. He's intubated and attached to two or three other machines; it's hard to tell with all the wires. I haven't seen him like this since he first went into the ICU during my sophomore year of high school—except now his skin is gray, and the life has been sucked out of his formerly happy chubby face. I hold his hand and tremble at its cold touch; he's not dead, but his body feels like it's on its way. A doctor finally enters the room and explains the seizure, unsure of the cause. He says the prognosis is poor given how weak the

Parkinson's has rendered him. He assures me my father should be fine (read: he won't die) through the night and suggests I get some rest. I retain very little as my eyes gaze at my father's body; his skin appears more translucent by the moment.

The doctor leaves the room, and I don't want to be alone. With the last bit of battery in my phone, I text Meg and ask her to please come to room 53, and she's there within two minutes. It is her first time ever seeing my father in person. He would be devastated to know someone who had never met him before saw him for the first time when he was in such a state. I can almost feel the shame seeping out of his body.

I use Meg's phone to call my mom and ask her to pick me up. I hadn't even realized that in the rush of this afternoon, I never informed her what was going on. She arrives around a quarter to eleven, and Meg takes my car back to her apartment in the city.

Over the next few days, the situation changes constantly. The doctor explains to me that my father has developed pneumonia and the severity of his overall condition continues to worsen. He remains in the ICU. Some days, he is hooked up to more machines than the day prior. Other days, the doctors say he will be home soon. It's hard to keep up.

73.

Somehow, just one week after being admitted, one week of this nightmare, my father is stable enough to discharge from the ICU; and he's placed on a medical floor in a shared room. I breathe relief at this turnaround, no longer fearing an imminent death. Pete accompanies me one day to visit. My dad seems to be in much better shape now—he's just groggy and half-asleep, really. When the ICU doctors removed the intubation, the process wreaked havoc on his throat, leaving his voice painfully hoarse.

"I want to meet your parents soon," my father says to Pete softly, scratchily. "I'll buy them dinner."

"They would love that. Let's make it happen," Pete says, then subtly checks his watch. "I'm sorry, I have to get back to Boston now." He kisses my cheek.

As Pete leaves, my father says with a gurgle, "Nice to see you."

My dad tells me that in just under a month, on July 28, it is Peruvian Independence Day! We talk about how we *have to* celebrate by going out to eat—maybe even finding a Peruvian place so I can finally try the cuisine. How have we never done this before? Meanwhile, I spoon-feed him hospital cranberry juice cocktail with an added thickening agent to prevent more fluid from inadvertently entering his weakened lungs.

As more days pass, he stays put on the medical floor. I continue bouncing back and forth between my place and my mom's. It seems my father will be home in a few days, and I vow to myself I will visit him the day he is released and as often as I can between jobs and class for the rest of the summer.

74.

My phone rings around 10:30 p.m. It is Gerardo, and instantly, I freeze. Why would he be calling me now?

"Erika, hi, this is Gerardo. I'm sorry to call so late, but your father has been moved back to the ICU, okay? I wanted to let you know right away."

My heart skips. "Thank you, Gerardo. Don't worry about the time. I'm always up this late, but . . . what happened? The last time I saw him, he was doing better, and the doctors said he'd probably be going home soon."

"Yes," Gerardo says. "That's what they thought. But earlier tonight, more fluid went into his lungs, and it's causing an infection. I don't want to scare you, Erika, but the doctors say it's serious."

"Okay." A long silence as I try to register this information. "Thank you again for calling me. I'll call out of work tomorrow so I can visit first thing."

Then with the same seriousness as the nurse who called me a week and a half ago, Gerardo gulps and says, "Erika, we may need to make some decisions in the next few days."

What does he mean? Decisions about next steps? Readmitting him to a rehab center or nursing home? Once the doctors cure the infection and he's ready to discharge, I would absolutely be on board with him receiving more around-the-clock care than a single health aide is able to provide in his home. I know my dad would be devastated to live in a nursing home full-time, but it may be the only option given his worsening condition.

It's as if Gerardo hears my thoughts, my questions. "What I'm trying to say is . . . Things aren't looking good for him . . . for his future. He is suffering."

Oh.

Gerardo is so gentle, and I realize that when he said "decisions," he did not mean if my dad will be in a nursing home. He meant if my dad will *be*. Although he never uses the words "end of life" or "pull the plug," his wording and his calm, somber tone make it obvious that he is suggesting that in the next few days, I may have to play a part in the decision regarding whether my father will live or die.

When I'd received that first call from the nurse, I'd convinced myself that my father's death was imminent and began to just barely wrap my head around some level of acceptance . . . And now the idea of me having to *decide* his fate is unbearable. My chest crumples into itself; my legs go numb. I grip the phone tightly, my hand turning white.

Gerardo tells me he will call me whenever he has more information from the hospital; and I realize that as my father's health-care proxy, he knows *a lot* more than I do, which prevents him from living in the denial that the doctors can *just fix this* and send my father on his way.

I fight tears in order to drive safely, and head home and talk with my mom until half past midnight, soaking in her comfort. What is happening? Am I about to lose a parent? Am I about to be the one who has to make an *end-of-life decision* about a *family member*? I'm twenty-two fucking years old. This is too much, this is not possible, this is not normal. I toss and turn all night on my mom's couch, wondering if this is a really terrible dream that I—and my dad—might wake up from someday. Maybe someday soon.

In the morning, I visit the ICU, staring at my father, comatose in his hospital bed. Then I rush back to the city in time to be at camp for my afternoon shift. I struggle with wanting to be the perfect daughter and the perfect employee—honoring one seemingly makes me bad at the other. Unlike the compassion and understanding my office-job bosses have afforded me, one of my supervisors at camp has started to drop hints that she is annoyed by me suddenly needing to take days off—little sighs here and there, a subtle, but undeniable wince when I say I need to arrive late or leave early. After an hour of being there, though, I realize that maybe it's a good thing I'm here. After a morning of watching my unconscious father breathe through a tube, spending the afternoon dancing and playing with kiddos is actually the perfect antidote.

But once all the little kids are picked up, once it's time to head back to my apartment, as much as I try to avoid thinking about my conversation with Gerardo from last night, the words "We may need to make some decisions" echo over and over in my head as I zombie my way through the rest of the evening.

75.

I roll out of bed the next morning after pressing "Snooze" two or three or ten times because I have been asleep for maybe five hours. I hop into the shower, let the warm water run over my body, shampoo my hair, skip the conditioner since I'm running late, wrap myself in the towel hanging on the door, grab a wrinkled black shirt to wear that complements my white capri pants, slip into sandals, spray and scrunch my hair, and I'm out the door. I forget breakfast, which is a very rare occurrence in my life, but my body is running on some kind of crazy adrenaline today, so I don't give it a second thought. I feel like I have to keep shaking my head in one quick motion from side to side to really establish my presence and recognize that I am awake, I am alive, this is real, this is hard, but I'm going to make it through the day even if I'm completely checked out.

I enter the education school building, and it's as though I'm watching myself from a distance—a sad, disheveled girl trying so hard to look put together but failing miserably. I walk into the office and force a smile. When I know I look like shit, it's harder to make myself appear *happy!* and *fine!* But I do my best. I wave hello to my coworkers and knock on my boss Tricia's door. I have the foresight to warn her, "I may be getting a phone call later . . . It'll be about my dad . . . Is it okay if I take it?"

"Yes, of course, do what you need to do," Tricia replies with a warm smile, which I reciprocate as I thank her and get to work.

I check my email, as per usual, but so badly want a distraction from talking about my life that I avoid chatting with friends online—a normal staple in my workday. I focus on the Program of Study and Transfer of Credit Request forms before me, taking my time with these because it's a Friday, which means there's not a lot to do, so I need to drag this out for as long as possible. I don't want to think about the reality that exists outside the four walls of my workplace. I don't want to face the potential impending tragedy, the impossibility of The Decision. I remember a past conversation with Megan where I'd mentioned feeling lucky to never have experienced anything tragic.

> *E, are you kidding me?*
> *No. I mean, seriously, Meg, I haven't had any tragedies, really. I feel bad whenever I complain because I know I've been so fortunate, and some people really have it bad and—*
> *Erika, your dad has fucking Parkinson's disease, for God's sake. You're allowed to be upset. Dealing with that is traumatic in and of itself.*
> *I mean, you're right, yeah . . . You're right. I guess I just—*
> *That's what I mean when I say you're empathetic to a fault. You're always so concerned with other people and their lives. But once in a while, love, you need to focus on yourself and your own obstacles. It's okay to be sad about your dad, and there's no need to brush it off, telling yourself it isn't tragic. Because it is, and it's harder to face than so many people can even imagine.*

As validating as our conversation had been, I don't want to think about it right now. I want to be here, having a workday, breathing and functioning like a normal human being.

Don't let your mind wander today. Don't let your mind wander today. Focus on these forms. Focus, focus, focus, I say to myself over and over.

Surprisingly, it works.

The exit from flashbacks and the subsequent return to the present moment is a sensation I can actually feel. Like when you drink caffeine and you can literally feel your brain waking up—like it has wiped the sleep from its eyes and has emerged into a real, awake, alive, busy, happy human brain again, little flowers blooming in the space between your ears and beneath your skull. My brain has that snap. Suddenly, I'm bustling around the office, joking with my coworkers Gregory and Martín, chatting with Cara while we prepare our morning coffees; and everything is better. Why focus on what *might* be bad, what *might* be scary and insurmountable when everything in this moment is still okay?

The coffee hits hard, and caffeine pumps through my veins, my pupils dilating by the millimeter; and I am on a roll with these forms. *Enter student's last name, first name, confirm academic program, check graduation date, print, initial, scan, click "Complete"* . . .

Ring.

I look at my cell phone.

Ring.

It's Gerardo.

Shit.

My heart stops. I try to lean into staying present, staying positive . . . Maybe it's just an update. Maybe suddenly, miraculously, my dad has improved—just like how every time the past few weeks I have thought he was going to die on me, he made it. Maybe this has nothing to do with The Decision.

I rush out of the office with my phone. I don't want to be having this conversation where people can hear, no matter what news he has for me. I run out into the beautiful entryway to the school, the glistening wooden walls and photographs of smiling, happy students and professors protecting me. Here, I am safe. Here, nothing can hurt me.

Nothing can hurt me until Gerardo reiterates what he said two nights ago—that we have to make some very big, important decisions. Nothing can hurt me until he says, "You need to come to the hospital as soon as possible," and explains that a doctor called him before dawn to discuss ceasing life support, and Gerardo told them to keep my father in the ICU and The Decision would be made later. Nothing can hurt me until my heart drops in my chest, until it skips a beat, until my stomach feels like hurt is seeping through it; and that's what's driving me—no food, just dread in my stomach, digesting and spreading into my bloodstream and to my brain, telling me to get moving, to complete a series of tasks: go back to work, tell Tricia, go to my other job, explain why I can't be there today, go to the car, drive home, you know how to get there, you've driven this road hundreds of times, park and walk into the hospital . . . Then the fear sets in. What the hell is going to happen once I get there? I'm frozen; but somehow, the fear motivates my body to move from the school entrance, taking the steps I've outlined for myself.

I saunter back to the office. Time has slowed down; everything around me looks blurred, though I'm not crying. I offer a shaky smile to Cara or Gregory or whoever is sitting in the first desk when I walk back into the office, I don't even register who it is. My mind is too clouded. I go into Tricia's office and tell her what's going on and that I have to leave. It is 11:30 a.m. I start to cry a bit because I am so scared, so *fucking* scared of telling camp—not even about the fact that my father is maybe about to fucking *die*, but because I am so nervous about what camp will say. I know they will be mad. I know that until he is dead, they are going to continue to grow frustrated with my constant absences (constant? Three and a half, including today). I try to calm myself. Tricia puts her hands on my shoulders and tells me to not worry, to get my stuff and to leave now, that I do not have to come back after telling camp. I say, "No, no, no, I want to come back here. I know this sounds weird, but this needs to be the last place I am before I go. I can't go from camp because I know they're going to make this even harder than it already is." I walk out and pass Martín, and he asks if we are getting lunch like we had planned, and I say, "I have to go. I'm sorry, I can't today," and I walk out of the graduate office and into the camp office across the way. No one is there. *Are you kidding me?* I think to myself. *I have to go searching for someone?* I pray to God I can find Adam, the fun boss, and tell him because he is more understanding than my other boss, June. But the way this day is going, of *course* I see June outside, and Adam is nowhere in sight. I call her name three times. Nothing. I run up to her, and she looks at me, and my eyes are damp, and my breath quivers. I don't even know what to say, what to explain. There are kids around; they don't want to hear about impending death. They want to be protected from ever realizing that one day Mommy and Daddy will die. I muster up the courage, take a deep breath, and say, "I can't be here today. I'm sorry."

"Hmm, what's going on?" she asks, looking up at the sky and not at me.

"I just got a call from my dad's friend . . . He says we need to make some decisions . . . It isn't looking good . . ."

In her defense, things have ended up being "fine" with my dad on the other days I've had to skip camp.

In my defense, this is my father's actual life, not a fucking "I overslept again and may be running late to work" type of excuse.

"Okay," she says. She pauses, then cocks her head a bit, the campers playing soccer and tag and kickball a blur in the background. "But, Erika, you do have a responsibility to camp . . ."

Are you *kidding* me? *Are you kidding me?* I am baffled. THANK YOU, my lovely boss, for actually causing me to feel a tickle in my throat, like when you want to laugh but know that doing so would be incredibly inappropriate. My father is probably about to die, and you're reminding me of a contract I signed.

She continues, "Are you going to be able to uphold your commitment?"

I'm instantly nauseous. Confrontation scares the shit out of me. Somehow, I remain outwardly calm.

"June, I really can't help this and couldn't have foreseen this . . . I mean, he's been in the hospital for weeks, and right now, I'm a bit more concerned with my commitment as a daughter. I'm sorry, I really think that's my prevailing concern . . ."

That is what I say. My mind is screaming, *Are you* fucking *kidding me?!* Tears fall from my eyes while a child in the background mirrors my cries upon tripping and skinning his elbow on the pavement. I am baffled by what possibly went through June's head that made her think it was actually a good idea to remind someone that they have a job and a paycheck when they are about to lose someone they have loved since the day their tiny baby body entered this world.

She says, "I know, I know it's so difficult for you. I understand." She is sincere. "But it's also very difficult and stressful for *me* because of staffing concerns and camp ratios . . ."

ARE YOU KIDDING ME?

Sadness and fear of what is to come turns into anger. What does she expect me to say? *Oh, okay. You're right, June. Never mind, I will stay—I can just say my farewells to the most important man in my life once the kids are done playing, once he's maybe already dead.*

ERIKA VARGAS

I swallow my anger and offer a half-assed apology again, mustering up some fake sincerity, but actually feel sorry for her lack of empathy and tact.

I am quietly sobbing as I walk back to the graduate office. I call my mom on the way and tell her briefly what's going on and what happened with June, asking "What the hell?" and feeling strange that this plagues my mind more so than what I'm about to face. In a way, it serves as a distraction—something to focus on, something to be angry about instead of letting the unbearable thought of The Decision pervade my mind and cripple me.

Back at work, Cara asks me if I'm okay. I have stopped crying, but I can imagine my expression is fairly indicative of the hurricane inside me. I gather my things; and my boss's boss, Jeannette, calls me into her office, says nothing, and just hugs me so tightly. I soak her shoulder with my sadness the way you do when someone offers you the exact support you didn't realize you needed until you're releasing everything. It's clear Tricia has filled her in. As Jeannette rubs my back, she offers to drive me to the hospital. I should probably take her up on the offer as I am definitely not in any condition to drive (1) because of the news, (2) because of the anger, and (3) because now it is noon and all I've consumed today is enough coffee to give me the shakes and heighten my already-skyrocketing anxiety.

But I don't want Jeannette to drive me because she would have to see my car. I have a feeling about this day. I have a feeling that unlike other days over the past few weeks, I will be home for a while. It will be a few days, not a few hours. And campus police will tow the car if I leave it parked in the school garage overnight. I'd have to move the car to my apartment, and in the process of doing so, Jeannette would see it. And last night, I put a dent in the car. Meg, hoping to distract me with something good, took me out for froyo. As we were taking our last half-melted bites, I heard a ding come from my purse, and fear struck me like lightning—my phone the liaison between the safe world inside the yogurt shop and the scary world inside the hospital. *What if it's Gerardo?*

It turned out to be a text from Angela: "Hey girl, just saying hi!" I said nothing to Meg, hoping the feeling of panic would float through my body and quickly leave. But after we got in the car to go home, I accidentally backed into a pole because my hands were shaking. The dent is large and covered with a black trash bag to prevent rain from getting inside it. It is impossible to miss. It exposes a vulnerability I'm not willing to share.

So I tell Jeannette, "No, no, thank you. No, I'm okay." I accept one more hug, grab my bag, give everyone a half smile goodbye, thank Tricia for understanding, and walk to my dented car.

I call Pete and am actually relieved when he doesn't answer because I know he's likely too busy to come with me. His new business has been picking up; and while I'm proud of him, I've been feeling neglected, disconnected. I cannot get into that argument right now. I leave a message letting him know I'm heading to the hospital and am not sure what the day will look like.

I drive in a daze for thirty minutes, then turn onto the road to Leonard Morse Hospital. "Second Chance" by Shinedown is on the radio; my stomach drops at the lyrics about saying goodbye.

I park, wanting to stay in the safety of my car forever, but I force myself to get out. I walk into the lobby, my head held high, upholding my commitment not as an employee of some day camp, but as a daughter. I call Gerardo, and he directs me to the unit. When I arrive, he's sitting around a table with Camila, her son, and Manuela in a large room adjacent to what I imagine is my father's intensive care room. There are several other tables and travel-size cardboard boxes of tissues everywhere. This place was designed for death.

76.

Gerardo immediately stands up to greet me and wraps me in a hug, holding on for longer than usual.

The doctor in charge of my father's care has just left for his lunch break. The five of us sit there in silence for a half hour, twenty feet from the door of the room that holds my father's failing body.

When my mom walks in, my tightened chest feels a slight relief. I'm not sure what to expect, what today is going to look or feel like, and I know I will need her in a way I never have before.

A nurse with kind, sympathetic eyes comes out of my father's room and asks if we would like to see him.

We rotate going in the room—first me, then Mom and me, then Gerardo, then Camila with her son, then Manuela, then just me again. Each of us is unsure what to do or think or say during these mini visits. Are we saying goodbye? Are we praying for a miraculous recovery? Without the doctor there to tell us otherwise, it feels like there is still a tiny glimmer of hope.

The doctor returns, wiping crumbs off the side of his lip; it is clear he rushed his meal in order to get back. We all return to our seats and wait for him to speak.

"I'm so sorry your family is going through this," the doctor says, making eye contact with each of us. I feel a twinge of anger that he refers to us all as "family" when, really, I'm the only one directly related to my dad. I feel possessive of my father, of my experience, but I don't correct him.

"As you know, José's condition continues to worsen. We had some promising moments the past few weeks, but unfortunately, the pneumonia has advanced. And to be completely candid"—his tone softens—"given his overall medical state, at this point, there isn't any indication of hope for survival without life support." He pauses, allowing our brains to catch up with this information. It feels as though lightning has struck my body.

After a moment, the doctor continues, "How familiar are you with his diagnosis?"

I speak up, electricity still shooting through my veins. "I've been told he has Parkinson's . . . well, Parkinson's disease dementia?" I don't know why I say it like it's a question, like I'm seeking confirmation of something I already know.

"Yes, I reviewed his chart, and this is accurate based on his overall symptomology and presentation. Unfortunately, with Parkinson's patients, pneumonia is one of the leading causes of death."

Death.

He continues, "I'm sure you've struggled greatly with witnessing some of the other symptoms common in Parkinson's. Have you heard the term 'Lewy body dementia'?"

He is staring at me when he asks this. I shake my head no.

The doctor speaks slowly, clearly. "While technically Lewy body dementia can't be diagnosed before an autops—" He cuts himself off, seemingly afraid to use such a painfully blunt word. "Until after a patient has passed, José's symptoms suggest that this may be what is happening in his brain."

He senses our confusion; this is a new term to us.

"Why don't I explain it to you a bit more? You, of course, have watched José's struggle and are much more familiar with his symptoms than I am. Some families find that more information helps to provide closure. I want you to have all the information to help inform your decision."

He waits for our consent; we offer nods, and he continues, "Lewy bodies are abnormal proteins that show up in different parts of the brain, either affecting someone's mobility or cognition first. Usually, with Parkinson's disease dementia—one of the types of LBD—the impaired movement precedes the cognitive decline. But in dementia with Lewy bodies—the other type of Lewy body dementia—the cognitive decline typically appears first."

My brain struggles to organize all of these new words and definitions. I try to think back and remember the timeline of my father's impairments. The depression—was that resulting from specific events (the death of his good friend, my growing up), like I'd always thought? Or was it, perhaps, in response to his impaired movement, worsening by the day? Could his depression have started when the Lewy bodies, unbeknownst to him, began attacking his brain? His difficulty driving—was that due to his physical or mental decline?

My mind interrupts itself, reminding me that either way, this doesn't really matter right now.

I tune back in to the doctor's explanation.

"Many Lewy body patients also experience visual hallucinations, seeing things that aren't really there."

A memory: *One of the nurses has a knife.*

"Similarly, another common and, of course, unfortunate symptom is that sometimes patients with LBD experience delirium, which can lead to a misinterpretation of reality. For example, they may think people in their lives are different from who they really are. They may then assign a different personality to that person, which can change their relationship for better or for worse."

My mom and I glance at each other. I feel Gerardo's eyes on us as well, but he quickly looks away. No one, not even Dr. Rose, has explained it to me quite like this before. It makes perfect sense—this may be why suddenly, out of nowhere, my dad seemingly hated my mother and me, especially her. Who had my mom become in his mind? Had anyone ever explained to him that this may have been what was going on? Would he have been well enough to understand?

The doctor keeps talking, listing more and more symptoms that are spot-on with my father's presentation over the past five years. It seems as though the doctor doesn't want to stop talking because he knows that what comes next will be incredibly hard for all of us in the room and is procrastinating that difficult moment. He explains that death typically occurs, on average, five to eight years after the onset of Lewy body dementia. We are at about year 5 at this point, depending on what is considered *the beginning*. Tears well in my eyes as I think back to my junior year winter break when the visiting nurse had said, "José, you have a long life ahead," reassuring us that he would certainly accompany me down the aisle someday. What would have been different if someone, anyone could have known that "long life" would turn out to be only nineteen more months?

I wonder how much Gerardo knew about these things—the details of Lewy body dementia and life expectancy, the assigning of different personalities. I try to decide whether I'm angry or relieved he hadn't shared this level of detail with me. My thoughts trend toward the latter. I know he wanted to protect me.

After a short pause and a long sigh, the doctor states that taking my father off life support may be the best decision at this point. He explains that this is his recommendation, but ultimately, it is up to us. He then completely stops talking and again makes eye contact with each of us. I had taken such comfort in the sound of his voice, the distraction it created, the fact that it bought us a few more minutes before we had to dive into the inevitable moment of The Decision. After what feels like a nauseating hour but is only a few seconds, Gerardo speaks up. "I believe that ending life support is what needs to be done."

He looks at me.

Impossibly, I nod.

A few months ago, Gerardo and I had been at my father's apartment sorting through paperwork and organizing some of his things. I'd stumbled upon a copy of my father's will, and its presence had smacked the severity of his condition right in my face. The will probably wouldn't be hanging around on his dining room table if there wasn't any indication he might die relatively soon. I'd flipped through the pages, and my eyes zeroed in on one line: "Please do not implement extreme life-saving measures if I am in a condition where I would no longer be able to interact or communicate with my friends and family." In this moment in the hospital, those words flash through my head, validating my nod to Gerardo. This is the situation we are in, and this is what my father had expressed he wanted.

The doctor explains what is going to happen, and my ability to focus waivers, as though I'm in and out of consciousness. I hear words like "morphine" and "blood pressure." I hear him say that the removal of life support will take about an hour, though it may take up to a day for my father's life to actually end.

He asks us again to confirm our plan, and I look to my mom's eyes, filled with tears; she gently reaches for my hand and gives me a knowing look, as if to say, "Honey, we both know this is what's best." I look to Gerardo, and he offers a singular nod, shutting his eyes to hold back his own tears.

"Yes," I say aloud, raising my chin to trick myself into thinking I am confident in this decision. "I think this makes the most sense."

We sign some legal paperwork, and the doctor informs the nurse of the plan. The six of us remain in the waiting area, not sure what to do with ourselves. We pace, stare out the window, try to stay busy so time will pass more quickly, even though part of me wants things to slow down so the final moment never comes. There is mention of grabbing food—none of us has eaten for hours, but our appetites are all an all-time low. My mom and I decide to pop into the hospital cafeteria, but as soon as we stand up to leave, the nurse opens the door. "We've removed some of the systems that have been sustaining him," she says. "Would you like to come in again? He looks better without all the wires . . ." My mom and I enter the room; she holds my hand the whole time. My father is still intubated, but otherwise, he looks slightly better—less sick, even though logically we know that is far from true. We stand there for a few minutes, and my mom's quiet sobs turn into an uncontrollable bawl. This is the man who gave her her daughter; and despite everything that changed over the course of their relationship, particularly these past few years, I know she will always love him. She kisses his hand and asks me if I want a moment alone. I do.

I sit on the bed beside him and take his hand, which is growing colder but still retains enough warmth to let me know that he is still alive, still there.

I thank him for our Friday glory days. The irony hits me that today is a Friday too.

I tell him I'm going to visit Peru in his honor. I don't know when, but I'm going to make it happen. I tell him I want to learn Spanish and raise my kids to know the language as a tribute to their late grandfather.

I tell him I'm sorry. I'm so sorry. For not being there more, for the way his illness changed everything, for his hurt that made him so angry, so sad, so confused.

I tell him I wish I had understood, I wish I had known more about what he was going through, and that I wish he had known too.

I head back out to the waiting area, and within a half hour, the nurse lets us know it is time to remove the final tube. My mom and I move our chairs outside the door to my father's room to be as close to him as we can, but shortly thereafter, we wish we hadn't. The sounds are horrible. Gagging and scratching and what I imagine is intense pain, though I know he is on enough morphine that he feels nothing. I try to sit there as an act of solidarity, an act of showing my support for him as he goes through this pain, as a last act of kindness and dedication to him . . . But it becomes too much. I walk to the other side of the room, just out of earshot, and decide I'm ready to tell my friends what is happening.

First, I call Megan, who tells me she is renting a Zipcar immediately and will be in Natick within the hour. Then Angela, who will be leaving work in forty-five minutes and plans to meet me at the hospital or my mom's or wherever I am at the time. I try Pete again. He answers this time. "Just come whenever you can, no rush," I say but don't mean. I don't want to burden him, but at the same time, I want him here, need him here, and hope he will hop in his car right away to come be with me. I need the comfort that his arms, his scent, his love provides me.

I see the nurse step out of the room and know this must mean the sounds are over. She provides another update, explaining that my father's blood pressure has dropped significantly.

We sit.

We sit longer.

We pace.

Forty minutes pass.

She comes out again, opening the door slowly, as if with trepidation. Before she opens her mouth, I know by the look on her face what she is about to say.

"It's over. I'm so sorry."

AFTER

77.

Even though my father hadn't lived with us for over two decades and had never set foot inside my mom's current home, her apartment feels empty when we get there. Our world has one less soul in it, and we feel his absence instantly.

Angela arrives shortly after we do, a brightly decorated fruit tart in hand. As soon as our eyes meet, she quickens her gait, drops her handbag, and offers me what feels like an endless hug. We stand outside in front of the open sliding glass door, and I feel her tears start to fall. My dad truly loved her, and she him.

Megan shows up moments later, a sealed envelope and a gift bag in her hand. She kisses me on the cheek and tells me to read the card later when things slow down and I need support. I open the bag and find a blue hairbrush, hair ties, lavender-scented lotion, and a vanilla sandalwood candle.

"You need to keep taking care of yourself, E. The next few weeks are going to be especially hard. These things won't take away your pain, but they might help."

We light the candle, order a pizza, and sit around talking for a few hours. The conversation shifts from reflecting on memories of my dad to sharing stories from college. It feels good to laugh. I glance at the clock; it's nearing 11:30 p.m. They don't see me notice their yawns.

"Guys, you should go. It's late . . . I'll be okay," I offer.

Megan and Angela exchange glances.

"Uh, where's Pete?" Angela asks. "I thought he'd be the first one here . . ."

It hadn't occurred to me that his lack of presence is odd until she pointed it out. I mean, I *had* told him he could take his time . . . But I suppose I didn't realize he would be quite this long. It's almost tomorrow after all.

The girls stay until Pete arrives just a few minutes before midnight. I'm too tired to be upset, so I kiss him hello, hug the girls goodbye, and we go to sleep.

78.

My mom and I meet with the staff of a funeral home, where the director tries to sell us on a *state-of-the-art* solid oak casket for a few grand. I hold back a giggle as I imagine my father telling me it's too expensive and rolling his eyes. Though he enjoyed high-quality things, he was frugal and not easily cajoled.

"The steel casket will be fine," I say.

We have to choose a burial plot, and in doing so, I'm asked if I'd like to purchase an additional plot for myself so I can be next to my father when I inevitably pass. Jesus Christ. I *just* lost my dad—I'd love to not be smacked in the face with my own mortality. The decision feels impossible. I struggle for minutes and wonder how the cemetery manager handles regularly having this conversation with tearful, grieving people. Ultimately, I decline.

Cards arrive daily; my phone rings hourly. After the first few calls, it's easy to turn off my emotions during the conversation. I become a pull-string doll with a few key phrases:

I'm fortunate to live so close to home.

I'm glad he isn't suffering anymore.

Thank you for calling. I'm lucky to have so much support.

Acquaintances offer, "Erika, just remember . . . everything happens for a reason."

Tell me, I want to say. *Tell me the reason why my father died at age sixty-five. Why I lost my father at age twenty-two. Why he spent the last five years fighting an illness that robbed him of his personality and his body and changed his relationships so dramatically, so beyond repair. Tell me.*

But I bite my tongue and thank them for calling.

Before I know it, it's the night before the final goodbye.

79.

It's an odd feeling, waking up knowing you'll be burying your parent.

Getting ready brings about a strange sensation. Why put the effort into looking nice, applying makeup, and finding a decent outfit? There won't be pictures—will there?

Why look put together on the outside when you're falling apart inside?

My mom, Pete, and I head to the funeral parlor. What an odd name for a place; it sounds so appealing when in reality it is anything but. The July heat is in full force, and I am anxious about how much I'm sweating. I'm going to have to hug a lot of people today—and soon. For a moment, I smile to myself, sarcastically thanking my father for passing along the hyperhidrosis gene.

My coworkers from the graduate office are the first to arrive. This whole event is a learning process for me as I have never been to a funeral for someone in my own family. It's weird to plan an event and have absolutely no clue who is going to show up. It's not like something you send invitations for: "Acquaintances and friends, come one, come all . . . Watch me sob while telling stories about my recently deceased father!" I had asked Pete to inform people from college, Angela to inform friends from home, and Megan to inform anyone in between. Upon seeing my coworkers filter into the room, tears fill my eyes. Almost all of them are there.

"Who's running the office?" I ask. I'm too stunned by the turnout to thank them for coming. I think (and hope) it's implied.

"Cecily and Justin," Jeannette tells me through the first hug of many I will receive. "They're so sorry they couldn't be here, and they send their best."

There are now nine people in the room. The silence is awkward, but what is there to say? Asking me "How are you?" probably feels silly. *Me? Oh, I'm just starting to navigate the five stages of grief, how are you?* I am at a total loss of what to say to them. I've worked with these people for just shy of two months. I am overwhelmed by their loyalty in this moment and speechless as a result. We look down and shuffle our feet as the slideshow the funeral home prepared rotates a collection of memories in the background—photos of me with my father when he was a strong, healthy, happy man.

I introduce my coworkers to my mother, which feels strange given the circumstances. The intolerable silence continues. All I can think about is how badly I want to quell the discomfort in the room.

"WOW, check out those *ears!*" Like clockwork, my coworker Cara breaks the awkwardness. After an initial gasp, everyone—including me—erupts into a much-needed fit of laughter. A photograph of my father holding me on his lap while sitting on the steps of our first home shines on the parlor screen. I'm six months old, and my ears are too big for my head; it's likely the first thing people notice when they see the picture but generally don't acknowledge out loud. Unless they are Cara. She will never know how much I needed her comic relief in this moment.

More guests filter in, some I don't recognize. A few introduce themselves as old friends of my father's, men who worked with him at Exxon. Their presence offers me a clarity and reminder of how much of a mark my father left before Parkinson's stole his spirit. I have no idea how they found out about the funeral, but I try to focus less on the logistics and more on the fact that there is an outpouring of love standing in this funeral home that I have borrowed for the day.

My father's lawyer walks through the door. I look at her and remember how she referred to representing my father in court as "babysitting." Bitch.

I schmooze with the guests for a bit longer, and then the funeral director rings a bell.

It's time to say goodbye.

I sit up front with my mom, Angela, Pete, and Meg. I worry for too long about how my other friends might feel that I chose these particular people to sit up with me. This nagging feeling gnaws at me, but I know it's irrational. It's my father's funeral, and I'll sit with my best friends if I want to.

The opening events, run by the director, are all a blur. All I'm thinking about is delivering the eulogy. I've been working on it all week, but it still feels unfinished. How do you pay respect to someone who is responsible for half of your DNA—and so much more—in one simple speech? How can I sound genuine when I'm still scarred by the tumultuous nature of our relationship these past few years? I may have won a public speaking contest last year, but today, I won't be talking about steps to reduce cyberbullying and teen suicide. I won't care if I walk away with a cash prize and my name on a plaque.

The director calls me to the podium. I look out at the crowd of family, friends, and strangers whose lives were touched by my father. My godmother Donna, who is one of my father's oldest friends, sneaks in the back; and we meet eyes. Something about her sweet smile gives me the confidence I need.

I quell my shaking hands. Then I begin to speak.

"Thank you, everyone, for being here today.

"A little over a year and a half ago, a nurse was visiting my father at home and discussing his prognosis. Somewhere in the conversation, my dad said, 'I only need two more years, really.' The nurse assured him that he had more time left than that, but he continued. He said he needed two years so that he could see me graduate from BC and get married. I laughed and told him I would not be getting married that soon . . . Sorry, Pete. I'm just thankful that after a five-year battle with Parkinson's disease, although he couldn't be at my graduation in person, he was able to hit one out of two of his wishes.

"Many of you never had the opportunity to meet my dad, while some of you only met him when he was at his worst. It's been hard mourning the loss of my father twice—first, the loss of who he was before this awful disease robbed him of his mobility and his creativity. But when I look back, parts of who he always was still stuck even when he was mostly bedridden and had difficulty speaking. I want to introduce him to anyone who didn't get to know him well.

"My dad was born in Lima, Peru. He lived there for twenty-one years, then came to the United States. After learning English and overcoming other immigration obstacles, he worked for Arco and Exxon, first as a driver and then as a terminal operator. I have always thought of my dad as a 'self-made' man. He came from very humble beginnings and worked his way up—first with odd jobs, then Exxon, then with real estate and the stock market—to make sure he took full advantage of becoming a US citizen and living in a land of opportunity. When I think of my dad, I think of his love for NASCAR racing, the Boston Red Sox, soccer, Corvettes, *Seinfeld*, the Olive Garden, and anything related to Peru. Even though my parents divorced when I was still in diapers, we always spent Christmas and my birthday together, and they made sure I was never affected by their separation.

"Little girls love their daddies, but I was mad about mine. Friday was my glory day, when I could spend the afternoon and night with him. He would pick me up from school, take me anywhere—a playground, the grocery store, or the mall as I got older. He was always making sure I had fun and being the best dad he could be, even when I was too little to remember it or old enough to not always appreciate it.

"Growing up, he taught me how to play soccer, practicing with me in his side yard, and was always proud of me even though I scored two goals in my entire soccer career—one of which was on the wrong team. He still supported me when I forfeited soccer to participate in the town drama workshop. He taught me to drive stick shift and remained patient even when I stalled out. And when the time came, he sent me to Boston College, which was his dream school for me. Luckily, it was also mine. Ever since I was younger, my dad had said, 'I promise I will send you to BC.' I know if my dad were here, he would say that this was one of his biggest accomplishments.

"My dad was the hardest worker I have ever met and was incredibly generous, often to a fault. He taught me how to mow the lawn when I was in high school but would still come by many weekends to do it himself. When he first started to lose a ton of weight and grow visibly sick, he often apologized for not being able to mow anymore, which, of course, was a ridiculous apology—but he never saw it that way. He also used to come over at six in the morning to snow-blow the driveway, even when my mom and I were completely prepared to do it ourselves. I remember when he would bring a friend and me to Canobie Lake Park every summer, and he would never go on the rides with us because he was afraid of heights. At Exxon, though, he had to climb really tall ladders up the sides of oil towers and never complained, although I can't even imagine how scary this would be for someone with such a fear. He did everything he could for that company. I have vivid memories of bedtime stories growing up. He and I always loved reading 'The Grasshopper and the Ants.' This story taught me all about today's hard work paying off tomorrow. The fable is a great descriptor of my father's life and work ethic. He was the perfect person to read and to teach me this story.

"He always wanted to meet everyone in my life and even strangers. He used to ask waiters where they were from so he could speak Spanish with them and hear their stories. Ever since I was little, he has taken several of my friends out for meals to make sure he got to know them. He spent so much time with Angela that she was almost a second daughter to him. In his sickness, it became very easy for him to forget things. Even so, the last time he saw Angela, he asked her how she was enjoying business school and how her sister and brother and parents were doing.

"Even though he changed so much mentally and physically, dropping weight by the day and becoming more and more immobile, my dad was still in there at times. Several people in the past week have described him as 'always lively' and commented on the constant laughter he brought about over the course of his life. At the end of a visit a few months ago, I told him to call me if he needed anything. Although he was half-asleep and suffering immense physical pain, he mumbled, 'A Corvette?' Even in his weakest state, he cracked the occasional joke.

"On July 5th, Pete and I visited him at the hospital when he was temporarily discharged from the ICU. He was on some sedatives, so it was a short visit, mostly during which I fed him some thickened juice, and he asked for help changing the TV channel. When Pete left, my dad, who was feeling especially weak and had been half-asleep because of the medicine, lifted his head, smiled, and said, 'Nice to see you.' This sounds so simple, but this is the perfect example of a time when he was more concerned for others than he was for himself. He wanted to make sure Pete knew that he had genuinely enjoyed his company.

"He never asked to get sick. He always said to people, 'Never get sick. This is just a shame. I never abused alcohol. I never did drugs. I stopped smoking as soon as Erika was born, and I don't know what I did to deserve this.' He really never did deserve it. No one does. All he did was care.

"He always found a way to smile even when he was sick and hurting. Whether it was over a holiday card, a little gift, a Dunkin' Donuts coffee, or a Red Sox win, he found it.

"The past few days, everything has reminded me of my dad. I think this is a testament to how much we did together, especially for seeing each other only one and a half days a week growing up. I am leaving my dad with a little goody bag to be buried with him. Inside are all the things he loves: a red toy Corvette, a packet of Dunkin' Donuts sugar, an Olive Garden menu, a model of Dale Earnhardt's race car, one of his old work gloves, a Good Humor Popsicle stick, and my BC Superfan shirt. He went too soon, and no speech can do him justice. Anyone who ever met him can attest to how hardworking, loving, giving, and genuine he always was. I just wish I'd had a little more time with him."

I don't want to stop talking because that means the goodbye is even more imminent than it already was, but I do. I walk back to my seat; my mom puts her arm around me and whispers "I love you" into my ear. The director returns, thanks me for speaking, and the service ends. A college friend kneels in front of my father's casket, saying a quiet prayer and crossing himself. I am offered hugs and watch people leave, and before I know it, it's time to go.

The same group of people who were there in my father's final moments—plus Pepe, Angela, Meg, and Pete—head to the cemetery for the burial. As four sweaty men carry my father's casket to the site, I notice his name is misspelled on the plaque atop the casket—they engraved "Varges" instead of "Vargas." What are we going to do, though? Make them correct it and delay his burial? It's not like it's on the headstone; no one will ever see this again. Although I know it wouldn't make sense to change it, a strong pang of guilt shoots through my body—it feels like this is another way in which I've let him down.

We stand in silence. Each of us tosses a single flower on his casket, and we watch as he is lowered into his final resting place. I toss a second flower, wanting to have the final interaction with him.

Then we say goodbye once more and head home.

80.

Jeannette and Tricia had told me to take all the time I need, but after a week out of the office, I'm back at work.

Real life keeps me busy, focused, distracted. My office mates are great at welcoming me back and don't ask "How *are* you?" too many times with solemn looks on their faces, knowing that could break me. At camp, June greets me with a giant smile every afternoon, overcompensating for how she handled the day my father died.

Camp pickup time is extremely hard, harder than I imagined it would be. Watching the campers, especially the little girls, light up when they see their daddies' faces and run into their strong arms, instantly being showered with kisses, causes me to stare off blankly into the distance, trying to ignore the explosion of love happening next to me every two minutes. It doesn't get easier. I just get better at ignoring it. I don't have a manual on grief. I don't know when I will heal. I don't know how long I'm allowed to be sad.

Time goes on . . . just without him.

81.

With every passing week, people seem to stop asking how I'm doing, which I'm fine with—it gives me a break from thinking and feeling. Sure, if I started to cry, everyone would stop what they're doing and offer support. But if I seem okay, I must be okay. And truly, I am feeling okay—not *all better*, but *less bad*. I hold my head a little higher. I spend less time crying in the bathroom in the middle of the workday. I even smile as I watch one of my campers jump into her father's arms.

I think I'm pretty strong. I think, *Wow, this is what it's like. Someone dies, and you cry your eyes out, and then you move on.*

It's the hottest day of the summer; sweat pours from our faces as Angela and I walk along Newbury Street, mostly window-shopping but occasionally popping into a store for cool relief. After hours socializing in the sun, I return to my boiling apartment, both refreshed and exhausted. I pull my sticky hair into a ponytail and stand in front of my window box fan for a few minutes until I'm ready to wind down with some mindless reality TV and a Popsicle.

Only something stops me. When I go to the kitchen and open the freezer, I lose my breath.

My roommate has brought home a pack of Klondike bars. My heart skips a beat, maybe two. You'd think I just saw a dead animal in there.

Tears erupt like they haven't since the day my father died. I shuffle to my room, collapse on the bed, and let it all out. My dad and I ate Klondike bars together all the time; they often found their way into our Friday glory day dessert rotation. I never really ate them with anyone else, and I haven't had one for years—not since he was alive, healthy, hungry. Memories of us sitting on his couch, fingers covered in melting chocolate while we laugh at cartoons and try not to drip cold, melty vanilla ice cream on the couch flash through my head. I want that again—I want it just one more time.

But I can't have it. A terrible illness has taken him away from me, and we will never again eat ice cream together, and he will never know what I do for a living, and he won't hold my firstborn child.

My roommate peeks in on me, then comes in and lies down beside me—her presence all the comfort I need. Eventually, I fall asleep.

That fucking Klondike bar.

82.

Camp has ended for the summer, so I switch my office shift to afternoons. I love sleeping in. I've never been a morning person, and my brain and body need the extra rest now more than ever.

The office cleaning lady comes every day around half past three. She is a petite older woman from Colombia. She wears bright purple eye shadow painted up to the midpoint of her underbrow. She always comes in smiling, saying "hello!" to each of us as she empties our bins into a larger rolling barrel, meticulously separating the recycling from the garbage.

This has been the routine for weeks now. I'm usually distracted around the time she arrives, scrambling to finish up my work for the day before I head to my 4:30 p.m. class. I always say hi, but that's usually about it. Occasionally, we comment on how beautiful it is outside, which feels silly as both of us are clearly stuck indoors. A handful of times, she has shared with me short anecdotes about her children and her home country.

Today, I am more distracted than usual; I'm done with my *work* work, and frantically editing a paper about Gestalt group therapy and what qualities make me a competent therapeutic leader. I am aware of her presence. I hear her cheerful "hello!" to my officemates, but I don't turn around to greet her as I usually would. I have to finish the paper. I'm running out of time.

I hear her head to the door directly behind my desk, and I decide to turn around and wave hello. *It will only take a second, Erika*, I think. *Come on, the paper is fine. Relax.* We make eye contact. She smiles, waves goodbye to me, and leaves.

I quickly do a double take.

I just looked into the eyes of the cleaning woman in our office and saw my father waving hello. This is what I scribble on a pink Post-it note so I can record the moment, capture it. I write it so I have validation that it is real and I did not make this up. I see the words. I believe them when they are in print. I can't share this with anyone in the office; it feels weird, vulnerable, inexplicable.

I saw him. Her eyes had changed to his for a moment—to his happy brown eyes that grew smaller with age and illness but always remained beautiful despite his decline. Her hand had resembled his fragile wrinkly hand and the way he would softly wave to me when I arrived or left the rehabilitation centers or hospital rooms he was in. She had flashed me his tender smile, where the very ends of his mouth would curl up without showing any teeth—the most genuine smile I have ever seen. She had a knowing look when it happened. It gives me chills, butterflies, an overwhelming feeling of comfort starting in my stomach and spreading outward through my entire body. He was here, just checking in to say "Hello, I love you, I am thinking of you."

Last month, my friend Will called me when he heard the news of my father's death. He had lost his father to cancer a little over a year prior, and we had a really good talk about loss and how grief can be similar, yet so different for everyone. I asked him if he ever saw his dad places right after he died. Will had asked what I meant, and I told him that every older man I saw seemed to look like my father in the weeks following his death. I feared this would never go away, and I would be constantly blinking back tears whenever I happened to see a man over the age of sixty.

Will told me that while he had never quite experienced this, he had experienced a more figurative way of seeing his father. On a cruise with his family, his sister had hoped to see dolphins. Shortly after she expressed her wish, a large group of beautiful dolphins jumped out of the water. Will saw his father then.

A few months later, I see my father again while visiting New York City for the weekend. I'm at Rockefeller Center and cannot seem to find the Peruvian flag. When I finally find it, I want to take a picture of it; and immediately, the wind blows. The Peruvian flag proudly waves above me for several minutes. I know my father is with me in this moment.

Our loved ones never really leave us; they're here even when they're gone. We can't try to find them. We have to let them find us. They will.

83.

Right before Christmas, Pete and I break up. He had been a rock in my life for so long, showering me with love and comfort and encouraging me to join the organizations that offered me a sense of purpose. I'm not sure how I would have otherwise survived BC. But toward the end, our relationship had become too broken in too many ways. He put his guard up after my infidelity and my resistance to recommit to our relationship for half of senior year. I put mine up after he began working so much when I needed him most in my father's final weeks and when he wasn't there sooner on the day he died. I wonder if I've been hanging on to Pete even when our relationship began to break because I've been too afraid to navigate everything with my dad without something solid in my life—something I haven't allowed myself to do since before freshman year. I wonder if Pete felt he couldn't break up with me given what I was going through. Who dumps a girl with a dying father?

84.

In the months immediately following my father's death, I'd experienced mostly sadness and longing; a blessing of his passing is that it allowed me to remember the hero he was before dementia changed him. Eventually, though, this feeling shifts as my brain forces me to remember the challenges we faced during his illness and consequently how much I'd struggled these past few years.

Some things don't go away, won't go away. Like the guilt, warranted or not, of not being there for him the way he wanted me to be, the constant "Erika, everyone asks why you aren't here taking care of me . . . They have big hearts, but not you." Every time that statement echoes in my mind, his sullen expression flashes in my memory, and my stomach sinks.

Although I don't admit it out loud, there is a bit of a relief in his passing. He, of course, is no longer suffering physically or mentally . . . and neither am I—at least not in the same way as I was before. I no longer have someone telling me how ungrateful I am, that I'm not doing enough, that I'm heartless. I can be more present in my life without the constant guilt that I should be elsewhere. I volunteer for a local non-profit that provides support for women navigating poverty and depression. I travel more. I train for and complete a half-marathon. I form lasting friendships with the other mental health counseling students. Explaining to anyone how my life has, in many ways, changed for the better feels impossible—how can I feel anything but sadness that my father has passed away? Doesn't that just make me the bad daughter he told me I was? So I keep it in.

My father died on July 17. I visit his grave on the seventeenth of every month for a year. Each time, I write a letter and read it out loud to him, filling him in on my life and what has changed, asking how he is doing and who he spends time with in heaven. Some of it is update, some apology.

Shortly after the one-year anniversary of his death, I have to make a decision. I'm entering my second year of grad school; and between my clinical internship at a crisis center, my job at the graduate office, classes, and living a half hour away, I can no longer commit to visiting every seventeenth. As much as this makes sense, I can't shake the feeling that even in his death, I have failed him. I live with an intense, but brief guilt for not sticking to my monthly ritual. Fortunately, with time, I am able to look at this more rationally and understand it is okay to value my own life and priorities. I visit his grave whenever I'm in my hometown, usually around the holidays.

While carpooling to the crisis center office one morning, one of my fellow interns shares that she lost her father the same year I lost mine.

"He had Parkinson's disease," she says. Her eyes are fixed on the road, so she doesn't see my mouth gape open.

"Mine too," I say finally; and when she looks over at me, both of us have tears in our eyes. I am filled with both connection and regret as I realize I was never alone in this; had I opened up more, I may have found others who shared parts of my story as I was living it.

85.

Just shy of two years after my father's death, I graduate with my master's in counseling psychology. I walk across the same stage where I received my undergraduate degree and wish, again, that my dad was here to watch. Later in the year, I use some of the money my father left me in his will to travel to Peru for the first time. I spend three months in Cuzco and Lima taking Spanish classes, teaching English to blind adults, and, of course, visiting Machu Picchu. My father had a large print of the ruins hanging in his bedroom and visited the site many times throughout his life. I hike to the top of Huayna Picchu, a steep mountain on the Incan citadel, and stare down at the other tourists bustling below me as small as ants. I sit there for an hour, tranquility washing over me as I feel deeply connected to my father.

While in Lima, I contact my aunt Chela, my father's younger sister, who I haven't seen or spoken with in over a decade. My host family helps me communicate by phone to schedule a visit, but when I arrive at our planned meeting spot on the steps of Iglesia Virgen Milagrosa, Chela isn't there and never shows. A flutter of shame ripples through my body. *She knows I was a bad daughter. She doesn't want to meet with me. I'm not trying hard enough. I've let my father down yet again.* I remind myself, *I don't have to feel that way anymore.* But the echo remains, albeit quieter.

86.

A month after returning from Peru, I am hired as a therapist at an eating disorder clinic, working with adolescents and their families. I understand firsthand why many of my clients self-harm, and I help them find safer, more productive outlets. This career path brings me the same joy and purpose I felt as an RA. Using a narrative therapy approach, I constantly preach to the parents that if they can separate the eating disorder from their child, they will feel relief. Their child's illness will manipulate them, but they will feel it is their child manipulating them. Remembering that the disorder has temporarily taken over the mind and spirit of their child is key in helping them fight the demon and navigate recovery. Only after several years of preaching this will I realize why I find such comfort in this conceptualization. I knew this through my father's illness, but knowing it and believing it are different things. It was his illness that hated me at times, not him. It was his illness that berated me for not being good enough, not him. Unlike with eating disorders, with Parkinson's and Lewy body dementia there was no goal of full recovery, no way to rid him of the demon. The goal was for me to understand and accept how his life was forever changed by Parkinson's disease. I wonder how much easier things might have felt had I achieved that understanding and acceptance sooner.

87.

On my twenty-fifth birthday, my mom gives me a handwritten journal she has been keeping for me since the day I was born. She wrote to me every time something significant happened: my first word, my first day of school, my college acceptance, some of my heartbreaks, a few arguments she and I had ending in tearful apologies, and sometimes just about how much being a mom changed her. It is beautiful. But I can't read it without sobbing to the point of nausea, so I stop. In response to an uptick in my anxiety last year, I'd started seeing a new therapist, Dr. Miller. I bring up the journal in one of our sessions. I realize that reading this journal is further triggering my fear that my mom will die. I hadn't realized how deep my fear was until reading my mom's words didn't turn into appreciation for her, but instead exacerbated my unbearable anxiety that something will happen to her and I won't have adequately reciprocated her love for me. Dr. Miller helps me see that the function of obsessing over the idea that my mom may suddenly die is to feel like I am somehow keeping her safe—if I obsess over it, if I reassure myself out of every possible scenario, everything has to be okay, right?

"Worrying about it won't prevent it from happening," Dr. Miller says gently, but it cuts into my ego like a knife as I realize that on a subconscious level, I thought I could control it. It also sets me free when I realize I can't.

I stop reading the journal for a while and return to baseline.

Months later, I treat a client who lost both her parents by the time she hit adolescence. That abominable pit returns in my stomach. I thought that was impossible. I thought I had an invincibility cloak once I lost my dad at twenty-two, and that meant my mom couldn't die until I became an adult with three grown children and a white picket fence. How is it possible that the world can be so cruel? Working with this incredibly resilient teenager shatters my sense of invincibility and helps me to accept the reality of life and the unknown. We control so little.

Acceptance becomes the hallmark of my therapeutic approach. It can be unsettling, as a therapist, to imply to my clients that bad things *can and will* happen, though I know that helping them stop trying to make sense of the nonsensical and instead relinquish perceived, but false control is a way of setting them free.

88.

Five years after my father's death, my mom is admitted to the hospital for a minor, but unexpected surgery. I am sick with guilt that I'm working and cannot be there for her the first night. She reassures me that it's fine, that she had a close friend with her, that she was sleeping for most of the evening anyway. But the guilt continues to grow. The body does not forget. It is instant, visceral.

I visit a few times over the week and stay with her for her first weekend home. Because I am, evidently, masochistic, I ask her if anyone said anything about me not being the one to pick her up from the hospital upon discharge. "Yeah, Louise did," she shares. "She's always just *so* negative."

My stomach is in my throat as I bubble over with shame. I'm mad at my mom for telling me, but later in the week, Dr. Miller points out that I *literally* asked for the information. I think I wish my mom knew my brain well enough to understand that this was a very loaded question given the history with my dad, but I don't think she sees the two as related. For her, sharing that information (again, after I'd literally asked for it) was a way to vent about her coworker's negative attitude. She was not saying she wished I'd picked her up or that I was a bad daughter for not doing so. The epithet of "unreliable, careless daughter" is awakened within me for a few days, then slowly retreats.

89.

Even after six years without him, I still have moments when I forget my dad isn't here anymore. Whenever I have a chunk of time when I ordinarily might have called him, I find myself unlocking my phone to make the call until I inevitably remember. His number remains in my phone until I get a new one and lose all my contacts in the process, though I will always have it memorized by heart.

In a tourist shop in Reykjavik, I see a souvenir I know he will love. It is a little red toy car that mimics a Corvette; a Viking wearing sunglasses sits in the driver's seat. It takes a good fifteen seconds before I remember he isn't alive anymore to accept it.

90.

Almost seven years have passed. During one of my visits to his grave, something feels different. The cemetery is sandwiched between a main road in Natick and a somewhat-busy side road. There is usually a fair amount of background noise when I am visiting, whether it be the swoosh of cars, the occasional horn of a disgruntled driver, trees swaying in the breeze, or children playing in their backyards.

Tonight, it is silent. The winter cold is biting, the neighboring lake is still, and no one is on the roads. Initially, I am jarred by the silence, which says something about the world we live in—we feel most uncomfortable when we are most still.

I've mostly stopped crying about my father's death when memories pop into my head. Of course, there are moments when emotions overwhelm me: a sappy television show about a father-daughter relationship; seeing a middle-aged man shoveling snow, the childhood image I held of my father shouting "Erika, I'm coming for you!" appearing every time I blink; driving past a For Sale sign in the front yard of a house, still attracting my eyes like magnets as I'm transported back to the fun we had driving around house hunting before everything changed; preparing for my wedding while acknowledging that my father never had the chance to meet my fiancé.

The silence begins to feel peaceful, as though my father is here, silencing the world around us and being with just me. There are no words. I don't have a letter to read tonight—just myself and my thoughts and his spirit. The sobs start in my stomach, work up through my throat, and catch me off guard as I pour salty tears into my gloves—the sounds of my sadness and grief interrupting the quietness of the night.

Minutes pass, and I walk back to the car. Ryan, my soon-to-be husband, is waiting for me. He hugs me extra tightly, then starts to drive. There is no need to ask if I am okay. I am fine, I am sad, that makes sense—my father died. But my dad was here tonight, sitting with me in the silence of the cemetery, grieving the life we lost together.

Epilogue

I wish I could change the way it played out. I want to wheel him into a Red Sox game on a hot summer day and buy him a Fenway Frank. I want him to teach me Spanish and have a special phrase we say to help him cope with his pain. I want to understand his medications. I want copies of his medical records. I want to be more involved with his treatment and get him the best medical and psychiatric team possible.

I would have gone to Peru with him. I would have worked harder to get him to my college graduation. I would have read books about Parkinson's and dementia and ambiguous loss and gone to support groups.

I wouldn't have changed the four-month break, though. As hard of a decision as that was, as much as my guilt skyrocketed at times throughout, ultimately, I think it saved us.

Only through ongoing therapy do I recognize that I've built some pretty big walls to protect myself from emotional pain. If I keep the people I love the most at an arm's length, if I don't let myself love fully, then it won't hurt as badly when they die . . . right? Parkinson's created a distance between my father and me; and, albeit unintentional, that's what protected me from experiencing an even deeper sadness when he died. But this can't be manufactured. There is a cost to not loving. You cannot fully live if you refuse to fully love in anticipation of unpredictable grief that doesn't have a specific timeline. I realize this. I talk it through with my therapist, but it is deeply ingrained in me—it serves as a comfort and defense mechanism and, simultaneously, a thief of joy and love and life.

Is this what my father did with me? Instead of letting himself love me the way he had for the first seventeen years of my life, did his subconscious shift his focus to what I *wasn't* doing, to how *bad* I was so that the idea of him leaving me too early didn't feel so crushingly unbearable to him?

I wonder how different things would have felt if I could have leaned into the sadness of his illness instead of the guilt of my role. Sadness turns us inside out, exposes us, leaves us feeling like a fish out of water, struggling to breathe, to live. We are desperate to avoid it. Guilt, though debilitating and crushing to our egos, at least gives us some semblance of control: *If only I'd done more, then this would be all better.* But maybe that isn't true. Maybe just the same as it felt easier to hate and berate me so he could have someone to blame for his pain, to point his finger and say, "It's your fault. You—*you* make me depressed. *You* make me suffer," I did the same thing to myself . . . and at times to him. But no one is responsible. He didn't choose the illness. The illness chose him. Parkinson's is a soul-crushing, spirit-crushing disease dripping with sadness. If I had let myself feel that, feel the unbelievable, heavy sadness of losing my father slowly, confusingly, maybe it would have prevented so much of the pain and suffering the guilt brewed.

But that isn't how it happened. The guilt is paralyzing. Although it never fully disappears, the less I act in accordance with it, the more it starts to fade away. I grow more capable of making decisions that are more balanced between my own needs and the needs of others rather than doing whatever I feel I must do to prevent a deep and nauseating guilt in anticipation of letting someone down.

With time, I begin to believe that I did do my best, even if my idea of my best and his idea of my best were incongruent. I begin to accept just how little control he had over the things he said and did when his brain was sick. I begin to forgive myself for not understanding what I couldn't have understood.

. . .

Dear Me (age 17),

I wish I could go back.

Actually, never mind—I would never go back. Those years were hell. Unless it was to see him again, to hug him, to kiss his cheek, even if only for a moment. But I do wish you could know what I know now.

You are young. Your teens and early twenties are an incredibly fragile time. You will gain perspective on this when you, as an adult, work with teenagers and are exposed to the raw painful emotions of adolescence. You need to give yourself some more compassion. How can you navigate his brain-altering disease when your own brain has yet to fully develop?

Today, at work, a parent was giving advice to another parent about his child's eating disorder treatment process. He said, "Make sure you do what you can. That's the best you can do. When your head hits the pillow at night, you just need to know you did what you could, even if you can't fix it right then."

Someone will tell you this too, but you won't understand it fully. It's okay. You are doing what you can. You are there as best you can be. You can't see how much you're doing; instead, you're focusing on what you aren't doing.

You will fight this for years. Be easy on yourself. You love him, but he will tell you things that make you feel terrible, and you will believe them. It's okay to take a break so you can survive.

Try to be less afraid of vulnerability. The more you speak about your pain, the more others can hold it with you.

Thinking of you. I would give you a hug if I could and hold on for as long as possible.

Love,
You (age 29)

Acknowledgments

I started writing this memoir in 2007, when I was twenty years old. At the time of publishing, I am thirty-six; and my life has, as expected, changed in so many ways. It has been sad, bittersweet, humbling, and cathartic to reflect on this time in my life when emotions were so fragile. I truly could not have survived my high school and college years without so many people, and while I cannot name them all here, they deserve acknowledgment. To the people behind the names (Meg, Brendan, and the real Pete, Julia, Angela, and Jim), you were my lifelines through college, even during times of conflict. Each one of you holds a very special place in my heart. To the real Gerardo, you offered me a sense of calm during an otherwise stormy time. You recently told me you feel a connection to my father whenever we chat; that feeling is mutual.

So many thank-yous: To my early readers/favorite bookworms Maggie and Lacey, thank you for your honest feedback, but mostly for being incredible women with whom I entrusted this book before I felt emotionally ready to allow it to exist in the world. I love you. To Brad, for your support and expertise in portions of the medical chapters. To Julia Pastore, who provided me with a thorough developmental edit of my first draft. To my beta readers, Andi and Nicolette, for your kind and thoughtful feedback. To Word-2-Kindle for copy editing, publishing, and cover design support. To the NeuroDiverseFamily Etsy shop owner, Clinton, who graciously allowed me to use their gorgeous artwork for the front cover.

To my first-grade teacher, Mrs. Maranian, who, after I completed an assignment entirely incorrectly, pulled me aside to give me a special notebook for my writing. She encouraged me to continue thinking outside the box and to foster my creativity, thus awakening my love for writing.

To my husband, Ryan, for being one of my earliest readers, for pushing me to write when I otherwise felt stuck, for supporting me when I dipped into our savings to pay for professional support with edits and revisions, for hanging with our babies while I wrote and rewrote, and for not watching any of our TV shows without me on the nights I needed to prioritize writing. As I said in my wedding vows, you are reserved, yet silly and incredibly hardworking, which are qualities you share with my father. Even though you never got the chance to meet him, I know without a doubt he would have approved of you. I love you, and without you, I'm not sure I would have finished this memoir.

To my babies, Skyler and Mari. Skyler, there are moments I see the beautiful parts of my father in your smile. Mari, my *mariposa*, your name is inspired by my father's native tongue. I am in awe of you two, and I can't believe I get to be your mom. I hope to pass on the resilience and strength I can proudly say I've developed from what I've gone through. I love you, I love you, I love you. Thank you for making me constantly smile and laugh. You make every day better.

To my late father, I love you with my whole heart. You were my hero and source of belly laughs, my buddy, the man who made me beam with happiness on our Friday glory days. I will never forget who you were before Parkinson's stole you away. It breaks my heart that my husband and my children didn't get to meet you and feel your warm smile or witness your sassy sense of humor.

They would have absolutely adored you. I hope you are resting in the sweetest peace, driving a red Corvette, and eating Olive Garden breadsticks every single day.

And last but certainly not least, to my mom. This memoir is dedicated to you. Without you, this book would truly not have been possible. Without the logs you kept of every single detail until those very final moments, without your vulnerability in letting me read through the raw emotions of said log, I would have a story to tell, but fewer details with which to tell it. So much is a blur, but what I remember the most is that you showed up for me every single time I needed you; and when my world was spinning out of control and I was plagued with guilt, you let me cry on your shoulder. I love you so, so much. MWA kbte.

About The Author

Erika Vargas owns a private psychotherapy and consultation practice, where she specializes in the treatment of disordered eating, anxiety disorders, sexual trauma, and perinatal mental health. Erika lives in Massachusetts with her husband, pup, and the sweetest children in the world. This is her first book.